AIRSHIP NAVIGATOR

AIRSHIP
NAVIGATOR

ONE MAN'S PART IN THE BRITISH AIRSHIP TRAGEDY 1916-1930

by **E A Johnston** OBE FRAeS

SKYLINE

First Published in 1994 by Skyline Publishing
Chapel End, Littleworth, Amberley, Stroud,
Gloucestershire GL5 5AL

Designed by John Christopher, Designworks
Printed in Great Britain by Bookcraft

ISBN – 1 874180 01 6

CONTENTS

Many people have written about the tragedy of the airship *R101* but none, I think, with my own unique involvement in the story. I was born with one ear cocked to catch the sound of engines of airships returning from patrol, and between 1925 when I was seven years old and 1930 when I was twelve I lived in the airship community at Pulham and Cardington. I was then a precocious youngster with a passionate interest in all things aeronautical, and most of all in my Father's two airships *R100* and *R101*. Those five years and the people who inhabited them are still very vivid in my memory.

I was stimulated to write this book as a result of Sir Peter Masefield's own *To Ride The Storm*, a most authoritative, detailed account of the 1924 Airship Programme and its tragic demise. There are, however, some important aspects of his interpretation of the events leading to the *R101* disaster with which I disagreed. Over several years he and I discussed our differences in voluminous correspondence and I am deeply grateful to him for many kindnesses and for putting me in the way of much useful background information.Through his influence I was able to participate in a fascinating computer study of the motions of *R101* under various flight conditions carried out by Professor Alan Simpson of Bristol University, some of the results of which are discussed in my Epilogue.

While collaborating with Sir Peter and Professor Simpson in an attempt to write a joint pamphlet describing the outcome of our lengthy study of the *R101* disaster, I came to the conclusion that I had a deeper tale to tell than could be contained within the format of a technical paper. *To Ride the Storm* looked at the airship saga from the point of view of a Minister of the Crown; Captain George Meager wrote the story of *R100* from a pilot's point of view in his classic work *My Airship Flights*; and my tale is told from the point of view of my Father and the people I knew best, the senior Management at Cardington and the Officers of both airships.

E.A. Johnston
Seaford

CHAPTER ONE

FROM SEA TO SKY

When Ernest Livingston Johnston knocked a drunken airship crewman to the ground in the shed at Cardington his friend and colleague the First Officer of *R101* remarked acidly "Very Merchant Service." But Lieutenant Commander Atherstone RN (Ret) was right: Johnston was the scion on his father's side of a line of merchant shipmasters from the Tyne and the Forth ports stretching back for more than 250 years, and on his mother's side a dynasty of Wearside masters at least a century old. He was born at North Shields in November 1891 and, like the preceding generations baptised in the Scottish Church there, for his great-grandfather was a Fifer born and bred. After excelling as a pupil at Tynemouth High School he was apprenticed in 1904, despite strong objections from his widowed Mother, to the Stag Line, a bulk carrier fleet which had been started by the Robinson family in North Shields around 1846.

The Robinsons were one of those fine little family firms in the northeast who, by careful attention to tramp building and owning, ensured that the highest standards were brought to bear on the construction of bulk cargo carriers that were at once cheap, roomy, economical and seaworthy. They insisted that their Masters concerned themselves with training schemes for the apprentices, they nurtured sound Officers and they treated them fairly. Their vessels were run by British Officers and manned by Lascars. When Ernest Johnston sailed out of North Shields as the junior of two apprentices, the typical complement of a Stag Line steamer was Master, Chief Engineer, two Mates and two Engineers (these keeping watch and watch about), half a dozen lascar seamen under their serang and two tindals, and rather more firemen and trimmers. The two apprentices bunked and fed alone in a dog-hutch of a cabin of their own, and each was allotted to the watch of one of the Mates. The first duty of an apprentice was absolute obedience, for he had come to sea to learn and he could only learn by obeying. Whilst all too often in those days, as in the preceding generations, the premium apprentices were treated as inferior, cheap labour and driven harder than any others of a ship's company at the more uncongenial tasks of running a vessel, Ernest was fortunate to sail under a conscientious Master who felt himself in honour bound to see that his apprentices were properly schooled. For his part, Ernest was from the very first smart and eager to learn. Capable of his fair share of devilment ashore, he had a natural habit of ready and cheerful obedience afloat, an alert and well-tutored mind and the unashamed initiative to inquire what he might usefully do. From the serang of lascars he quickly learned the lingua franca of the native seamen – "lascari bhat"– and acquired a fine fluency to curse in it. As junior apprentice he rated lower than a lascar ordinary seaman and must take his tutelage in the basic skills of a seaman from the tindals – something of a change from being a star pupil at Tynemouth High School. Nevertheless it needed more than the ability to curse in lascari bhat, more even than a proficiency with his fists for a lad fresh from High School to establish a commanding position in a crew of jabbering lascars and among the dockies who swarmed all over the ship when she was in port. His mentor the Second Mate conscientiously taught him the professional lore of a mariner, but he reckoned it was no job of his to help a boy stand on his feet and become a man. In a tramp ship east of Suez there was no Master-at-Arms backed by a company of Marines to enforce discipline, but only professional knowledge and skill, in which Ernest was at first deficient, allied to strength of character and a powerful pair of fists, both of which he possessed in plenty. By the time he reached Bombay the well-read, cultivated schoolboy was on the way to becoming a tough-minded driver of men.

With one short visit to Tynemouth in 1908, Ernest's sea education proceeded over the next four years in a series of voyages spanning the Indian Ocean, the Arabian Sea and the Bay of Bengal, taking in Mombassa, Aden, Karachi, Bombay, Calicut, Colombo, Calcutta, Rangoon, Moulmein, Penang and Singapore. On completing his indentures in December 1910 while his ship was lying in Bombay, Ernest appeared before a number of grave and senior Master Mariners who severally examined his competence to hold a Second Mate's certificate. He satisfied them at his first attempt, whereupon his own Master signed him on immediately as Second Mate – who, he soon began to feel, was the hardest-worked man on board. When the ship was at sea he not only kept his watch on the bridge four hours on and four hours off, but was also the ship's navigator with special charge of compasses, charts and chronometer; and in port his place was in the holds seeing to the stowing and unloading of cargo and coping with native stevedores whose one aim in life was to do nothing, or failing that to do wrongly the least amount they could get away with. The proper stowage of cargo was as essential for the safety of the ship as was the proper navigation. It was a filthy job; nevertheless photographs of him on deck at this period invariably showed him as a somewhat dashing figure in immaculate white ducks.

Back in North Shields in the early summer of 1912 Ernest obtained his First Mate's certificate and then, in order to acquire sufficient qualifying seagoing time, shipped as Second Mate again for a further eighteen months east of Suez. Early in 1914 he sailed out of the Tyne again, this time as First Mate of the Stag Line steamship *Stephanotis* (4,000 tons). By then, he held a Sub-Lieutenant's commission in the Royal Naval Reserve as well, for like most of his generation he perceived the shadows of war looming closer. As Mate, Ernest now had responsibility to the Master for the overall running of the vessel and the discipline of the crew while at sea, as well as standing watch and watch about; and in port he had the entire conduct of the ship's business on board as distinct from that which the Master must needs perform on shore. His was the job of looking after the shipment of all cargo, examining bills of lading, and tallying while his second saw to the stowage below. When the ship lay alongside a wharf in a foreign port his overworked life was full of trouble, with a lascar crew devoting all its cunning to doing as little work as possible, a motley gang of stevedores capable of working only under the strongest and most constant compulsion, and a horde of touts, crimps, runners and idlers of one sort and another to keep at bay. Like the generations of his forefathers who had served as Mates before him, his work must be done in an environment where personal abuse and violence on the part of drunken seamen bearing a grudge, or dockrats caught stealing, was commonplace. He could retain mastery only by knowing when to apply diplomacy or when to throw a punch to quell trouble before it overwhelmed him. The training he had as Mate of a tramp steamer in the Indian Ocean brought out all his sterling qualities - courage, patience, persistence, intelligence and the orderly application of thought, the ability to get obedience from men in a tough environment, enthusiasm for doing a job well, personal endurance of physical hardship, the enjoyment of comradeship and, in the quiet moonlit watches on the gentler seas, an abiding sense of destiny.

While at Bombay in July 1914, Ernest obtained his Board of Trade Master's certificate in steam. During the year, *Stephanotis* carried five cargoes of coal from Calcutta to Bombay, three to Penang and one to

Calicut; then in May 1915 she loaded 6475 tons of wheat at Karachi and sailed on the 12th for England. She arrived in the Humber on 15th June and Ernest, having seen his ship unloaded, took his discharge as soon as she arrived back in the Tyne to seek active service with the Fleet. In July he was appointed Navigating Officer of an elderly Torpedo-Gunboat *HMS Spanker* doing duty as a minesweeper out of Harwich and served in her until March 1916. Ambitious, enthusiastic, articulate and handsome as well as being a hard driver, he had already discovered in himself not only an outstanding aptitude for practical navigation but also what was much rarer, particularly in the deck officers of his day, a quick and intuitive grasp of the theoretical and mathematical basis of the art.

Spanker's minesweeping operations during the latter half of 1915 in the coastal sea lanes and approaches to the London River brought her within purview of operations from the RNAS seaplane stations at Eastchurch on the Isle of Sheppey, and Felixstowe, as well as the airship station at Kingsnorth on the Isle of Grain which, since early spring of that year, had become the principal airship dockyard, centre of research and development, and major training establishment under the command of Wing Commander Neville Usborne, shortly to be killed while testing an aeroplane-airship combination as a potential anti-Zeppelin weapon. The Zeppelin raids on London in the autumn of 1915 and on Edinburgh and the industrial Midlands early in the following year, which seemed to add a wholly new dimension to warfare, made an enormous and lasting impression on the whole population of Britain. Ernest, always eager to explore new frontiers, was stimulated to respond with enthusiasm to the call from Wing Commander Edward Maitland, who was Superintendent of the Naval Airship Service, for Officers to volunteer to train as pilots of the expanding fleet of small non-rigids. And so on 16th March 1916 he transferred to the Royal Naval Air Service and joined the 'Awkward Squad' at Eastchurch for a short course of air gunnery before being posted to Wormwood Scrubs for his basic aviation training.

The RNAS had been formed in June 1914. Five non-rigid airships hitherto operated by both the Naval and the Military Wings of the Royal Flying Corps, together with their personnel, were then all turned over to the Royal Navy. The two original ships of the former Naval Wing, a French Astra-Torres and a German Parseval (designated *HM Airships Nos. 3 and 4* respectively) were allocated at the outbreak of war to coastal patrol duties; *No.3* was flown by Flight Commander W.C. Hicks with Flight Sub-Lieutenant I.B. Hartford, *No.4* by Flight Commander A.D. Cunningham with Flight-Sub Lieutenant G.C. Colmore. Their first war patrol was flown six days after the German invasion of Belgium: thereafter both ships flew extensive patrols to cover the shipment of the British Expeditionary Force across the Channel. Early in 1915 the Admiralty commissioned the construction of a large number of inexpensive non-rigid airships based on the *Willows No.4* (designated *Naval Airship No.2* in Admiralty service), for use in coastal anti-submarine work.

Ernest's Commanding Officer at the Scrubs was Major C.M. (Tim) Waterlow, late Royal Engineers, one of those Army Officers who had been transferred to the RNAS with the airships. Waterlow, who had begun his career as an airship pilot with Capper and Cody in the *Nulli Secundus* in 1907, was later to lose his life at Cranwell when, failing to let go of the handling guy of a rising airship, he was carried away and fell from a great height.

The course consisted of rigorous training in theoretical aerostatics, ground handling and rigging of balloons and airships, and other technical subjects prior to a practical course in free-ballooning; it was split between Scrubs (for ground training), Hurlingham (for ballooning) and Kingsnorth (for airship flying). "Although the usual thing is to go on to Kingsnorth from here, I understand that you yourself will be going direct to one of the operational stations as you are comparatively senior to the other trainees," Waterlow told Johnston. There was much to be learned and much midnight oil to be burned in studying such arcane subjects as the gas laws of Charles and Boyle and their application to Archimedes' principles of flotation before the Crossley Tender carried Ernest and his colleagues to Hurlingham for the practical work with balloons. There was also the art of transforming a pile of rubberised fabric and rope and wooden spars and great quantities of highly inflammable hydrogen into a manoeuvrable flying machine to be acquired; and the theory of the internal combustion engine and airscrews; the significance of Eta patches, valves, sleeves, crab-pots, petticoats and ballonets; meteorology; the peculiar skills needed for airborne pilotage and navigation; the construction and use of altimeters, statoscopes, manometers and airspeed indicators. Ernest attacked it all with his usual zest and emerged from Waterlow's frequent examinations with outstanding results.

There was at Scrubs a small man-lifting Spencer kite-balloon derived from the old German 'Drachen' design which had predominated until the famous 'Cacquot' was universally adopted during 1916. Its margin of lift was minimal and the design was, by Cacquot standards, wildly unstable. The aeronaut rode upon a plank seat suspended from the winching wire, his feet dangling in space. It was upon this contraption that Ernest first became airborne in a series of short lifts totalling less than an hour to cultivate 'air sense' - that is to say, in addition to orientation, a sense of the meaning of static and dynamic stability (or rather, instability). He took to it naturally.

Whetted by this experience, their brains crammed with theory, Ernest and his colleagues arrived at Hurlingham early one morning to begin their practical training as aeronauts in the tradition of Charles, Lunardi, Blanchard and Green. Jacques Charles, a young French Academician, invented the hydrogen balloon - his second, made of rubberised silk, first ascended on 1st December 1783 from the Tuileries Gardens carrying Charles and his engineering colleague Marie-Noel Robert; but the distinction of being the very first aeronauts belongs to Pilatre de Rozier and the Marquis d'Arlandes who, less than a fortnight earlier, had ascended in a Montgolfier balloon made of paper and lifted by hot-air generated by a fire of wool and moist straw. The design of Jacques Charles' balloon to all intents and purposes set the standard which was still in use when Ernest Johnston went to Hurlingham 135 years later, save that Vincenzo Lunardi, who made the first ascent in Great Britain in September 1784 using a 'Charliere' balloon, improved the design of the net and introduced the suspension terminating in a hoop from which the car was suspended. The only other development of significance was the adoption by the great British pioneer, Charles Green, of coal gas as the lifting agent in 1821. Nothing much had changed between Green's day and the spring of 1916 when Johnston and his mates stood on the Hurlingham ground confronted by a pile of rope and rubberised fabric alongside a wicker basket, under the sardonic eye of their instructor, Warrant Officer King.

The rigging and inflation of a gas balloon needed the attention of half a dozen people and took several hours. Upon a large protective ground-sheet, the hempen net was stretched out with the grommet for the balloon's gas valve set at one end and the eye for attaching the wooden hoop, from which the basket was to be slung, at the other. The envelope, which had been rolled up so that the neck of the balloon was outermost, was then unrolled inside the net towards the grommet in such a way that the valve seating ended up in position to be secured to the grommet by straps and buckles. To Ernest and his sidekick, another RNR Lieutenant named Seabrook, both of them ex-apprentices in the Merchant Marine, this operation presented no difficulty, but there was much laughter and horseplay among the young landlubbers who formed the majority of the class as, despite the patient Warrant Officer's instructions, they became hopelessly entangled in the mesh of hemp.

When the balloon was thus laid out, the end of the valve cord was secured to the valve with a good hitch and the end stopped, and the cord then coiled up clear and inserted in the balloon so that, as it filled, the end could drop through the neck. The valve itself was very carefully screwed into its seating. At this stage the handling party was posted for the operation of 'crowning', a complicated evolution involving seven men which ended with the envelope and its net spread out evenly in a circle with the valve lying on top at its centre. The balloon was then ready for filling.

Its neck was connected by fabric tubes to the high pressure gas bottles, the supply turned on; the slow process of inflation was begun. As the grey fabric bulged up from the ground under the constraining meshes the inflating party, having hooked sandbags evenly around the circumference of the net, moved them progressively outwards, first on the mesh and then, when the balloon was well developed, to the ends of the lift lines. If the gassing party possessed the proper skills, the result at the end of inflation was a near spherical balloon symmetrically located under its net with all eighteen lift lines of equal length terminating at the restraining bags of sand on the ground. Under Mr King's skilfull supervision in the calm morning this was readily accomplished. Inflation was usually done early in the day for two reasons: to avoid having to cope with wind at a time when the balloon was at its least manageable, and to give the gas plenty of time to warm up at least to ambient temperature before flight – this had an important effect on the amount of lift generated by the balloon.

While inflation was under way, Ernest and Seabrook prepared the basket for flight. The eight stout ropes which were spliced to the basket – one at each corner and one at the midpoint on each side – were toggled onto the suspension ring to which the lift-lines from the net would eventually be attached. The altimeter, statoscope and thermometer were taped to the rigging at a convenient height for use in flight, the trail-rope coiled, hitched, stopped and stowed, the grapnel put on board, and, finally, an appropriate number of bags of sand for disposable ballast was hitched around the periphery of the basket. When inflation was completed, the basket was trundled over, and one by one the lift lines were released from their sandbags and toggled onto the suspension ring. An anchor rope was also attached to the ring and run out to windward. The white line controlling the gas valve and the red ripcord falling out of the neck of the balloon were secured inboard.

After lunch Warrant Officer King took them to another balloon basket with the envelope, net and gear stowed in it, and detailed the class to inflate and rig it by themselves while he watched sardonically. Denied his deft skills, even in calm conditions the scope for chaos was enormous; now the afternoon breeze added an element of daemonic life to the balloon as the gas surged into the envelope. There was much laughter and sailorly language. Seabrook, who had served his time in sail, and Ernest, who had quickly developed an aptitude for juggling with lift and weight calculations, assumed between them the leadership of the group: order was imposed on the freakish monster, but they were weary and thirsty men who saw their own balloon swaying and bobbing in the wind that evening as it leaned on its anchor rope, basket correctly rigged and attached ready for flight.

The course laid down for Officers and Ratings qualifying as airship pilots consisted of four balloon ascents as passenger, in the last of which the pupil took charge under supervision; one 'passing out' ascent when the pupil took charge under observation; one solo run of at least an hour's duration; and one night ascent in which two hours had to be spent airborne between the hours of sunset and sunrise. A few days after the inflation and rigging exercise, Ernest made his first free-balloon ascent. He quickly realised that every balloon ascent is a unique adventure in which the unpredictability of things stimulates a mixture of apprehension and ecstasy in the aeronaut. Immersed in a largely invisible medium the ceaseless motion of which cannot be commanded, he can only react, and the only control he has is over the rate of ascent or descent, and that only within narrow limits set by his initial stock of gas and disposable ballast. Roughly, each 1,000 cu ft of gas provided 70 lb of surplus buoyancy, varying with changes of temperature and pressure.

When all was ready for the ascent, pilot and passengers manned the balloon. The neck was untied; the valve cord and ripping cord then dropped clear through into the basket. The pilot tested the operation of the valve, ensured that the valve cord and ripcord were not entangled, stowed the end of the valve cord in a white bag attached to the hoop and then stowed the ripcord in a red bag. Next, the balloon was 'ballasted up' – that is, sufficient ballast bags were removed so that she just lifted – where there was plenty of space to get away it was usual to lift off with a surplus of lift just enough to provide buoyant equilibrium at 500 ft, but in a constrained area, or if there was a lot of wind, they would ballast up to some 30 or 40 lb lighter than this. The amount of ballast remaining was then assessed and recorded, and two or three bags were opened ready for use to increase the rate of climb should there be any risk of hitting obstructions.

Once free in the air, the balloon rose to equilibrium height, the gas expanding as pressure dropped and blowing out at the neck until an amount had been lost equalling the surplus lift with which the ascent started; and there it would remain floating until something happened to disturb the equilibrium. If she leaked, or the valve was opened, she would descend. If the sun warmed the gas above ambient air temperature, she would rise; or if the gas cooled in the shadow of a cloud, or the balloon ran into denser air, she would sink. Moisture accumulating on the envelope would also make her sink. If for any reason the balloon began to sink after reaching equilibrium height, she would continue to fall to earth unless ballast was discharged; in which case, once the fall was checked, she would take up a new point of equilibrium above the previous one. A reserve, known as 'landing ballast', was calculated on the basis of the maximum height reached, the all-up weight of the balloon and a weather factor, and was kept for control of the final descent and alighting. Otherwise, after leaving the ground the aim was to allow the balloon to rise gently throughout the duration of its flight by the gradual disposal of ballast until only the landing ballast was left, when she was allowed to fall gently, checking any high rate of descent by use of the landing ballast.

Flying low down, particularly in preparation for alighting, the trail rope was lowered so that it dragged along the ground providing a more or less automatic height control, for if the balloon rose it had to lift a greater weight of the rope, or if it fell the ground bore a greater proportion. The working of the ballast during final descent required nice judgement. It was too easy to build up a high rate of descent that could only be checked by throwing out a large quantity of ballast which, once the downward momentum had decayed, might be enough to make her buoyant again. Ideally the ballast was thrown out by handfulls as she fell, with such judgement that the small loss of weight caused by the trail rope coming into first contact with the ground was enough to check the descent.

In the early days, when a suitable landing place (preferably in the lee of a wood) presented itself, the anchor rope was dropped and the anchor let go so that, when it held, the balloon came down clear of obstructions. The valve was momentarily released to compensate for the loss of the anchor's weight; then as soon as it was clear that the anchor was holding, the balloon was rapidly valved down to the ground – or, if the wind was strong, the ripcord was pulled. After landing and deflation, the balloon was methodically packed up into its basket for manhandling onto a cart for its journey to the nearest railway station, whence it travelled by train at the rate of 2d per ton mile. With experience, if he had inherited the instinct for it, the aeronaut could develop a cunning ability to sense what the wind was doing or likely to do to his path over the ground to such an extent that he was more likely to cause his landing to take place in a country gentleman's estate than in an urban sewage farm; and such a one was Lieut Cdr C.F.

Pollock, the patient and kindly instructor under whose aegis Ernest next came at Hurlingham. Pollock held Aeronaut's Certificate No 1; between 1899 and 1910 he crossed the English Channel by balloon eleven times; he was a man very much in the sporting ballooning tradition. In the next few weeks Ernest, although wartime frugality denied him the hampers of champagne and cold chicken as he floated over the springtime countryside, readily learned the art of concluding his flight with afternoon tea in the drawing room of a good country house never too far from a railway station. It was an introduction to a life style new to a man who had spent most of his life at sea, and he found it congenial.

Most of the Hurlingham balloons were about 60,000 cu ft capacity and bore the names *Swallow*, *Plover*, *Salmon*, *Shrimp* and *Seahorse*. After his four flights under Pollock's instruction, Ernest went off solo and finally completed his training with an uneventful night flight. Altogether the free-ballooning phase of his training occupied about twenty hours in the air. The vagaries of wind and weather, however, were such that this agreeable sport was spread over five or six weeks, so that it was not until early July that he received orders to proceed to Naval Airship Station Llangefni in Anglesey to assume the duties of First Lieutenant and for airship flying training.

CHAPTER TWO

SUBMARINE SCOUTS

As Ernest had learned at Hurlingham, the inability of a free-ballooning aeronaut to influence navigation by any other way than waiting for the wind to seem to hold promise of blowing in the right direction, becomes increasingly frustrating for a man with a goal. As far back as 1784 Jean-Baptiste Meusnier, a Lieutenant in the French Corps of Engineers, had come to the same conclusion and established for all time not only the proper shape for a dirigible balloon, but also the solution to the problem of maintaining that shape despite gas losses. He placed within the gas-filled envelope a small air ballonet which was kept supplied with air from a pump in the car. This principle was later applied to all non-rigid and semi-rigid airships. He could not, however, solve the problem of propulsion, and it was not until Daimler produced his petrol-driven internal combustion engine in the 1880s, light, powerful and reliable, that the frustrated aeronauts' prayers were answered. Nevertheless its application to dirigibles was not made successfully until the late 1890s. The non-rigid dirigible can be said to have arrived with the remarkable flights made by Alberto Santos Dumont between 1898 and 1901, whilst the rigid airship burst upon an astonished world as a reality in Count Zeppelin's third remarkable creation in 1906 (the year when Ernest began his apprenticeship at sea).

By comparison with what went on in France, Germany and even Italy, British efforts in the lighter-than-air field were laggardly and, for the most part, ineffectual. Stanley Spencer in 1902 became the first Englishman to construct and fly a dirigible; it carried only one man and its 3.5 HP engine was inadequate. Between 1903 and 1905 Dr F.A. Barton, the father of one of the ballooning instructors at Hurlingham, built a 230,000 cu ft non-rigid, but it came to grief on its maiden flight through being underpowered. E.T. Willows, whose firm had been making balloon envelopes for many years, built his first of a successful line of dirigibles in 1904; his fourth became the prototype of the Submarine Scout which Ernest was going to learn to fly at Anglesey. The backbone of British operating experience was built up by the Army in 1910 and 1911 with its small non-rigids *Beta* and *Gamma*, designed and built by the Balloon Factory at Farnborough, and subsequently with *Delta*. The driving force in developing both piloting techniques and practical applications at this time was Major E.M. Maitland, a brilliant, brave and gallant Officer whose personal influence on the Officers and men of the Airship Service became legendary even in his lifetime.

The Admiralty, bemused by the Zeppelin story in Germany, embarked on the fiasco of the rigid airship *Mayfly* which never did, and fell far behind in operating experience until Captain Murray Sueter RN revived the Naval Airship Section in 1912 (it had been disbanded after the destruction of *HM Airship No 1* in 1911). He attached it to the Royal Flying Corps to enable the Naval personnel to gain experience in flying *Beta*, *Gamma* and *Delta*. His persistence resulted in 1913 in the ordering of a German Parseval non-rigid and a well-tried French Astra-Torres non-rigid, both of over 300,000 cu ft capacity; the latter became the progenitor of the Navy's later *Coastal* and *North Sea* ships. Murray Sueter also played a large part in causing the formation of the Royal Naval Air Service in 1914.

In February 1915 the Board of Admiralty accepted the recommendation of the First Sea Lord, Admiral of the Fleet Lord Fisher, for the construction of a sizeable flotilla of inexpensive little airships for coastal patrol work. On 28th February Fisher sent for Commander Masterman, who had been in charge of the *Mayfly* project, and Lieut Commander Neville Usborne, the brilliant experimental non-rigid pilot, and told them he wanted at once some small, fast little airships for anti-submarine patrols. Usborne went straight down to the Royal Aircraft Factory at Farnborough where he talked over the requirement with Flight Commander T.R. Cave-Brown-Cave and Mr F.M. Green. Between them, they conceived the design of the SS class. In six weeks, the *Willows No 4* (*Naval Airship No 2*) envelope, a *BE2c* fuselage and a Renault engine were put together as *SS1*, the prototype of a class of ships of which about 150 were subsequently built, including advanced variants known as *SS Zero*, *SS Twin* and *SS Pusher*. The prototype modified *Willows* entered service in March 1915 designated *SS1*, the letters standing for 'Submarine Scout', but a couple of months later she was destroyed by fire in a night landing incident in the hands of Flight Sub-Lieut Ralph Booth near Folkestone. By the time Johnston joined *HMS Spanker*, airship stations for the *Submarine Scouts* had been set up at Capel, near Folkestone, Polegate and Marquise near Calais, while others were being prepared at Luce Bay near Stranraer and in Anglesey, and by the end of

September the *SS* airships were operating at all of them. The successful evolution of the *Coastal* type of non-rigid from the *Astra-Torres* led to the planning of further airship stations at Pembroke, Pulham, Howden, Long-side, Mullion and East Fortune to become active during 1916. By the time Ernest Johnston reported to the Naval Airship Station at Llangefni, there-fore, although the history of the practical dirigible had spanned barely fifteen years, the Admiralty's airship programme was in a state of very exciting growth and experimentation.

His Commanding Officer at Llangefni was Flight Commander George Herbert Scott. 'Scottie', educated at the Royal Naval Engineering College, Keyham, had forsaken the real Navy for general engineering as a civilian but had been attracted into joining the RNAS shortly after its formation in 1914. His mental grasp of the arcane science of lighter-than-air flight brought him to the forefront of the band of airship pioneers at Kingsnorth, and his natural aptitude for piloting airships led early in 1915 to his appointment as captain of the largest and most sophisticated of them, the 290,000 cu ft Parseval, *HMA No 4*, at Barrow-in-Furness until he moved down to take charge of the new station at Anglesey in September. He was a man of singular charm with a brilliant technical mind who was to achieve interna-tional distinction as an airship commander. He and Ernest were both immensely cheerful and enthusiastic, both were sound, practical men of keen, innovative intelligence. The widely popular Scottie combined an air of modesty with a tendency to laziness which are so often allied with pioneering genius; Ernest was a bluff, commanding seaman who demanded of himself and others instant compliance and the highest standards of achievement. As Commanding Officer and First Lieutenant they made an excellent team: this was to result later in a close linking of their careers. Early in 1917, however, Scottie moved back to Barrow to become Captain of *No 9*, the first British rigid airship to fly, when she was handed over to the RNAS by her makers, Vickers, after acceptance trials in April.

Having arrived at Llangefni and put up at the Bull Hotel where some of the flying officers were messed, Ernest was taken by Scottie to the air station, a cluster of creosoted weatherboard huts nestling in the lee of a large airship shed on the edge of a wide, desolate field. In the small wardroom he was introduced to several of the Officers – Lieutenant Charlie Swayne, the First Lieutenant whom he was about to succeed, and Flight Sub-Lieutenants Plowden, Underhill, Scroggs and Best, the station's pilots, among them. "I'll put you in Chichele Plowden's hands," Scottie said. "He'll show you the ropes on the air side, and you will find him a very good instructor." After lunch Plowden and Johnston walked over to the airship shed where the four SS ships were housed – SS18, SS22, SS24 and SS25. "SS24 and 25 are fully operational at present," Plowden explained, "but as you see, SS22 has had her car unrigged from the envelope so that she can be deflated for a major overhaul of her fabric and rigging. That heap of fabric under the net alongside her is my ship, SS18; she's had an overhaul and is waiting to be inflated."

These beautifully streamlined little ships had a total capacity of 70,000 cu ft, scarcely more than some of the larger balloons at Hurlingham. The car slung on wire bridles underneath, derived from the stripped fuselage of a BE2c aeroplane, accommodated a pilot, observer and wireless operator. The streamlined shape of the envelope was maintained by keeping the gas at a pressure above that of the ambient air equivalent to some 25-30mm of water; this was achieved by controlling the flow of part of the propeller slipstream into two internal ballonets each having a maximum capacity of 6,000 cu ft. The single Renault 8-cylinder Vee engine driving a four-bladed airscrew developing up to 75 HP could keep the ship flying at a speed of 40 mph for sixteen hours. These indeed, in their simplicity, were patently dirigible balloons.

Ernest's first question was, "When can I get up into the air?". Plowden explained that his ship would very likely not be ready for a week, but Ernest would have plenty on his hands helping with inflation and rigging. The two serviceable ships were fully committed to a hectic operational commitment and it was unlikely that the CO would spare them for training,

In fact, Ernest made his first flight on 13th July. Immediately after lunch he took an opportunity to fly in SS18 for half an hour with Underhill in the vicinity of the aerodrome. As they landed, SS25 was being ballasted up for flight. Scroggs, the pilot (later First Officer of R32) called to him that he was just going off to do a couple of hours patrolling off Holyhead and invited him to occupy the observer's seat behind the pilot. Two days later he flew as navigator to Best in SS18 on a patrol of the Holyhead-Dublin mail route; they were airborne at 10 am and took three and a half hours to reach Dublin, flying all the way at 300 ft; the flight lasted seven hours. On 18th July he again acted as navigator, this time for Plowden in SS18, on an eight hour patrol of Liverpool Bay between the Skerries and Barrow.

The navigation of an airship over the sea was markedly different, Ernest discovered, from the navigation of a surface vessel out of sight of land, though the principles were the same. In the air the ratio of the ship's speed to that of the wind was far lower than that of a surface vessel's to the current, with the result that the drift (the aeronautical equivalent of leeway) was usually very large by comparison: for example, the drift of an airship cruising at 30 knots in a beam wind of 15 knots was about 26 degrees. The airship's heading was indicated by the compass, in this case a Creagh-Osborne liquid filled type usually installed either at eye level in front of the pilot, or sometimes down between his knees; and its speed through the air by the airspeed indicator on the pilot's dashboard. The speed and direction of the wind had to be applied to the heading and airspeed to establish the groundspeed and the course made good over the ground, as the basis for plotting the dead reckoning position. There were at that period only the most primitive means of measuring the drift due to the wind, so everything depended on the navigator's ability to gauge the wind by eye. The wind blowing over the sea leaves characteristic markings on the surface, by means of which it is possible to do this very accurately indeed with experience.

On the afternoon of 19th July, under the guidance of Plowden, Ernest sat in the front seat of SS18 and took the controls for the first time, and spent half an hour handling the ship in the air. The open cockpit of the SS contained a large wheel mounted to the right of the pilot, by means of which the elevators were controlled, and a foot-operated rudder bar for steering. On the dashboard in front of him were a rev-counter, a gas pressure gauge, an aneroid altimeter, an airspeed indicator and a statoscope that indicates whether the ship was rising or falling. In the rigging above the car there were a number of toggled control lines by which the pilot could operate the gas valve, air valves, ripping panel and crab-pot valves. There were also various cocks and taps for the fuel and oil systems as well as a hand pump for each. Ernest took his first lesson in basic piloting – maintaining height by use of the elevator wheel, steering, adjusting engine speed and controlling gas pressure and equilibrium. Plowden demonstrated how, unlike a free-balloon, a dirigible could utilise positive or negative dynamic lift to compensate for minor changes of static lift by pitching the nose upwards or downwards relative to the line of flight. For small amounts of pitch the elevators were used; but if a large or sustained amount of pitch was required, it was better to trim the ship by varying the proportion of air in the fore and aft ballonets.

Later, in the calm of the afternoon, Ernest made three short circuits and landings, under Plowden's guidance from the observer's seat. Afterwards in the dusk Plowden said, "Righto, I think we'll arrange to send you solo as soon as possible, before you forget how to do it." By this time, Ernest had spent altogether less than an hour at the controls.

The next evening when the first ship, SS25, came back from patrol, he was waiting eagerly to fly her. It was flat calm. After she was refuelled, he climbed into the pilot's cockpit and carefully and methodically ballasted her up a little light, and by blowing air into the aft ballonet while releasing it from the fore one, trimmed her slightly down by the stern. Then, precisely at 8.15 pm, he raised both arms above his head and ordered "let go" to the ground handling crew. The ship rose gently a few feet into the air. As Ernest opened the throttle and wound back on the elevator control wheel the ship, picking up speed, pitched up and climbed steeply to 300 ft, her equilibrium height, where he levelled her on elevator, adjusted the static trim and brought her round in a wide circle to port onto a heading for the Skerries, where he spent a happy hour manoeuvring and trying out the effect of the various controls. Then he headed back to the aerodrome. The handling party in sight, he gradually took all way off the ship and brought her down to a couple of hundred feet, trimming her and ballasting her up carefully. When he was satisfied that she was perfectly buoyant with no way on, he dropped the trail rope and headed slowly towards the handling party with just sufficient negative dynamic lift to bring her down to their hands.

For his next flight, Ernest was despatched as captain of SS25 on a four hour war patrol in Liverpool Bay with Air Mechanic Curtis as his wireless operator. This time, in addition to flying the ship, he was responsible for navigating her, and his hands were full. His training continued with a five-hour patrol with Plowden in SS18 and some short gunnery and bomb-dropping flights interspersed with short solo patrols. On 14th September Flight Commander Hartford accompanied him on his first night flying sortie which consisted of half an hour's circuits and landings. This was his final training trip; with a total of fifty-six hours of airship flying he was certified as a qualified practical airship pilot and recommended for gradu-ation. For this, he returned to Wormwood Scrubs to sit his final examina-tions on 3rd October; his certificate of graduation on this day was signed by Major Waterlow, the Wing Commander.

Having put his pilot's brevet on his left sleeve, Ernest found that the tempo of his flying slowed down, particularly because the impending relief of his C.O. Scottie by Squadron Commander Corbett Wilson threw a heavier load of administration onto the First Lieutenant. Although he flew one six-hour night patrol between Holyhead and Dublin and one short night patrol between the Skerries and Barrow in the third week of October, he was forced to restrain his flying in the main to the shorter patrols, to test flights and to the occasional flight giving instruction to new pilots.

In December he was able to take a spell of leave to marry his childhood's sweetheart Janita Daisy Wood at Rugby. Now twenty-three, Daisy was a strikingly beautiful young woman, generous, light-hearted, mercurial and gregarious with a happy-go-lucky manner that nevertheless concealed a large measure of courage, common sense and shrewd under-standing of humankind. She made a gay, stylish and warmly devoted consort to her handsome, dashing new husband. When they returned to Llangefni she was an immediate success with Ernest's fellow Officers and their ladies. From that time forward she filled with zest her role as wife and, later, mother, forswearing for good the theatre to which she had been brought up; but she continued to sing occasionally as an amateur, appear-ing for the last time less than a year before her death in a concert at her son's school, when she and one of the most popular of the Masters, singing Noel Coward songs in a sophisticated duet at the Grand Piano, brought the house down.

Ernest, back at Llangefni in January 1917, found himself heavily engaged in the duties of First Lieutenant on the ground. During February *SS18* was replaced by *SS33* equipped with a Maurice Farman car, and he took the opportunity to carry out its initial flight post acceptance. A couple of weeks later he gave flying instruction on *SS33* to Flight Sub-Lieutenants T.B. Williams and George Nicholls – the latter returned the compliment after the war by becoming the family's Solicitor in his office at 1 Lincoln's Inn Fields. At the end of March Ernest was told that he had been selected to fly *Coastal* ships at East Fortune, and on 7th April he made his last flight at Anglesey with Corbett Wilson in *SS33*. In the ten months which he had served, he had flown just a few minutes less than 175 hours.

Shortly after the end of the war the 'Anglesey Old Boys' Association' was formed by the surviving Officers, Petty Officers and Ratings who had served there. They elected Ernest as their first President, and when he resigned on going back to sea they elected Scottie. After the loss of *R101* when both the original Presidents were killed, Captain George Nicholls was appointed President, a position which he held until 1968, when Captain T.B. Williams was elected as his successor.

CHAPTER THREE

COASTALS

Ernest was delighted with his posting from Anglesey to RNAS East Fortune for full flying duties. He arrived there in the middle of April 1917 to discover a larger, more active and more exciting place than Anglesey had been. His Commanding Officer was Wing Captain Roland Hunt. There were two standard sheds to accommodate the non-rigids and a vast shed under construction, scheduled to accommodate two rigids of the 23X Class then being built by Vickers. East Fortune was the last station to be commissioned in 1916; its function was to provide not only anti-submarine patrols but also air cover for the Grand Fleet. For this it was initially equipped with the *Coastal* non-rigid type developed from the *Astra-Torres, HMA No3*, under the direction of Cave-Brown-Cave, who had become responsible for design, construction and testing of non-rigids at Kingsnorth. The first one flew at Kingsnorth in May 1915. Altogether thirty-two were built.

The essential feature of the *Astra-Torres* envelope and its derivatives the *Coastals*, the *Coastal Stars* and the *North Seas*, was the tri-lobe cross-section which permitted the greater part of the rigging for suspending the loads to be within the envelope, thus enabling the car to be slung close up and reducing the drag. The gas capacity was 170,000 cu ft, and the envelope contained four ballonets of air for controlling the gas superpressure. In shape the *Coastal* envelope looked like a bunch of bananas; the cross-section was the same for most of its length with a blunt taper at each end.

The class was designed to meet the demand for more speed, lift, endurance and reliability than the *SS* was capable of. The car was an adaptation of two Avro seaplane fuselages placed back to back, with an engine and its associated fuel and oil tanks at each end. In between them were the four cockpits. Foremost was the coxswain's cockpit, containing the rudder control wheel and a duplicate elevator control wheel. Behind the cox'n was the pilot's cockpit containing the primary elevator control wheel and all the other controls and instruments. Aft again was the W/T Opera-tor's station. From it there was a wire ladder up to the tube in the hull which gave access to the Lewis-gun position on top of the envelope. A second Lewis gun was carried on one of two optional mounting posts on the footrails along the sides of the car. The generator for the wireless was operated by an auxiliary engine which could also be used to run an auxiliary blower to maintain ballonet pressure in the event of loss of main engine power. The wireless operator had a continuous-wave valve transmitter with a range of just over 200 miles, a receiver, an auxiliary transmitter with a range of seventy miles, and an Aldis signalling lamp. Right aft was the engineer's cockpit. All the engine controls and switches, however, were in the pilot's cockpit. In later ships a fifth seat was provided for an Observer who could assist the Commanding Officer with the navigation. Later it became standard practice for this type of ship to carry a second officer trained as a pilot, thus relieving the captain of the ship from the actual duties of piloting.

The original power units were two 150 HP Sunbeams fitted fore and aft in the car, operating through a two-to-one reduction gear which was a constant source of trouble. In very cold weather the carburettor throttles of the aft engine occasionally jammed, which could be an embarrassment when the pilot required to slow down the engine for landing. The propel-lers, made of mahogany, were four-bladed. In 1917 a 220HP Renault superseded the aft Sunbeam and some ships then had a 100HP Berliet forward. The Renault/Berliet installation increased the capabilities of this ship enormously: her duration rose from a little more than that of the SS to a normal patrol of twelve to fourteen hours and permitted of the ship flying and being handled on the ground in much more adverse weather condi-tions.

At first Ernest was teamed up with Flight Lieutenant Sugden in C15, and from the first flight onwards took his regular share of the controls. He immediately found her to be much more difficult to steer than the handy little SS, and much less responsive on the elevator controls. Unlike the SS, the operation of the elevator and the rudder controls was divided out between the pilot and a separate coxswain, and Ernest discovered that it needed a lot of practice to get the engine speed right so that the coxswain in the front cockpit could steer and the handling party get control of the ship cleanly while landing.

On ascending from the ground it was most important to have only a little up helm on the elevators and not to speed the engines up too much until a height of at least 40-50 ft was reached, as the elevators acted as a large brake and tended to drive the rudder plane into the ground, and it was desirable to avoid over-running the car party and hitting them with the after propeller. It was customary to start with the pressure at 15mm; the climb to 1,000 ft brought it to 35mm, and this was used as a yardstick when about to land. The best pressure in flight was 25mm, though it was found desirable always to raise the pressure to 30mm when making a large alteration of course, to reduce as much as possible the strain brought upon the internal rigging curtains.

As East Fortune lay a few miles from the sea, some pilots preferred to rise to only 200 or 300 ft, so as to valve as little gas as possible before reaching the coast, and then to lower the WT aerial. Others preferred to rise at once to patrol height, and to fly to the sea at this height in order to verify the force and direction of the wind before reaching the sea. In the patrol area the forward engine was shut down if not needed, to reduce the discomfort of the slipstream to the crew so as to allow a better lookout to be kept.

In good weather, airships of the *Coastal* type took very little handling, and could fly for long periods without attention. In bad and bumpy weather considerable skill was required to keep them on the required course, and it was essential, in order to attain this object, to meet the pitching motion in good time with opposite helm. As she became light, so she became bow heavy, and vice versa, and to make piloting easier it was essential to keep the ship properly trimmed by means of the ballonets. When diving steeply the elevator controls tautened, and at times it was necessary to ease the engines in order to bring the ship out of the dive quickly. The ship then lost way and started to become level of her own accord. Although the *Coastals* turned rather slowly, this defect could be considerably ameliorated by slowing down the engines shortly after the turn had begun. If the ship lost way before the turn was finished, the engines were speeded up again. It was inadvisable to allow the ship to become very light (say 500 lb) as this involved either flying very fast to keep fairly level or running slow with the bows well down, in which case the engines were likely to oil up. The average full speed endurance of a *Coastal* was about 9.5 hours. It was customary to let the middle tank run down to about 30-40 gallons and then to refill as necessary from the top tanks, so as to keep tally on exactly how much fuel was burnt and how much remained.

Before landing, it was necessary to 'ballast up' the ship, which was generally better done over the sea at the same height, or as nearly so, as the landing ground was above sea level, because over the sea fewer 'bumps' were likely to be experienced. Sometimes, however, it was necessary to ballast up again closer to the sheds, as the ship's equilibrium, particularly in summer, was affected by the difference of temperature over the land. To 'ballast up', the ship was trimmed horizontal and let to lose nearly all headway, when it could be seen at once, either by the statoscope or combination of the manometer and aneroid, whether the ship was light, in equilibrium, or heavy. If very light, air was blown into the forward ballonet so as to blow out gas as well as make the ship a little nose heavy; and if heavy, then whatever could be dispensed with was let go to maintain sufficient height.

Over the landing ground the landing pennant was hoisted and the ship brought down to about 50 ft off the ground, and the trail rope dropped as near the landing party as possible. The forward engine was stopped whenever practicable before dropping the trail rope. Landing could be tricky, especially on a bumpy day. When the air was turbulent, pilots considered it essential to land high; there was then a risk that the ship would fall off the wind before she could be hauled down by the trail rope, not infrequently taking charges, with consequential damage to the landing skids. Later, long foreguys were fitted to enable ships to land without the use of the trail rope, so that the landing party could take immediate control of the ship in gusty conditions. On early ships, air to the ballonets was taken by a scoop from the forward propeller, and this also created landing problems. Either a high pressure had to be obtained before landing on the after engine, which was impracticable in a strong wind, or the foremost engine had to be kept going, with the high risk of the propeller fouling the mooring gear and being broken. Moreover the forward scoop obscured the view of the cox'n. Later Coastals were modified to take the air into the ballonets from the after engine. As a pilot became more experienced, he found it decidedly advantageous to land with only the forward guys, as the ship was at once got under control by the landing party, but in bad weather it was necessary to have a large car party too.

On 9th and 10th July Ernest acted as second pilot to Flight Lieutenant W. Warneford in C25 on a flight that lasted 24 hours and 10 minutes which at that time created a record endurance for the type. They left the ground at 9.20 pm and the two pilots worked three-hour watches throughout. Warneford's ship C25 was one of the later models with a specially constructed car, larger in size, heavier in design and incorporating improved protection for the pilot. On this patrol they were covering the movement of elements of the Grand Fleet – Warneford was the leading light in developing techniques for operating airships with the Fleet at sea. He and the Johnstons became close friends while they were at East Fortune.

Ernest made his first solo on type on 12th July, in C15. He flew in her again for the last time on the 14th, the day before she was wrecked in an experimental attempt to refuel from *HMS Phaeton* during exercises with the Fleet.

In August he was appointed Captain of *C20*. Straight away he found the routine of patrols from East Fortune far more taxing than those from Anglesey. Not only was the duration of each patrol twice as long, but weather and sea conditions were markedly worse. The complexity of airship operations, particularly in cooperation with units of the Fleet, had made accurate navigation even more essential, and he discovered that the duties of the captain were enlarged by the continuous attention necessary to be paid to surface craft. He required a thorough knowledge of the behaviour, duties, capabilities, disposition and appearance of the surface craft patrols in his area, and he had to have a full grasp of what other craft in the vicinity were doing. The success of Fleet-airship cooperation lay on his decisions about the disposal of his ship; he had to be adept at using International and Naval codes for composing the main wireless communications and it was vital to organise his crew to allow instant communication by semaphore or flash lamp. And he was still responsible for the flying of the airship throughout.

On 5th September Ernest carried out his first Fleet escort sortie, carrying as his second pilot Flight Lieutenant H.C. Irwin, later to be captain of *R33* and *R101*. Irwin, a recent arrival, already had a fine reputation as a pilot; he had been flying *Submarine Scouts* of the Airship Expeditionary Force in the Eastern Mediterranean, initially in support of the Dardanelles campaign. The intention was to undertake a maximum endurance flight, but they were recalled to base because of bad weather, and Ernest made his first night landing of a *Coastal* after being airborne for only eleven hours.

On the afternoon of 16th September, he set off in *C20* for his second Fleet escort, this time without a second pilot. The day was heavily overcast with very low clouds and frequent showers. Owing to the low purity of her gas, the ship left the ground heavy and had to use high engine power to keep aloft, with the result that after some four hours of flight Ernest decided that it would be prudent to return to base to refuel. The Senior Naval Officer afloat having given permission, Ernest set course for May Island at 7.15 pm: with the wind at 12 mph from the southwest; he expected to pick up the land at 9.30 pm.

The weather now became very squally with frequent extremely heavy showers of rain. At times the ship, flying at 1,500 ft, made practically no headway. At 10.30 pm Ernest glimpsed a light briefly through the mist, which he took to be May Island light. At about 11.45 pm he decided to take

C20 down slowly to see whether she was over land, until at an indicated 500 ft he saw through the mist the dim outline of the coast, and identified it as being probably inside the Firth of Tay.

Intending to follow the coast, he ordered the cox'n to turn to port, but immediately they lost sight of the land as the airship went into dense white cloud. She hit the water at 11.50. The aneroid was then reading 400 ft. The error was caused by the considerable drop of barometric pressure which had taken place since the ship left East Fortune. (As a result of this incident airships were warned by wireless of any marked change in the barometer so that they could adjust their aneroid accordingly.)

When the ship hit the water, her for'ard propeller was broken and the after engine was brought to a standstill. Ernest released the remaining water ballast and the ship lifted off the sea. The after engine was started up at 800 revs, but made such an unusual sound that the engineer concluded that the crankshaft must be bent. As the ship drifted downwind, Ernest ordered a wireless distress call to be made. Verey lights were fired. He decided to try to land east of Arbroath, but the rudder control became jammed in the wind and, owing to the blackness of the night, he gave it up as being too dangerous. At 12.30 am (on the 17th) the after engine seized up and stopped. As the aircraft was drifting over the sea, Ernest ordered the drogue to be bent onto the trail rope and cast overboard. The towing bridle fouled a skid, however, so the ship did not ride very satisfactorily. The gas pressure rapidly subsided, and the auxiliary blower was kept running in order to keep the envelope inflated.

At 1 am the ship was pitched up in a squall and the drogue was lifted out of the water. In the darkness, however, Ernest thought that the drogue had been carried away and lost. Free-ballooning in the wind, *C20* then rose to 2,000 ft. As soon as the blower was stopped, the pressure subsided again. The ship was now pitched 20 degrees down by the stern. As the after ballonet was full, Ernest deduced that the forward ballonet was punctured. By continued blowing, the pressure of the envelope was maintained at 5mm. Ernest ordered all available weights to be disposed forward, the crew sitting on the forward engine and the petrol in the after tank being forced forward by pressure; also the water from the after tank was used as ballast. The ship was eventually trimmed 12 degrees by the stern. This was flying in the dark with a vengeance!

When daylight was just breaking at about 4.30 am, it was found that the drogue was still dangling on the trail rope. Ernest immediately brought the ship down until the drogue was in the water, and, the bridle having cleared itself, the ship rode very well in the 15 to 20 mph southwesterly wind. The rudder controls were cleared and the water carried from the forward radiator to the after one. The engine was again started up at just over 800 revs, which was sufficient to give her help with the helm when necessary. Its main purpose was to keep the pressure up, as the auxiliary blower was hot after working all night. The puncturing of the forward ballonet was confirmed, but now, riding to the drogue, it was easy to keep the ship on a level trim with the elevators.

At 4.45 am a searchlight was sighted and was answered with the Aldis lamp. It proved to be *HMS Ulysses*, who intercepted *C20* at 6.15 am about 70 miles east of Aberdeen, and picked up the drogue and took the airship in tow at 12 knots. A course was set for Peterhead, but as it was across wind, the airship yawed considerably, so much so that the tow parted. Ernest requested a tow right up to the wind. The Captain of *Ulysses* agreed, and when the tow was picked up again the course was made for Aberdeen at 8 knots. At 8am the after engine stopped and all efforts to restart it were unsuccessful.

C20 was towed into Aberdeen Harbour at 12.50 pm and at 2.15 pm the tow rope was transferred from *Ulysses* to two paddle boats which towed her out of the harbour again to Nigg Bay, where a landing party of RNAS men from Longside, assisted by troops from Balnagask camp, were in attendance. The end of the trail rope was passed ashore by a motor boat and, just as she was being hauled down, the long-suffering auxiliary blower seized up. Then, almost in the hands of the landing party, the after ballonet was punctured on a telegraph pole. By 3.15 pm, however, the ship was landed, and shortly after was packed up for return by rail to East Fortune.

On a black night over a black sea, with the airship pitching at all sorts of angles, the barometer in error, and the drogue dangling at the end of the trail rope, it was decidedly one of the more exciting sagas of the airship service, and there can be no doubt that Ernest and his crew displayed commendable courage and resourcefulness in appalling circumstances. His own logbook entry for this twenty-four hour marathon was laconic: "Ship totally disabled at midnight 16th-17th. Towed to Aberdeen and deflated on the beach."

It was during this month that East Fortune received *NS3*, the first of the scheduled six of the latest mark of non-rigid airship, the *North Sea* class, 360,000 cu ft capacity, the apotheosis of the non-rigid. They were conceived as being capable of carrying out flights of very long duration; their primary role was to be daylight screening of the Fleet at sea. The three at East Fortune and the remaining six built in 1917 proved disappointing because of persistent engine trouble which caused the loss of several of the class and resulted in a re-engining programme; this delayed completion of the plans to build a dozen of them until well on in 1918.

During October 1917 East Fortune also received its first rigid airship, R24, under the command of Squadron Commander Spurling. Her First Officer was Flight Lieutenant R.S. Booth, later to become captain of R33 and R100. He and Ernest became firm friends. R24 was the second of four ships of an improved design based on No 9; their prime task was to have been long range Fleet escort at sea. The crews, trained in No 9 by Scottie at Howden, were an elite with high expectations of their ships; but the first, R23, proved disappointingly heavy in her trial flights at Pulham under the command of Sqn Cdr Little. R24 at East Fortune and R25 at Pulham in October confirmed the serious shortfall in performance, as a result of which a substantial programme of modification was initiated on the uncompleted R26. The role of R23, R24 and R25 was consequently restricted merely to training, experiment, convoy escort and anti-submarine patrols. R25 in particular was an unsatisfactory ship as she suffered from gasbag surging which made her seriously unstable.

Although the experience of July and September Fleet exercises had indicated that the *Coastals* operating from East Fortune and Longside had severe limitations for this sort of work, the failure of the *North Sea* class and the rigids to live up to expectations meant that the *Coastals* would have to continue to escort the Fleet until well into 1918 despite insufficient radius of action, difficult control characteristics when under tow for refuelling at sea, and lack of strength to withstand the sort of weather conditions which the Fleet expected to encounter in the North Sea during much of the year.

After her forced deflation at Aberdeen it was nearly three months before C20 was ready to fly again. During the first week of November, however, in the absence of C24's regular captain, Flight Lieutenant Pritchard (who was later to have the unique distinction of being the first man ever to arrive in North America by parachute), Ernest took her over for four long patrols, including an eleven hour Fleet escort in fog and snow. Then on 9th December, C20 was back in the air again for a test flight under Ernest's control. All was well, so on the next day she proceeded on the 'Middle Patrol' from East Fortune, but landed back after only four hours because of a cracked water jacket. Her next trip was on the 21st, when again she was forced to return early from her escort task because of broken bracing wires.

On the 22nd C20 took to the air at 8 am to escort the Grand Fleet. At 4 pm on her way back to East Fortune both engines stopped because of fuel starvation. The ship free-ballooned to the southeast on a thirty knot gale and was lucky in the last remaining daylight to pass a tow rope to a destroyer. Shortly after 6pm, however, the rope parted. In the darkness, Ernest wrote a message on a Government Pigeon Service flimsy, attached it to a pigeon, and let her go. The message read: "From *C20* 22 December 1917, 6.30pm. Tow rope broken adrift from destroyer FN. Am free ballooning. Petrol finished in all tanks except from under chassis and pressure does not work. Am endeavouring to get petrol by draining tank from aft skid. Probably manage enough to run engine and keep pressure." The date stamp shows that the message was received in London on 27th December. Fortunately the crew did not have to wait all that long, for visual contact was established with *HMS Oriana*. *C20* was ditched; the crew took to the water and were picked up by *Oriana*'s boats. *Oriana* then destroyed the crippled airship by gunfire.

On the last day of the year Ernest was promoted to Flight Commander, put in charge of all four *Coastals* at East Fortune, and took command himself of Warneford's old ship *C25*, Warneford having been selected to command *NS11*. From her first flight under Ernest's command on 5th January, *C25* was plagued with engine trouble. The winter, moreover, produced particularly bad weather on the northeast coast. The log of successive flights reads:

> 16th January, returned owing to mist and frozen jets
> 17th January, returned owing to fore engine failure
> 31st January, engine trouble– water in petrol
> 1st February, engines stopped. Free balloon landing at Scrynie.
> 1st February, endeavoured to return on one engine. Engine
> stopped. Made free balloon landing at Balmachie. Moored out.

Ernest's actions on this day displayed yet another example of airmanship of the highest quality. *C25* remained safely moored in a field for forty-eight hours whilst the crew worked on the engines. A local army detachment was organised to transport gas cylinders from Longside to replenish the ship and provide additional manpower to help secure the ship as she swung on her tow rope mooring at the bow. Warneford came over by rail from East Fortune to give Ernest what assistance he could. By 3rd January they had managed to achieve full power from the water-cooled after engine, but the forward air-cooled engine remained totally unresponsive. Ernest therefore made the decision to fly back to East Fortune on the one engine before the wind changed for the worse.

On the morning of 7th February, after a satisfactory two-hour flight to test the engines, *C25* set out to search for a reported U- boat; barely was she over the sea before both engines failed. After free-ballooning for a while, one engine was restarted and she managed to return safely to base. The next few trips proceeded satisfactorily apart from the foul weather, but on 5th March she had to return from a Grand Fleet patrol owing to a broken rocker on the fore engine. On the 10th and 11th she made a couple of long engine test flights, on both of which the problem was loss of water from the radiator.

Ernest did his first merchant convoy escort on the 12th - a twelve hour flight covering an outbound Scandinavian convoy. Between the 13th and 17th he carried out four more such escorts averaging twelve hours each, and on the last, although he completed the planned flight, he reported frequent trouble with both engines. During the rest of March and all April he flew a demanding schedule in strong winds and much sea fog; many of these sorties were curtailed by wireless messages recalling the ship to base.

1st April 1918 was the day the Royal Air Force was born out of the RFC by the RNAS; the airships and their personnel, however, remained with the Admiralty until May 1919, so it was a routine day with a nine and a half hour patrol in fog and rain, and Ernest continued to wear his Naval uniform. May also was a heavy month, with another engine failure on the 5th to put up the pulse-rate. On the 18th, Ernest flew a seventeen hour convoy escort during which he sank a mine by gunfire fifteen miles northeast of Farne Island.

On 23rd May he had a break from operational flying in order to familiarise himself with Irwin's new ship, *Coastal Star 1*, having been told that he was going to be appointed Captain of *C Star 7* then under construction at Kingsnorth. As its name implied, the *Coastal Star* was an improved version of the *Coastal*, designed mainly for greater endurance. Early in May Irwin and his crew of four had flown *C Star 1* for over thirty-one hours, on a continuous convoy escort during the daylight hours followed by a special patrol east of May Island during the intervening darkness. When it was recalled to East Fortune owing to deteriorating weather, *C Star 1* still had over 200 gallons of petrol on board on landing.

Experience with the *Coastal* ships and a more complete knowledge of the requirements of anti-submarine patrol and prolonged escort duty made it clear that an airship of considerably improved capabilities was required to carry out these functions adequately; and the indications were that a very much enhanced reliability, speed, endurance and radius of action could be obtained without increasing appreciably the dimensions of that class or departing too far from the special features of the *Coastal* which were already familiar to pilots. The design ultimately developed to fulfill these conditions comprised a streamlined envelope of 210,000 cu ft which secured an increase of about one ton and a quarter in lifting capacity. The *Coastal* type of car, while falling very far short of the ideal, had in practice proved to be not ineffectual. It was decided not to depart from it, but to modify it. The fabric covering of the sides was replaced by three-ply wood, and four circular port-holes glazed with triplex were provided on either side of the car to facilitate observation. In the floor of the pilot's compartment a triplex glass window was introduced and it was intended to place a bomb sight there. Generally the cars were rendered more comfortable for the crew. In all other essentials the car and its equipment – controls, instruments, wireless installation etc – remained identical to the Coastal car. Two Lewis guns were carried in the car, the position on top of the hull having been deleted. The maximum endurance of the *C Stars* at their full speed of 56 mph was about ten hours. The rate of ascent was 1 min 19 sec for a climb of 1,000 ft. A turn of 360 degrees in either direction was accomplished in 1 min 11 sec, diameter of turning circle 680 ft. The NS petrol storage system was fitted; the petrol was carried in tanks slung by bridles from the rigging girdles inside the envelope, giving the advantage, inter alia, of more space in the car and also a gravity fuel feed.

After his final trip in *C25* on 1st June – an uneventful Mid-patrol of nine hours – Ernest travelled down to Kingsnorth to pick up *C Star 7*. Here, for the first time, he met the brilliant young Engineer Officer, Flight Lieutenant Michael Rope, who had established his reputation with the design of the immensely successful *SS Zero* class. He spent two days getting to grips with the technical details of his new ship. He flew as second pilot on her maiden flight on 8th June and then took command of her for a three-hour acceptance trial. The improvement in control effectiveness and general handling qualities resulting from the lower drag of her nicely streamline shape was very noticeable. Minor rectifications were completed in time for him to fly her to Pulham on the 12th, where weather held him up until the 16th. Pulham was the principal experimental station for rigid airships, as Kingsnorth was for non-rigids, and many old friends were there including Scottie who, as the Chief Experimental Officer, was carrying out fundamental work on mooring in the open which he had initiated when he was captain of *No 9*. Ernest night-stopped at Cranwell on the 16th and arrived at East Fortune the next afternoon, having taken twenty hours' flying time from Kingsnorth. He was delighted with his new ship.

He quickly settled into a routine of anti-submarine patrols and convoy escorts in the new ship through the remainder of June, July and August. On 29th July his old ship *C25* was lost without trace while on patrol. On 10th August Ernest made his last flight in a non-rigid and, indeed, his last wartime flight. By this time he had accumulated over 980 hours of war-time airship flying. His arduous tour of duty at East Fortune, marked by two extremely hazardous flights, a great deal of flying in bad weather and more than his fair share of mechanical trouble, had been carried out with courage and distinction; his leadership, persistence and bravery earned for him the award of the Air Force Cross.

During Ernest's last few months at East Fortune *R29* had arrived, commanded by Squadron Commander G.M. Thomas. Her First Officer was a brilliant *SS Zero* pilot from Luce Bay, Lieutenant Noel Grabowski (later Atherstone). *R29*, an improved version of the *R23* Class without an external keel, had the distinction of being the only British rigid to have an operational success in the war: in September she sighted and marked a U-boat off Sunderland, which was subsequently destroyed by the surface forces she called up. At the end of the war Atherstone reverted to regular Naval duties (he had served in the Grand Fleet before joining the airship service in 1917), but retired in 1920. He came back to airships at Cardington seven years later.

CHAPTER FOUR

COMMAND & STAFF

The old RNAS hands in the airship service had been casual about adopting their new RAF ranks, but now Ernest had no excuse, for he received a chit appointing him to the command of the Airship Station at Luce Bay, near Stranraer, in the rank of Major. He and Daisy took up lodgings in Northwest Castle at Stranraer, the home formerly of Sir John Ross, who had mounted the first expedition in search of the Northwest Passage into the Pacific Ocean. It was here that their first child Ernest Alfred was born on 9th October 1918.

Luce Bay was equipped with the *SS Zero*, the most successful and popular variant of the *SS* class, which had been developed under the direction of Flight Commander Cunningham at Capel in 1916 to meet a special towing requirement at sea. The design work had been in the hands of Lieutenant Michael Rope. The main feature was a very trim little boat-shaped three-seater car powered by a remarkably reliable Rolls Royce 75 HP Hawk engine, all slung under a 70,000 cu foot streamlined envelope. To his disappointment, however, Ernest found himself fully committed by his duties to Mother Earth, despite an able First Lieutenant in Noel Astley. As a result of experiments at Mullion in Cornwall in mooring blimps out at advanced landing grounds, the airship service took up the concept of operating them from sub-stations. Consequently Ernest's major concern on arriving at Luce Bay was setting up forward operating sub-stations at Ramsay, Larne, Machrihanish and Doagh Island. The purpose of these was not only to widen the operational area of the *SS Zeros* but also to provide flexibility so that the flying effort and ground support could be concentrated quickly where it was most needed.

The arrival of the Armistice in November put a sudden end to all but a few airship operations. The airship service was run down very rapidly; most of the 103 non-rigid airships in commission were deflated and 'deleted' within weeks. Some few were retained well into 1919, principally for mine-hunting, and to this end in Spring, when Luce Bay was closed down, Ernest moved north to take over from Lt Colonel Robinson the command of Longside, near Peterhead in Aberdeenshire. There a small clutch of ships was still operating, including *NS11* commanded by Ernest's old friend and colleague from East Fortune days, Warneford. Underhill, who had given him his first airship flight at Anglesey, was also there, and he found his old ship *C Star 7* deflated in a corner of the shed awaiting the deletion that came to her in October.

In July *R34*, commanded by Major Scott, made her brilliantly success-ful flight with thirty people on board from East Fortune to New York, 3,130 nautical miles against the prevailing wind structure – the first crossing by air from east to west. After replenishing, she flew back to Pulham to complete the first double crossing of the Atlantic. The success of this remarkable achievement set a seal of pride on the entire airship fraternity, and provided enormous impetus for schemes of airship transportation over the next decade or so. But the triumph was converted to tragedy a couple of days later when *NS11* was struck by lightning, set on fire and lost with Warneford and all hands off the Norfolk coast. The airship service mourned the loss of a brilliant non-rigid captain. Captain Elliot, who died with him, had been a colleague of Ernest's in the early days at Llangefni. At the *NS11* Memorial Service held in St John's Church, Longside, Daisy Johnston "contributed two vocal solos to the programme, 'Father in Heaven' (Handel) and 'O Correct Me' (Handel), her cultured singing being admired by all."

During the summer of 1919 Ernest was beginning to be seriously concerned about his own future. The airship service, quite apart from the almost complete rundown of the non-rigids, was in the throes of a major power struggle between the Admiralty, who still owned and controlled the airships, and the Royal Air Force to whom all the personnel had belonged since May. All forward thinking revolved around the employment of the rigids which were now coming into service in increasing numbers, but Ernest was not one of the select fraternity of rigid pilots, and with no more than a wartime commission in the RNAS his turn for demobilisation must soon arrive. The last thing he wished to do was to have to go back to sea. At the end of August, however, to his delight he was offered, and accepted, a short service commission in the RAF in the rank of Flight Lieutenant; his career took a new direction and he and his family turned their faces towards London and, if not to fortune, certainly in the long run to a fair modicum of professional renown.

The control of the airship service was not transferred from the Admiralty to the Air Ministry until October 1919. That September, shortly before taking over the rigid airship stations at Cardington, Howden and Pulham, the Air Ministry put forward a scheme for the operation of a commercial air service to India using *R33*, *R36* and *R80*. It came to nothing; nevertheless Ernest found himself seconded to the brand new Controllerate-General of Civil Aviation to advise on navigation requirements for long range airship services. In the higher echelons of the RAF there was neither enthusiasm for airships nor any intention to spend any money on them if it could be avoided. Air Commodore Maitland, whose personality and powerful drive as Superintendent of Airships had been largely instrumental in the Admiralty's decision to continue to build one new rigid airship every two years, was, after a short spell at the Air Ministry, put out to grass as Commanding Officer of the airship station at Howden. With him out of the way, the Air Council was able to save funds for the rest of the RAF by disbanding its airship service in January 1921. It terminated the construction programme, with the exception of *R38* which, almost completed, was sold to the United States Navy; and it hired out first *R32* and later *R80* to them for crew training at Howden. *R33* and *R36* were handed over to the Contoller-General of Civil Aviation for evaluation of the potential of airships in commercial aviation. Major Scott had already quitted the RAF to become the first civilian airship pilot and to work on the development of a new mast mooring system at the Airship Works.

During 1920, Ernest found he had much time on his hands in Whitehall, and he began to write a civil *Manual of Airship Piloting*. The surviving, uncompleted manuscript, with much mathematics and many tables and graphs, makes heavy reading, but some excerpts give a feel for the arcane theory of handling airships and are germane to the arguments in the Epilogue.

"**LIFT**: The gross lift in pounds per 1,000 cu ft is equal to the total volume x the percentage full x the purity of the gas x the pressure (millibars) x 0.3462 divided by the absolute temperature, if the gas and air temperature are equal.

"The term 'purity' of gas is used in the ratio (density of air – actual density of gas) divided by (density of air – density of pure gas), the gas and air being supposed at the same temperature and pressure.

"**PRESSURE HEIGHT**: A ship is said to be at or near her pressure height when the gasbags are just full. This height depends on the total mass of gas in the bags, the volume of the ship, the temperature and pressure of the atmosphere at various heights at the particular time and place, and on the difference between gas and air temperature. It is, therefore, a somewhat vague quantity. The 'relative density' of the gas at which the gasbags will become just full is, on the other hand, quite a definite quantity depending only on the volume of the ship and the total mass of the gas (assuming all the bags become full at the same time). 'Relative density' is the ratio of the actual density of a gas to its standard density at sea level. If we know this we can refer to a graph of relative density and height of the 'standard atmosphere' and give the 'pressure height' for standard atmospheric conditions and equal gas and air temperatures. The quantity 'pressure height' is extremely useful in practice since, when gas and air temperatures, purity and ship's volume only are known in addition, the lift of the ship is known.

"It is now desirable to write down a general formula for lift, making use of the quantity 'pressure height' to take account of the fullness of gas bags. One can either treat with the actual densities of the displaced air and of the gas, and multiply them by the total capacity of the ship and again by percentage full/100; or one can treat with the air and gas densities corresponding to the pressure height, and multiply them by the total capacity of the ship. Let D stand for the relative density of the gas at pressure height; then, if gas and air temperatures are equal:

Lift per 1,000 cu ft = 72.765 x purity x D.

"If the ship rises above pressure height, the lift is found from the new pressure height and can be predicted from the standard curve of relative densities or from any contemporary information.

"**SUPERHEATING**: When an airship is flying through a warm sun, the temperature of the gas is raised above that of the surrounding air. This condition is termed superheating, and in British practice is measured by the number of degrees Fahrenheit between the temperature of the air and the temperature of the gas. Thus a 10 degree superheat means the gas is heated 10 deg F above the surrounding air. The lift of gas is increased by superheating. The increase in lift due to superheating is calculated by multiplying the lift without superheating by the degree of superheating divided by the absolute air temperature; this quantity is known as 'false lift'.

"A condition occasionally arises when the gas temperature is lower than the air temperature; the decrease of lift in this case is known as the 'latent lift'.

"In most cases superheating is due to the direct heat from the sun, and this depends on the sun's intensity without respect to the surrounding air. The expression for correction to lift for superheat can also be written thus:

(Gas temp – air temp) x 78.2 x D divided by air temp.

"Consequently the whole expression for lift per 1,000 cu ft including superheat is:

[0.9305 x purity + (Tg–Ta)/Ta] x 78.2 x D

"It is worthy of notice that the extra or false lift due to superheat is independent of the purity, other conditions being the same. A practice which has been in use to some extent is that of estimating the lift due to superheat as:

the total lift for no superheat x (Tg–Ta)/Ta.

"This underestimates the change and leads to quite an appreciable error if the purity is too low and the difference between air and gas temperatures high, but it is convenient for approximate calculations.

"Superheating is not always a drawback, as if a ship leaves the ground during the heat of the day when lightly superheated and lands again at night with no superheating, the loss of lift due to the false lift which disappears after sunset will partially or wholly counterbalance the weight of petrol consumed, so that little or no gas need be expended.

"**VARIATION OF RESISTANCE WITH SPEED**: The resistance to forward motion of an airship has not yet been measured very accurately. The resistance of models has been accurately measured, but the relation between model and full scale is as yet only approximately known. The law assumed as a basis to which corrections may be applied is that the resistance of a given form of ship varies as the square of the linear dimensions and the square of the speed. This is probably quite close to the truth for variations such as from 250 to 1,000 ft in length and from 30 to 70 knots, but cannot be trusted from model to full scale. Actual figures are of little interest to the pilot, but the general effects of the law are of interest. From the well known fact that the resistance varies approximately as the square of the speed, it follows that the effective thrust horse-power required varies as the cube of the speed, since power is the product of thrust and speed. If then the engine and propeller efficiency were constant, the fuel burned in unit time would be proportional to the cube of the speed, and therefore the fuel burned in unit distance would vary as the square of the speed. That is to say, reduction to half speed would increase one's range four times.

"The most economical air speed (i.e. the speed giving greatest range) in calm air would be dead slow, and in a head wind would be 1.5 times the wind speed. Several important factors modify these considerations in practice. The most important are:

(1) The effect of attitude on resistance and controllability.

(2) The variation of fuel efficiency of the engine with load.

(3) The variation of propeller efficiency with 'advance per revolution', and, therefore, with number of propellers running.

"Dealing with these in order:

(1) Owing chiefly to variations of superheat a ship must frequently be flown light or heavy, and therefore must be maintained at such an attitude as to provide the necessary dynamic lift. This affects the drag and therefore the thrust required to maintain a given speed. A curve can be drawn that shows the variation in thrust with dynamic lift for several speeds, approximately only, because the elevator angle necessary to maintain the attitude depends partly on the static trim and also affects the drag. It is clear that the higher the speed, the less is the relative increase in drag due to lightness or heaviness. Consequently the economic speed is usually increased by departure from static equilibrium.

(2) The fuel consumption per HP always increases with reduced load, though the extent to which it does varies considerably with the particular engine and carburettor (this is an inherent feature of the internal combustion engine). Thus one gets more shaft horsepower hours for a given weight of fuel by running a reduced number of engines at normal full power than by running all engines throttled down.

(3) The advance per revolution of the propellers and their efficiency can be shown to remain practically constant so long as the revolution speeds of all the propellers are varied proportionately. If some of the propellers are stopped the advance per revolution of those doing the work is decreased, or the slip is increased, and the efficiency is decreased. It is true that the design of propeller may be so chosen that the increase of slip increases the efficiency up to a point of optimum slip, but limitations of airship design tend the other way. However, the amount of reduction of airscrew efficiency due to

running, say, one half of all propellers, does vary considerably with design.

"Whilst (2) shows an advantage in favour of obtaining reduced speed by running a reduced number of engines at normal full power, (3) points to the opposite practice of throttling all engines alike. Experience hitherto has shown a definite balance of advantage for the former, which curves show for the *North Sea* and *R33* classes. Both considerations (2) and (3) also tend to increase the economic speed of flight.

"FORCES ACTING ON AN AIRSHIP IN DIFFERENT ATTITUDES: The force on the ship due to the wind when the axis of the ship is inclined to the direction of wind is the resultant of a complex distribution of pressure on the surface of the hull. Two points are particularly noteworthy: first, the fact that the resultant force is so far forward on the hull when the angle between axis and wind is small; and second, the fact that the direction of the force makes a large angle with the wind direction, so that a dynamic lift can be obtained, which is large in proportion to the additional thrust required in the direction of flight. In fact, the hull behaves like an aerofoil (though naturally it is not so efficient a means of obtaining dynamic lift).

"The line of action of this resultant force depends only on the inclination of the hull to the relative wind, and is independent (for practical purposes) of the speed. The magnitude of the force for a given attitude varies with the square of the speed (as for the case of axis parallel to wind direction). It is also directly proportional to the density of the air. The position of the elevator, or rudder, largely affects the position of the resultant force. We could break down the composition of the resultant force to show a force depending on the attitude of the hull and an additional force due to the setting of the elevator.

"DYNAMIC LIFT: The dynamic lift of an airship is defined as the component at right angles to the flightpath of the resistance of a ship moving through the air with its centreline inclined to the path of flight. It is the vertical component of this dynamic lift that is employed to maintain an airship at a constant altitude, or to drive her up or down when she is not in static equilibrium - that is, when the lift of the gas is greater or less than the weight of the ship and her cargo.

"A streamlined airship, if travelling through the air at a small angle to the axis of the ship, instead of tending to return to the direction with its centreline parallel to the line of motion, tends to increase this angle. This has a remarkable effect upon the controllability when the ship is being flown light or heavy. Thus when a ship becomes light she appears to be nose-heavy and conversely when she becomes heavy she appears to be nose-light. This effect acts in favour of the pilot at certain speeds, but at high speeds when a ship is more than a certain percent light or heavy the effect becomes so great that the elevators cannot cope with it and the ship, if heavy, will continue to climb or if light will continue to dive. The correction in such a case, should it occur, is to slow down the engines.

"In the event of the elevators jamming, this unstable property of a streamlined ship can be employed to pilot the ship back to her base; if the elevators jam down, trim heavy and nose light; if the elevators jam up, trim light and nose heavy."

In December 1919 the United States Navy Department signed a comprehensive Agreement for the purchase of R38, still being built at Cardington in the new Government Airship Works (created by the takeover of Shorts' airship factory), and for the training of US Navy personnel. Although R38 did not fly until the summer of 1921, Ernest was called on during her building to advise on the supply of navigation equipment and the procedures for the transatlantic delivery flight. He wrote:

"The supply of efficient navigation equipment to R38 will play no small part in the success of her flight across the Atlantic. She is being equipped with the most up-to-date instruments for aerial navigation which have revolutionised the time-honoured practice of navigation and indicate a new era in the means of position-finding and of rapid communication. All the instruments are especially designed for aerial work and are the outcome of patient research and experiment. No makeshift of any kind has been tolerated, and now the navigation of any aircraft over the sea or land or above the clouds has attained such a high degree of accuracy that it closely rivals that of the navigation of marine craft. Aerial navigation is closely akin to marine navigation inasmuch that the position is defined by observations of terrestrial and celestial objects, but owing to the greater development of speed and the vagaries of that unstable element the air, many of the old time-honoured practices carried out at sea have had to be discarded."

Ernest never did anything by halves. His interest in aerial navigation as a specialist subject took wings, and he dropped his work on the airship manual of piloting to begin a major work which, although not completed by him, was the basis of the first Air Ministry *Manual of Air Navigation*. With this for consolation, he remained earthbound right through 1920 and into 1921 when the civil airship programme began to get under way at last.

From the Armistice onwards, Vickers, who had undoubtedly been preeminent in the design and construction of rigid airships from *Mayfly* to *R80*, campaigned vigorously but unsuccessfully in favour of a new civil airship construction programme. Just when the future of airships was wholly in disarray, Commander Sir Denistoun Burney, an ingenious and enormously energetic man, discovered them and, although he had never flown in one, convinced himself that they were the answer to the problem of carrying people and goods between the Mother Country and India, Australia and New Zealand. Burney's main claim to fame, wealth – and status in Vickers' Head Office – was the invention of the Paravane for minesweeping during the War. Now he began a powerful campaign to build a fleet of civil airships to join the elements of the Empire together.

In February 1921 R33 was flown from Howden to Pulham under the command of Flight Lieutenant Thomas to begin mooring trials at the 100 foot mast which had been fitted with a mooring attachment designed largely by Scott at Cardington. It offered a fundamentally different solution to the mooring operation from that developed by Barnes Wallis of Vickers under the direction of Wing Commander Masterman at the end of the War. By mid-June when R33 went into her shed for overhaul she had made about fifty mast landings; she had spent 150 days secured to the mast and proved beyond doubt the practical importance of the mast conception general and Scott's application of it in particular.

Ernest was now delighted by the opportunities which the civil programme offered him to fly in R33 and R36. On 17th/18th March, as navigator of R33, he made his first flight in a rigid for a twenty hour aerial survey in the Croydon area, with Thomas in command. R33's total gas capacity was 1,960,000 cu ft as compared with the 218,000 of his old *C Star* 7, and he found the piloting of her altogether less demanding of attention to detail; she was slower to respond to controls, needed greater space for manoeuvring, and was in her motion as stately as any Dowager Duchess. On this flight, after returning to Pulham from Croydon in heavy rain, Thomas made a noteworthy landing at the mast in winds gusting up to 40 mph. During a mast landing, the First Officer's post was in the bows of the ship supervising the handling of the trail ropes and guys; the Navigator, in the

Control Car, assisted the Captain with lift and trim calculations and was responsible for air-ground communications.

R36, built by Beardmores, first flew on 1st April 1921. The next day she was flown to Pulham and secured to the mast. On her third, with Scott in command, she was damaged in flight and brought back with great skill to a night landing and put safely in her shed for repair. When she was brought out for a thirty hour trial flight on 10th/12th June, Ernest flying as navigator undertook responsibility for the acceptance-testing of all the navigation and wireless equipment. A week later he flew in her on a demonstration flight for Members of Parliament. On 21st June, after a thirteen hour trip, he was at his usual post alongside the Captain, Scottie, when she came in for what at first appeared to be a normal mast landing in almost flat calm conditions. Having too much way on, the ship overrode the mast and her mooring wire fouled the winch, bringing her up with a jerk that was strong enough to cause the inadvertent release of two forward emergency ballast bags. The bows pitched up sharply, and the lightened ship rose to be brought up standing a second time at the full length of her cable. The severe jerk caused the bows to collapse aft of frame 1. Later, Scottie observed that he had experienced jerks just as severe in R33 without damage. R36 was brought gently to the ground by valving gas, and while a small handling party manned the guys Scottie examined the damage and conferred with his Officers. He decided that it would not be safe to fly to the only vacant shed, which was at Howden. Alongside R33 in the Pulham shed was the German Zeppelin L64; work was immediately put in hand to demolish her to make room for R36. Unfortunately when R36 was halfway into L64's berth at 4.30 in the morning the wind rose sufficiently to blow her sideways onto the shed door and damage her port side amidships. She never flew again because nobody was prepared to spend money on her, and was dismantled in 1926.

R33 was flying again on 30th June with Ernest on board. On 14th and 15th July he flew in her for landing trials at a mooring mast which had been erected close to the civil aerodrome at Croydon. Shortly afterwards, this mast was taken down on the insistence of the aeroplane people who claimed that it was a hazard to navigation. On 16th July he flew on a demonstration flight for the Colonial Premiers, and made his last trip on the 21st with the Under Secretary of State for Air and a party of Members of Parliament on board.

R38 had meanwhile been completed at Cardington where she made her first flight on 23rd June. The first two flights showed up serious control overbalance which was remedied early in July by a ten percent reduction of the surface area of the controls. On her third flight, severe oscillations in pitch caused the failure of two girders amidships, and had her commander, Flight Lieutenant Pritchard, not personally taken over the elevator control from the height coxswain, she would almost certainly have broken up. Pritchard, with great skill, brought her safely back to Howden. He was the Admiralty's Acceptance Pilot for rigid airships, responsible for their flight clearance as they were taken over from the contractors, and had acquired the reputation of being one of the most capable and successful pilots in the airship service. As captain of *C24* at East Fortune in 1917 he had been a colleague and friend of Ernest's.

After being repaired, *R38* made her last flight on 23rd August. Flight Lieutenant A.H. Wann, another of Ernest's East Fortune colleagues, was in command. At 5.37 pm she broke in half while carrying out high-speed turns, the forward half being destroyed by fire and explosion. Maitland, Pritchard and her designer C.I. Campbell were among the forty-four who lost their lives. Only five, including Archie Wann, survived. Maitland's loss in particular was deeply felt throughout the tightly knit airship service. A man of handsome appearance and great personal charm in manner, voice and character, he combined an absolute honesty of purpose with unflinching devotion to the cause of airships, with which he had been continuously associated since the days of the Army's *Beta*. He commanded the wholehearted trust of all who served under him and was, indeed, a man who inspired a deep personal love in all whom he came into contact with. Other talented Officers as well as Pritchard died – Ivor Little of *R32* and *R80*, the navigator Montague, Thomas of *R33*, and the cream of the US Navy's seedling airship service. The rest of the airship community was left in a state of shock.

The Government immediately cancelled the whole airship programme; *R33* was flown to Cardington, deflated and slung, and for a while it looked as if she might be demolished. In the aftermath of the disaster, Ernest's short service commission was terminated, and with it his secondment to the civil aviation department. Despite his growing reputation in the forefront of aerial navigation, there was no place for an airshipman. With a wife and now two children to support, he was forced to rejoin his old company and go back to sea.

Robinsons' were glad to have him back as Mate of the Stag Line's latest acquisition, *SS Ixia*, at a princely salary of £21 10s a month, just about enough to pay the rent of the London flat that he and Daisy and the two children had been living in. He made four foreign voyages in *Ixia* in the following twelve months – North Africa, Mozambique, Seychelles and

Karachi. After she reached Avonmouth on 5th August 1923, having seen *Ixia* safely unloaded, Ernest took his final discharge from the Merchant Service to resume his flying career. The frustrations which he felt as Mate of a tramp steamer are clearly implied by the tone of the following letter which he wrote from *Ixia* in the winter of 1922 to Frederick Tymms, his friend and colleague with whom he had worked for nearly two years in the navigation section of the Controllerate of Civil Aviation. That had been a life infinitely removed in style and content from the sheer hard grind, and often brutality, and endless monotony of *Ixia*.

"So sorry I didn't get a chance to answer your very welcome letter from Port Said, but as a matter of fact we were there only for a few hours and I was terribly busy looking after the discharging and bunkering, and of course like all ships we put to sea at night after a hard day of it.

"The navigation tables you are enquiring about are Goodwin's *Alpha, Beta and Gamma Tables* published by J.D. Potter, price 8 shillings. My opinion of them remains the same and I've used nothing else since I came back to sea and have always obtained the best results with them. A further recommendation for these tables is that the 'Old Man', who is one of those rules of thumb fanatics who works all his sights to seconds of arc and steers course to half a degree, has NO use for them and won't even listen to me explain them to him, but nevertheless always has me take a sight alongside him morning, noon and night, whether it is my watch below or on deck, so as to check his.

"It is really remarkable though that the old blighter flatters himself as being a smart navigator – I'll admit that he is above the average tramp skipper – but for all that he works the old chronometer methods and won't listen to the position line and intercept method at all. He actually says he doesn't think it is so reliable as the chronometer sight. Ye gods! Man alive, it is wonderful how thoroughly stagnant some people become through sheer petty-mindedness. The other day he sprang a wonderful 'new' method of ex-meridian on me, more or less to take a feather out of my cap as we had been having a discussion on the navigation subject which arose from my extolling the prowess of aerial navigators who had never been to sea to learn navigation - and it hurt him badly. However, he was pleased to call his method 'Jeans's, the said gent having been an erstwhile teacher of navigation in the Navy - perhaps in the early 1840s. My popularity further decreased when I pointed out that it was really a direct method of spherical trig and nothing very wonderful about it. This proved the last straw and we parted brass rags, the 'Old Man' making some trite remark about not believing in new-fangled ideas. It's hardly credible, is it?

"I've never been over the ship's rail since we left home. Saving money, oh yes! Good God, it takes a whole month's pay to pay the rent.

"Do you think you could manage to get me the loan of an RAE bubble sextant for practical sea tests – you might pull the ropes and I'll know what to do when I get home. I'm awfully keen to try one at sea and I'm sure the results would be interesting, especially in foggy weather. You see there are lots of days when the sun is quite bright and the horizon awfully hazed, and in the Red Sea during the day the clearest horizon is useless owing to the abnormal refraction. I've had some very good sights this trip – even got a fix with the sun, moon and Venus one afternoon."

CHAPTER FIVE

DAIMLER & IMPERIAL AIRWAYS

Although Ernest Johnston was an airshipman through and through, by an odd quirk of fate he was destined to make a not inconsiderable contribution to the navigation of commercial aeroplanes. In order to understand how this came about, it is necessary to turn the clock back a little.

The Controllerate-General of Civil Aviation in the Air Ministry, to which he was appointed as a Staff Officer for the civil airship programme, was created in August 1919. At the beginning "nobody knew anything about civil aviation so nobody knew the direction in which it ought to be controlled or directed or fostered". But by the time Ernest reported for duty, civil aviation had actually begun. The fundamental legislation enabling national and international civil aviation was in place. The country's first commercial airline, Air Transport and Travel Ltd, was set up during the spring of 1919 with Major General Sir Sefton Brancker in charge of its organisation – he had previously played a leading role in the creation and development of the Royal Flying Corps – and commenced scheduled operations on 25th August, when E.H. Lawford flew the first service between London (Hounslow) and Paris. The aeroplane had been developed to a high pitch for purely military applications, and now the early commercial machines had to be evolved from them. Ernest was to enjoy from the centre of things three exciting pioneering years dominated by aeroplanes, for although his official duties were to advise the Controller of Communications on the airship service's requirements for radio navigation and communication aids, he was increasingly swept up into the exciting heavier-than-air aspects of the Department's work. His very considerable expertise as an airship navigator was increasingly in demand to advise all sorts of agencies on the development of navigational equipment and techniques. The job was what he made of it.

At the end of 1919 a Clerical Officer, Frederick Tymms, obtained a transfer from the Ministry of Labour to the Controllerate of Civil Aviation. He had been demobilised from the RAF with the acting rank of Captain and a good Military Cross won as an infantry subaltern on the Somme. On discovering that 'Tymmie' had completed the Long Range Navigation course at Andover earlier in the year, Ernest had no inhibitions about talking air navigation on level terms with the clerk. The two very diverse men, the bluff sailor-airshipman and the diligent, reserved ex-RFC Observer, formed a close friendship fostered by a shared enthusiasm for the arts of navigation.

At Andover Tymms had made friends with one of the pilots, Major George Woods Humphery, who shortly afterwards left the RAF to become General Manager of Handley Page Air Transport Ltd. As a result of this contact, Tymms got himself appointed navigator of their O-400 bomber in an attempt to win the *Daily Mail* Prize for the first aeroplane to fly from Cairo to Cape Town. Johnston was delighted to be able to give him every bit of support in preparing for the flight. The pilot of the Handley Page entry was Major H.G. Brackley DSO DFC, chief of the Air Department of HP Air Transport. They set out from Cricklewood on 25th January 1920, and in the next thirty-one days covered rather fewer miles than the airship *R34* had covered in her four-and-a-half day flight from East Fortune to New York; they ended up with a crash-landing in the desert some 200 miles north of Khartoum.

While Tymms was adventuring, Sir Frederick Sykes, the Controller General, delivered an important lecture at the Royal Geographical Society on the subject of Imperial Air Routes. The Prince of Wales was there, and so were Field Marshal Lord Haig and Mr Winston Churchill, then the Secretary of State for War and Air, and somewhere towards the back of the hall Ernest listened to the first exposition of an aviation policy which was to become his own guiding concept in years to come. "We have charted the Earth, we must chart the Air" was Sir Frederick's battle-cry. He emphasised the importance of Egypt as the great junction for Imperial routes from Britain to India, Australia and South Africa. The first subsidised Imperial route would be from Egypt to India, for the Cape to Cairo route (even though it had been surveyed and a chain of landing grounds established) was not likely to pay commercially for some years yet. The Atlantic route to Newfoundland and Canada would be the last to be developed because of the distance over water.

Tymmie the Clerical Officer returned to Air Ministry in March with a personal status enhanced by the glamour of his pioneering flight, and was permitted to transfer from his clerical grade in the Civil Service to that of

"Technical Assistant". Ernest and he, the airship man and the aeroplane man, working together exerted great influence in laying down the foundations of the practice of air navigation by the struggling commercial airlines. They formed a centre of discussion and writing which had immense influence because, above all, they both continued to be practising air navigators. Each immensely enthusiastic about the potential of his own vehicle, neither could foresee the extinction of the airship and the total domination of the aeroplane that was to come.

1920 was a desperate year for civil aviation. Nobody could make a profit out of operating two-seat and four-seat variants of wartime aeroplanes. Without wireless communications pilots could not fly regularly; and while it was essential to utilise aeroplanes for ten hours a day if they were ever to become profitable, it was still impossible to fly at night. By February 1921 all three British airlines had ceased business, leaving the country's aerodromes, wireless and weather services wide open to use by heavily subsidised foreign operators.

The Government was forced to set up a scheme of subsidies in a hurry. Handley Page and Instone resumed operations in the last half of March. In April a new British airline, Daimler Airways, appeared on the scene with the aim of pioneering a route between Manchester and Berlin. Its Managing Director was Frank Searle of AT&T, who had made a name for himself as the organiser of the London General Omnibus Company, and its General Manager was George Woods Humphery, ex-Handley Page Air Transport. This tough management team, aided by the newly designed De Havilland DH34 as the mainstay of its operations, was to have a major influence on the way airlines were run and to set ever greater standards of efficiency through intensive utilisation of its fleet.

Daimler opened its Manchester-Berlin service in the middle of April 1922. The schedule involved leaving Manchester at 6 am in order to reach Berlin, by way of London, Amsterdam, Bremen and Hamburg, before sunset. Straight away its policy of intensive utilisation was inhibited by navigational problems. In bad weather pilots believed implicitly in flying below cloud and following railway lines. Woods Humphery invited Tymms to fly the route, partly to look at the operating efficiency of the W/T Direction Finding installations and partly to assess the problem of training pilots in proper navigation procedures. Tymms recommended to Woods Humphery that he employ a specialist navigator to instill the right ideas and methods into the minds of his pilots. Knowing of Ernest's dissatisfaction with life at sea and grateful for his friendship in his early days in the Controllerate, he brought the two men together as soon as Ernest's ship *Ixia* docked in Avonmouth. Ernest did not hesitate for a second; he took his discharge from *Ixia* and within a week, on 23rd August, made his first flight in an aeroplane as navigator of *DH34* G-EBBS from Croydon to Berlin by way of Amsterdam and Hamburg: total time airborne 6 hours 34 minutes. The flight back was accomplished on the next day.

Mr A.J. Quin-Harkin, who was Daimler's Accountant, wrote half a century later:

"When we started up the London-Berlin service, something like 700 miles long, which was a tremendous distance in those days, we considered that we needed a navigator. The pilots were against it. They said that they knew the railway network and would have no difficulty getting there. We were lucky enough to procure the services of Johnnie Johnston, and they soon discovered that they knew nothing compared with him. He could tell them where they were, what courses to steer and what time they would arrive at the next destination: and he was always right. They became converted to his methods in no time at all".

G-EBBS, the prototype *DH34*, had made its first flight in the hands of A.J. Cobham at Stag Lane in March; it was destroyed when it stalled near the ground on 14th September while attempting a forced landing, killing the two pilots on board. The stalling speed, 63 mph (which was considered to be very high in those days), made forced landings extremely difficult. This class was one of the first successful purpose-built passenger aircraft designed for cross-channel services under permanent subsidy; the wing span was 51 ft 4 in, giving a total wing area of 590 sq ft to support a maximum all-up weight of 7,200 lb (tare weight 4,574 lb), and it had a range of 365 miles cruising at 105 mph. The cabin seated nine passengers in wicker chairs. The cockpit for the two pilots or pilot and navigator was positioned forward, ahead of the wings and behind the Napier Lion engine.

During the winter Ernest became involved in a programme of intensive flying in the *DH34*, mostly on the Berlin route; in eight months he amassed no less than 393 hours in the air in addition to his many responsibilities for navigational matters on the ground such as compass swinging, W/T D/F calibration, upkeep of maps, and training. They were not uneventful months. They also formed the basis of his lasting influence on the pilots who were, for the most part, barely conscious that they were laying the foundations of what was to become a highly respected profession.

On 5th December Ernest was aboard G-EBBX when she turned over on her back while making a forced landing on the beach at Coq sur Mer, near Ostende. The aircraft was later badly damaged by the incoming tide. On 11th January he was in G-EBCX when she forced-landed at Herzel on the way back from Berlin, but she was repairable and he was flying in her again three weeks later.

Arthur Hughes, the Principal of the pioneering firm of Henry Hughes and Son, makers of navigational instruments, with whom he had been closely associated as far back as 1920, invited Ernest to write an introductory chapter to a booklet on the firm's products. His final draft read:

"The high running costs of Civil Aviation demand that the service should be run on strict lines of economy and efficiency, and as every one mile saved means time and fuel saved, it is obvious that air navigation plays a very great part in the two factors of efficiency and economy. It is thus that now, more than ever, the obsolete rule of thumb methods and the practice of following the railways must be superseded by more accurate methods with the aid and intelligent use of instruments.

"Aerial navigation is classed under two categories – Air Pilotage and Air Navigation. Both these two categories are closely allied to Marine Pilotage and Navigation, but owing to the more unstable elements of the atmosphere and certain altered conditions in the speed and stability of aircraft, the art of Marine Pilotage and Navigation has had to be modified to meet the requirements of the aerial navigator. This modification is embodied more in the design and adaptation of the instruments than in the methods employed.

"As the issue is sometimes overlooked, it is advisable to state it explicitly: the object of the aerial navigator is to reach his destination in the shortest possible time with the greatest degree of accuracy.

"If the aviator was always flying over land and the country beneath him was always visible and his machine was stable, there would be very little difficulty in achieving this object. The efficiency and success of any transport business depends on regular running; therefore machines must be able to fly when conditions are unfavourable with the same regularity as when conditions are ideal. It is then that air navigation and air pilotage become the safety factor. The difficulties and dangers of flying in cloud or mist are only too well known to those engaged in aviation to emphasise them here.

"In air pilotage it is essential that the aviator be able to orientate his course, maintain his direction, estimate drift, determine his position, and calculate his groundspeed."

The Government made the introduction of the permanent subsidy system the occasion to reorganise the Civil Aviation Department as a Directorate, reporting directly to the Under Secretary of State. Sykes resigned. Sir Sefton Brancker was appointed Director of Civil Aviation in May 1922 and immediately slimmed his Directorate down into a tight technical staff with Lieut. Colonel Ivo Edwards CMG as his Chief Technical Assistant and Tymms as No 2.

While the pilots and navigators in their fragile machines were battling with the problems of low cloud, bad visibility, strong winds, inadequate instruments and mechanical unreliability, the politicians and businessmen were, during 1923, rethinking the operating structure for civil aviation for the future. Appointed Air Minister in 1922, Sir Samuel Hoare, at the start of an association with civil aviation that was to have a major impact on its growth and direction, set up the Hambling Committee which, reporting in the following year, recommended the setting up of Imperial Airways Ltd through a merger of the four existing airlines.

The formation of Imperial Airways under the Chairmanship of Sir Eric Geddes, with Col. Frank Searle as its Managing Director, was marked by the most crass mishandling of its most vital human asset, the pilots of the constituent airlines. Geddes, who came from the old North Eastern Railway with a reputation for ruthlessness, wholly failed to understand the psychology of airmen. At this period, aeroplanes were operating very close to their limits with the support of a minimal ground organisation. Even in the best of weather, completion of a journey depended entirely on what risks a pilot was prepared to take; and in the worst, the avoidance of a collision between machines flying in opposite directions along the route was often a matter of luck when the pilot's skill was wholly absorbed in navigating and handling his machine. The drive of Woods Humphery and Searle in Daimler Airways to take away from pilots their freedom of action on operations and to confine them to a fairly rigid timetable in order to utilise the company's assets efficiently, whilst it commended itself to Geddes and his Board, created resentment among many Daimler pilots and gave Daimler's management an unfortunate reputation among the pilots of the other airlines. The pilots themselves were young, courageous pioneers in skilfull and dangerous employment; their only experience of life was as pilots in war and peace and they felt that it was they, as much as anyone, who were making commercial aviation work. If a new National Airline was to be formed, they as much as anyone else should be consulted as to their terms of employment.

Greatly fearing difficulties on the two major issues of the General Manager under whose orders they would have to fly, and the rationalisation of the differing salary structures of the four existing airlines, they formed a Pilots' Federation early in 1924. F.L. Barnard, Chief Pilot of Instone (who had won the King's Cup Air Race in the previous summer) was elected Secretary; the President was Lt Colonel F. Minchin, a charming and honourable man who disappeared without trace three years later on an attempt to fly across the Atlantic from England. Ernest was not directly involved, for as the Company's sole Navigation Officer he was on a unique contract; nevertheless he felt very strongly, as an ex-Merchant Navy Officer with a much wider experience of the world than his young colleagues, that the pilots' decision to federate with the Trades Union Congress was a fundamentally bad one, likely to prejudice the standing of the pilots.

Imperial Airways, scheduled to commence operations on 1st April 1924, made no offer of employment to the pilots concerned until 31st March. The pilots therefore submitted their own proposals for the terms on which they would be willing to accept employment by the new airline. When Imperials made their own offer almost simultaneously, the pilots, having serious reservations about the mileage basis of remuneration, turned it down. To compound matters, the Pilots' Federation had earlier raised the issue of the appointment of the Company's General Manager: the Board turned down their nominee and appointed Woods Humphery, who was persona non grata to the members of the Federation. Ernest, on the other hand, had great respect for the man.

All Fools' Day 1924 therefore began with a new National Airline with the grandiose title of Imperial Airways Ltd, unable to employ any pilots. There followed twenty-four days of very unpleasant in-fighting involving some of the TUC's most notorious strike leaders, the Pilots' Federation, the new Socialist Secretary of State for Air Lord Thomson of Cardington, Sir Eric Geddes, Colonel Searle and Major Woods Humphery. In the middle of what was publicised as a strike – incorrectly, because actually the pilots were not contracted to any employer – for pay and conditions, the Federation submitted a written account of the pilots' objections to the appointment of Woods Humphery, who immediately issued writs of libel against Minchin the President and Barnard the Secretary. Whilst the matter of pay and conditions was settled on an hours-flown basis by 24th April, it was not until 2nd May that the management problem was solved. At heart, the issue was whether management was to be permitted to force pilots to fly in conditions which pilots individually considered to be dangerous to their passengers. Here, Ernest was at one with the pilots, for it was a very important issue indeed, bearing directly on their professional judgement, pride and status: it was probably much more important to these dedicated young men than the question of money.

The Board of Imperials stood rock-steady on their opinion that Woods Humphery was a fair and proper person to be Manager. In the end, Sir Samuel Instone suggested the creation of an Air Superintendent, being a man who was persona grata with the pilots and having direct access to the Board on all matters affecting them. Although this clearly put the General Manager in a difficult position, the compromise was accepted. That it worked out was due to the personality of the man appointed, and welcomed on both sides – Major H.G. Brackley, put forward as a candidate by Woods Humphery himself.

'Brackles', one of the great practising pilots of commercial aviation, had played a major part in the successful operation of the early continental services of Handley Page Air Transport as Chief Pilot, and after spending much of the summer of 1920 test-flying the *HP W8* he went out to Japan as Chief Instructor in the British Aviation Mission to the Japanese Navy. His return to England in the spring of 1924 was timely. Imperial Airways began flying operations on 2nd May with the Cologne service, and on 7th May, his first day as Air Superintendent, Brackley wrote in his diary "This morning I had to get out temporary agreements for all the pilots, sixteen in number." He appointed as Chief Pilot Franklyn Barnard from Instone, a charming man who was to lose his life three years later while testing an aircraft for the King's Cup Air Race. The others were: from Handley Page, G.P Olley, A.S. Wilcockson, F. Dismore, W. Rogers, R.H. MacIntosh and L.A. Walters; from Instone, O.P. Jones and F. Wolley Dod; from Daimler, W.S.R. Hinchliffe, Robertson and Robinson; and from British Marine, J. Youell, Bailey, Powell, Robins and Horsey.

Ernest started flying again on the 9th May, navigating the Handley Page *W8b* on the Cologne route until the end of the month. The three aircraft of this class, baptised *Princess Mary*, *Prince George* and *Prince Henry* (respectively G-EBBG, BH and BI), were twelve-seater machines powered by two uncowled Rolls-Royce Eagle engines. Contemporary with the smaller *DH34*, they had been developed from Handley Page's first purely civil transport for use by HP Transport on the Paris and Brussels services. The pilot and navigator sat right forward in an open cockpit. The wing-span of 75 ft provided a total lifting area of 1,456 sq ft for a maximum all-up weight of 12,000 lb (tare weight 7,700 lb). They cruised at a modest speed of 90 mph.

Throughout June, Ernest was back in the *DH34* fleet on the Berlin run, making four round trips – over fifty hours' flying – between the 6th and 17th. But by now thoughts about airships were stirring, and the dreams of

Imperial Communications that had been nurtured in the corridors of the Controllerate of Civil Aviation four years before looked as though they might be turning into reality. The problems of navigating long-haul airships were far more congenial to Ernest than the pilotage of aeroplanes on short-haul stages, as his prolific writings in the decade 1920-30 showed: moreover, the Imperial Airways operations were beginning to fall into routine. He sounded out his old colleague Scottie, who had just been appointed Officer in charge of Flying and Training for the new civil airship programme, with the happy result that he accepted the offer of a job as Scott's Technical Assistant, and at the turn of the year found himself oscillating between an office at the Royal Airship Works at Cardington and the skeleton airships in the sheds at Pulham.

CHAPTER SIX

AIRSHIPS REVIVED

Following the *R38* disaster the fate of airships hung in a very delicate balance; the Navy wanted them, the RAF had no time for them and the Government had no money to spare. Personnel were dispersed, the ships themselves were deflated and slung in the sheds and left to rot. With Maitland dead there was no senior airshipman left of big enough stature to shape the course of airships for the future, and it was rather on the rumbustious outsider Sir Denistoun Burney that the surviving professionals at the top focussed their aspirations – Scott, the brilliant and inventive aviator now in charge of the silent ships in their sheds at Cardington and Pulham; Lt Colonel Vincent Richmond the fabric and dope expert now in the Air Ministry's Directorate of Research under Wing Commander Cave-Brown-Cave; Squadron Leader Reginald Colmore the Airship Staff Officer in the Air Ministry; and the wayward, brilliant Barnes Wallis who, after playing a significant part in the construction of *No. 9* had gone on to design *R23* and *R80*, probably the most elegant airship ever built. Burney proposed to have these four associated with him in his Airship Guarantee Company when, early in 1923, he prepared for submission to the Government proposals for building a large airship as the first phase of his very ambitious commercial airship programme. Wallis refused to work with Scott, Richmond and Colmore under the conditions laid down by Burney, and in the end they did not join the Company, whereas Wallis was appointed Chief Designer with sole responsibility for designing the Company's ships. When he came to examine Burney's proposals in depth, Wallis concluded that they were wildly optimistic and expressed considerable doubt about the practicability of building a safe airship quickly in Britain. He thought that the Burney scheme needed a great deal more time for experimental work than Burney or his supporters might be prepared to concede. Indeed, initially he favoured approaching the Zeppelin Company for design and construction, and negotiations were actually opened by Burney.

Burney's genius for lobbying and publicity forced successive Governments to take his proposals seriously, for the concept of linking up the various centres of the Empire by means of airship services was one capable of firing public enthusiasm. In 1923 a Cabinet Sub-Committee was set up to consider the Burney scheme, and within the Air Ministry an Advisory Panel was convened under the chairmanship of the Air Member for Supply and Research, Air Vice-Marshal Sir Geoffrey Salmond, to deal with the technical and operational problems. Colmore, as the senior airshipman in the Air Ministry, was a member of this panel, and so was Sir Sefton Brancker as Director of Civil Aviation, and of course Burney himself could not be excluded. Salmond, conscious of the risk of imbalance arising from Burney's immense power of advocacy, sought a counterweight: his Secretary of State, Sir Samuel Hoare, recommended a retired Sapper Brigadier with radical political leanings but good connections, Christopher Thomson. His brief encounter with ballooning when he was a Subaltern apart, aviation was a wholly new world for Thomson. He became an instant convert to the cause. Within less than a year the first Labour Government took office under his friend Ramsay MacDonald, who offered him a peerage and the post of Secretary of State for Air. Such was his new-found enthusiasm for airships that he took the title 'Baron Thomson of Cardington'. Colmore, Scott and Richmond were not impressed by such pretension.

For all his failings, the outsider Burney did more than any other man to make possible the launch of the great civil airship programme; and by the same token it can be said of Burney's counterweight on the Advisory Panel, that for all his romantic good intentions, Thomson carried more responsibility than any other single man for wrecking it.

In October 1923 Sir Samuel Hoare announced that the Air Ministry had been authorised to proceed with a subsidised programme based on Burney's proposals for a fleet of six airships of five million cu ft each, to be used commercially on services between England and India, Australia, South Africa and Canada. Before any contracts with the Airship Guarantee Company were finalised, however, a General Election returned the first Labour Government and Thomson succeeded Hoare in office at the beginning of January. From the first Thomson was determined that the golden future of airships should be dominated neither by the Admiralty nor by Vickers. With the support of Air Marshal Sir Hugh Trenchard, the Chief of Air Staff, he presented a paper to the Cabinet proposing that the Air Ministry itself design and construct its own airship and build bases in Egypt and India so as to gain operational experience on which to plan the construction of a number of ships for commercial and defence purposes. The Admiralty and Burney contested the proposals with acrimony, and in the end Thomson compromised cleverly. The Government undertook to fund a three-year programme of research and development centred on the construction of two five-million cu ft airships to test their capacity for long-distance air transport. One of the ships was to be designed and built by the Royal Airship Works and one by a private firm, Burney's Airship Guarantee Company being offered first refusal. Scientific caution was to be the keynote of this programme. The specifics of the Burney scheme thus rejected, the possibility of a Vickers-Burney monopoly in airships was eliminated, and the Air Ministry, by retaining complete control of airship development, put the Admiralty firmly in its place.

Had there been no Burney, there would probably have been no airship programme. He had proved a powerful catalyst. The decision to embark on a carefully controlled experimental and development programme was absolutely sound, but the decision to build two ships of different designs to a common specification was unwise, for there simply was not the talent and experience in the country to do it. After the loss of C.I.R. Campbell in R38 and the departure of H.B. Pratt to other fields, Barnes Wallis was the only design engineer in Britain with long and up-to-date experience of designing and building rigid airships. Although he had his own doubts about the ability of his Chief, Burney, to carry through a sufficient experimental programme for the safe completion of his own scheme, Wallis was outraged by the Government's proposal to give the Airship Guarantee Company (and hence himself) a secondary role. The appointment of Vincent Richmond, for whose ability as an engineer Wallis had nothing but contempt, as head of the design team for the Government ship fuelled a bitterness in the rivalry between the Wallis team and the Cardington design team which found its jaundiced Memorial years later in the autobiographical Sliderule of Nevil Shute Norway. Norway, in the early stages of the design of R100, was Wallis' Chief Calculator; he became Deputy Chief Engineer in 1929.

A new Air Ministry Directorate of Airship Development, reporting to AMSR, was formed and located at the Royal Airship Works, Cardington. There being no airshipman sufficiently senior for the post, Salmond selected a first class administrator, Group Captain (later Air Commodore) P.F.M. Fellowes, as the first Director, and gave him Sqn Leader R.B.B. Colmore, who was an exceptionally experienced airship staff officer, as his Deputy. Richmond was put in charge of Technical Development, Scott in charge of Flying and Training. The Director and his staff were really part of

Air Ministry; their location at, and therefore identification with, the RAW was, perhaps, another mistake. It seemed that those whom the brilliant Wallis had rejected as being inadequate to be his colleagues on the original Burney scheme – Colmore, Richmond and Scott – were now not only rivals but also occupying positions which could prejudice the success of the new Burney ship; and in much subsequent literature about the airship affair this view was put about. In fact, only Richmond could be considered a rival, to the extent that Wallis was designing one ship while Richmond led the design team for the other; but Richmond was also responsible to his Director for all the technical aspects of the airship development programme as a whole – indeed, he played a major part in writing the Air Ministry specification to which both airships were designed.

'Dope' Richmond was no man's fool. A graduate of the Royal College of Science, he had worked on the engineering problems of dock construction before joining the RNAS in 1915, and by the end of the War he had made his reputation by inventing a fabric doping process for non-rigid envelopes which speeded up their production at a vital period of the war against the U-Boats. In 1920 he was assigned to the Joint Allied Commission of Control in Germany as the Officer in charge of the Sub-Committee responsible for superintending the surrender and dismantling of the German airships and seaplanes; here he was so deeply impressed by the magnificent Zeppelins that he became almost religiously converted to the cause of rigid airships. On his return to England in 1921 he exercised his determination successfully to obtain a post in the Air Ministry Directorate of Research to carry out research into rigid airship design and construction. In 1923 he became Lecturer on airship design and construction at the Imperial College of Science. By the time he was offered the job at Cardington in 1924 he had already established a high reputation for his learned papers on airship affairs. He was a first class organiser and a good picker of men. He chose as his principal assistant a serving RAF Officer, Michael Rope, probably the brightest technical star in the airship world outside Germany. If Wallis was a brilliant prima donna engineer, Richmond was a hardworking, intelligent and articulate team leader who knew how to surround himself with, and direct and use, a technical staff of high quality. Richmond died flying in his own ship; Wallis, by the time the construction of his ship had become a matter of routine engineering, had largely lost interest in it.

Towards the end of 1924 Scottie began to recruit his operational team. Ernest was the first to join him as his Technical Assistant, responsible for navigation, meteorological and communications studies and planning. R33 was to be recommissioned for experimental flying in connection with the design parameters for the two new ships; two of Ernest's old East Fortune colleagues were seconded from the RAF: Flight Lieutenant H.C. Irwin to command her and Flight Lieutenant Ralph Booth to be her First Officer. These two were designated to be the Commanders of the two new ships. Captain George Meager, one of the most brilliant non-rigid pilots of the war, also joined the 'club' at the end of the year.

On the morning of 2nd April 1925 the reconditioned *R33* was walked out of her shed at Cardington. Once airborne, she flew around the aerodrome for a couple of hours whilst everyone got the feel of her, and then departed for Pulham where she moored at the mast. During this flight Ernest calibrated the compasses and other navigation equipment. The next flight on the 6th and 7th, the first experimental sortie, lasted fifteen hours and he was kept busy. She slipped from the mast at 9pm, cruised along the east coast and up the Thames to London, and then cruised for eight hours above fog banks waiting for the weather to clear so that she could moor again at Pulham. She had been rigged up to provide full-scale aerodynamic data to complement wind-tunnel model tests; thousands of small diameter rubber tubes ran from holes on the equator, top and bottom of the ship to nests of manometers which were to be recorded photographically at different angles of pitch and yaw in various conditions of speed, trim and buoyancy.

This programme was seriously delayed, however, by the dramatic events of the following week when she broke away from the mast while riding a series of gales. Scottie, himself one of the immortals, said that the feat of Booth and his crew of eighteen in saving the ship and bringing her safely back to Pulham after thirty hours in the air was one of the finest ever carried out in airships.

Scottie's first reaction was to suggest, with Richmond's concurrence, that *R36* should be repaired, but after the damage to *R33* had been fully evaluated it was decided that the high-priority aerodynamic work would suffer less delay if efforts were concentrated on bringing *R33* back into service. The unfortunate *R36* was deleted in 1926.

On 5th and 6th October *R33* carried out pressure measurements in a nineteen and a half hour flight, mostly turning circles over Maplin Sands at various speeds and rudder angles in order to provide data to calculate the aerodynamic loadings on the hull and cover. Scottie was in overall charge of the flying programme; Irwin was in command of the ship; Booth was the First Officer; and Ernest and Meager were under instruction as pilots and watchkeepers, Ernest carrying out his function of navigator as required. Many of the *R101* design, calculating and drawing office staff were also

Ernest Livingston Johnston (1891-1930) - Navigator of *HMS Spanker*, 1915.

Submarine Scout, Anglesey 1916.

Newly wed Ernest and Daisy Johnston inside 'their' blimp, Anglesey 1916.

C25 at East Fortune, 1917.

Johnston *(second from front)* piloting *C Star 7*, 1918.

C20, engineless and under tow, approaching the beach at Nigg Bay, and *(below)* the last rending scene of her saga, 16/17 September 1917.

R33 damaged after breaking away from the mast in a gale at Pulham, April 1925.

Flight Lieutenant Ralph Booth and Sergeant 'Sky' Hunt aboard *R33* after bringing her back safely.

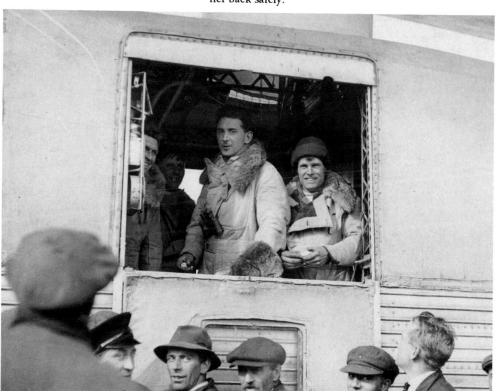

Johnston, Major G.H. Scott and Flight Lieutenant H.C. Irwin in the control car of *R33*, 1926.

Lieutenant Colonel V.C. Richmond with the author, the author's parents *(right)* and Mrs Richmond *(left)*, 1926.

The complement for the India flight, 1927, including *(left to right)*
Air Vice Marshal Sir Geoffrey Salmond, Captain F.L. Barnard (pilot), Lady Maude
Hoare, Johnston (navigator), and Sir Samuel Hoare (Lord Templewood).

After its arrival at Delhi the Viceroy, Lord Irwin, names the De Havilland Hercules
The City of Delhi.

Ernest Johnston, the Chief Mate, and Daisy his wife aboard *SS Ixia*, 1922.

aboard to participate in the experiments on this and on the five-hour flight of 9th October.

On the 15th, a short flight was made with the object of testing the feasibility of hooking an aeroplane onto the ship, following an initial drop. The first aeroplane drops had been carried out successfully from R23 in November 1918. For the R33 trials a DH53 Hummingbird was used. A trapeze bar slung under the ship could be extended to some fifty ft below her during flight; the aeroplane pilot aimed to engage it with a parrot-beak hook at a low overtaking speed. On the first flight Sqn Leader de Haga Haig slipped satisfactorily at 3,000 ft; then, attempting to engage prematurely, he damaged his propeller and had to glide to a forced landing (which he accomplished without any more damage). On the second flight, on 28th October, the drop was again successful but the pilot, Flt Lieutenant Junor, failed to re-engage because of too high an approach speed. On 4th December, however, all went well. Six successful hookups were accomplished at 45 knots between 3,000 and 4,000 ft. After the last one, the trapeze complete with aeroplane was winched up close under the ship and the aeroplane secured against pads. R33 was then ballasted up and landed with aeroplane attached.

After this flight R33 was deflated and slung in the shed at Pulham. The full-scale aerodynamic experiments which had been completed in her were correlated with elaborate small-scale investigations in the wind tunnel over the following two years, leading to the definition of the design parameters of R100 and R101. The construction of R100 at Howden and R101 at Cardington did not begin until 1927. There was a hiatus in the flying training programme as R33 was not commissioned again until October 1926, when it was decided to resume the aeroplane experiments, this time using a pair of Gloster Grebe fighters, each one very much heavier and of higher performance than the DH53 of the earlier experiments. Ernest was attached to the RAF Wireless School at Worthy Down for specialist studies when R33 was inflated in October, but he went to Pulham for the first flight in order to calibrate the wireless and navigation equipment for the subsequent flying programme. On the 21st she was walked out of the shed with the two Grebes, each weighing a ton, slung underneath. With Scottie in overall control of the programme, Booth was acting Captain for the first time; Meager was First Officer. The Grebe pilots were Flying Officers Ragg and Mackenzie-Richards. Both slipped satisfactorily from about 2,000 ft. Then a number of acoustic experiments were carried out using bomblets as a sound-source, one of which exploded too close to the ship and damaged the outer cover, fortunately without penetration of the gas bags. The ship landed rather heavily at Cardington, damaging certain struts and girders in the process – an eventful first solo for Booth. This flight ended Ernest's involvement with R33. Although, after repairs, she flew again twice in November, a subsequent examination of her framework showed signs of metal fatigue. Further flying was discontinued and she was scrapped in 1927.

The programme approved by the Government in 1924 envisaged a three-year span for research and development, construction and test flying of both of the five-million cu ft airships. Like nearly all programmes involving technological advances, it was wildly over-optimistic. In the event the construction of R100 and R101 did not begin until 1927. By late 1925 it was obvious that there was virtually no likelihood of collaboration between the Airship Guarantee Company and Richmond's technical team. Colmore, always open and friendly, never ceased hoping and striving for sensible liaison; in Whitehall Sir Geoffrey Salmond (AMSR) still hoped for some sort of collaboration, but he made it clear to the Secretary of State in August that Wallis himself did not believe in the possibility of cooperation because it would mean his handing over the results of years of work which belonged properly to Vickers. Whilst Richmond was from time to time ready to pass on to Howden the results of the Cardington experiments, Wallis continued to the end to despise the technical qualifications of the men responsible for R101. Wallis saw himself as an original creator solving all the problems of R100 on his own drawing board and in his own workshop on the shed floor, whilst Richmond, though many wondered how he had achieved his position, was a gifted organiser who saw himself as the manager of a multi-disciplinary design team – a team which included J.D. North, the technical chief of Boulton and Paul, who was made responsible for the design and construction of the girders of R101; and, among the juniors at Cardington, people like (Sir) Alfred Pugsley, Harold Roxbee Cox (Lord King's Norton), and Hilda Lyon, who were destined to achieve great eminence.

As for the relationship between the Director of Airship Development, Fellowes, and the Chairman of the Airship Guarantee Company, Burney, there was nothing but antagonism. Fellowes, a career Air Force Officer, disliked Burney and held him in contempt. "It seems to me", he wrote in a typical minute to Salmond, "that we are allowing Burney, because of his political influence, to cause us to spend an enormous amount of time and effort to placate him and to prevent his forcing his ideas on us. We know well that he has no practical knowledge whatever of airships or their possibilities." Fellowes regarded Burney as merely a contractor who ought to be brought to heel to fulfill his contract. His publicity stunts – and the extravagant atmosphere that he never failed to excite – offended against Fellowes' cool professional approach to a programme of exacting magnitude. It was easy for Burney to be theatrical and Wallis to be the brilliant 'loner', but the people at Cardington had the technical and financial responsibility for overall control of a complex technological effort which, year by year, proved to be more difficult than anybody (and most of all, Burney) had anticipated. By the spring of 1926 even Wallis' loyalty to Burney had come under strain. Privately, he tended to agree with the view that both Fellowes at Cardington and Salmond in Whitehall held, that Burney's record as a businessman was unimpressive, his optimism was wholly unbalanced, and he could not be relied upon to take adequate measures to ensure the fulfillment of his company's contract. By the time the construction of the two ships began in the following year, Burney's own people as well as the Air Ministry staffs came to share an unusually virulent dislike of him, but it only added to the tangle of jealousies, antipathies, obstructiveness and mere human inefficiency which bedevilled what ought to have been a healthy rivalry between the R100 contractor and the R101 design team. What Burney and Wallis (and their equally misguided minion Nevil Shute Norway) never seemed to grasp, was the dual function of the Directorate of Airship Development: on the one hand it was the Directorate responsible for the overall control of the airship programme, and on the other it was the parent of the Government factory designing and building a rival ship. This failure, particularly on the part of Norway, was to bedevil much that was written for popular consumption in later decades.

After the collapse of the first Labour Government in November 1924, Sir Samuel Hoare re-occupied the chair of Secretary of State for Air and kept it for the next four and a half years. As time passed, the controversy which had surrounded the birth of the programme seemed to grow rather than subside, fed by increasingly adverse publicity as delay seemed to follow delay, and it was naturally upon the so-called 'socialist' airship, R101, that most of the light of publicity fell. Both ships were nearing completion when another General Election brought the second Labour administration into power in June 1929, and Sam Hoare once again relinquished his seat to Christopher Thomson. Ten days after receiving his seal of Office as Secretary of State for Air, Lord Thomson was back at Cardington. "He was anxious to fly the ship to India at Christmas," Richmond noted laconically in his diary. The era of impatience was beginning.

Construction of R100 was completed at Howden in July. Sqn Leader Booth, who had been appointed her Captain, together with First Officer

George Meager, the Chief Coxswain Flight Sergeant Greenstreet and the three Assistant Cox'ns then had to show the staff of the Airship Guarantee Company how to inflate the first two gas bags before handing the rest of the process back to them; the operation began at the end of July and was completed in the middle of August. Engine running trials followed. Lift and trim trials were done on 11th November. Disappointingly, the trials disclosed a deficit of seven tons of useful lift. Booth and his crew took charge of the ship on 22nd November. Ernest, who had already advised the Company on the details of the layout of the navigation and communications equipment, spent a week at Howden to familiarise himself, as a future watchkeeping officer, with the flight systems of the ship. To form R100's permanent crew Booth, who had been at Howden for the best part of a year, had been able to select, in addition to the nucleus of old airship hands which he had recruited at Cardington, the best of the fitters and riggers from the Airship Guarantee Company's men and those who had worked on the installation of the Rolls Royce engines. All that now prevented her first flight was a combination of calm weather at Cardington to permit the transfer of R101 from the mooring mast into her shed, and weather at Howden calm enough to walk her out.

Although the construction of R101 was not completed until September, inflation of her sixteen gas bags began during July under the control of her Captain, Irwin, and his flight crew, so that all was ready by 30th September for her lift and trim trials. There had been omens of serious weight problems several weeks before, and it was a jaundiced Richmond who wrote that night "The organisation of this trial was rather poor and I am afraid that the result is not going to be very reliable. The various operations, owing to the fact that they had not been carefully planned beforehand, took considerable time to carry out. The filling of the gas bags took all the morning and I discovered that owing to the bad adjustment of the nets we were losing considerable volume. A hasty attempt was made to rectify this, but I am not satisfied that the best possible has been done. It was many hours after gassing operations were finished before the actual lift and trim were taken: meanwhile the temperature was slowly falling and I am not satisfied that the bags were 100% full at that moment. The condition of the various tanks was very irregular and it may be difficult if not impossible to compute the true amount of water and fuel on board."

The preliminary results worked out the following day caused much gloom: R101 was 23.5 tons heavier than the original target weight of 90 tons; the nominal disposable lift was 37 tons as compared with the specification of 62 tons. Richmond had to concede that his ship was incapable of flying to Egypt, India or Canada without a great deal of modification.

A comparison of the essential weights of the two ships (in tons) just before their first flights is illuminating:

	Air Ministry Specification	R100	R101
Gross Lift	152	157	149
Fixed weights	90	106	114
Disposable lift	62	51	35
Lift available for fuel & payload	32	31	15

By and large, the various elements of the fixed weights of the two ships tallied closely, except for the power plant installations. The decision to use Diesel engines in *R101* for safety in tropical temperatures imposed an eight ton penalty over the weight of the petrol engines in *R100*. The combination of Richmond's deep, stressed frames and Rope's clever gas bag wiring (designed to keep the fragile gas bags from contact with the hull) lost *R101* eight tons of lift vis-a-vis *R100*.

CHAPTER SEVEN

WAITING FOR AN AIRSHIP

During 1924 and 1925 the Directorate of Civil Aviation had tightened up on the navigational qualifications required for the commercial pilot's 'B' Licence, and finalised the requirements for the First and Second Class Navigators' licences. It was proposed that commercial aeroplane pilots on the longer routes should hold one or other of the navigation licences in addition to their pilot's licence, but at first the scheme was to be voluntary. In 1926 a dozen Imperials' pilots were coaxed – mainly on the initiative of the aviation insurance surveyor, Captain A.G. Lamplugh – into volunteering to sit the first examination, and Sir Sefton Brancker arranged for Ernest to be borrowed from the Director of Airship Development to coach them. They were F.L. Barnard, A. Wilcockson, W.S.R. Hinchliffe, H.J. Horsey, L.L. Leleu, L.A. Walters, D.H. Drew, W. Armstrong, W.F. Warner, F.D. Travers, E.H. Attwood, R.D. Howard and C.F. Wolley Dod. Tutor and students alike attacked the syllabus with zest and good humour; then Ernest and Entwhistle, the Meteorologist, were appointed as the first Air Ministry Board of Examiners for navigators' licences and in December 1926 there was a 100% pass rate for the first examination. In the course of time these pilots called themselves the Veteran Air Navigators: they were the rock on which the Guild of Air Pilots and Air Navigators was built. In 1928 when the examinations were resumed, Freddy Tymms took over and the pass rate fell drastically, but somehow civil aviation managed to survive.

During 1926 Woods Humphery, the General Manager of Imperial Airways, asked Sir Sefton Brancker to arrange for the loan of Ernest's services to act as the navigator and wireless operator for their first commercial flight to India, and to stay on in Egypt for a few months to supervise generally the arrangements for navigation on the Cairo-Karachi sector and to initiate navigation training of Imperials' pilots flying on the route. The Director of Airship Development readily concurred with this proposal.

The Royal Air Force had carried the mails between Cairo and Basra since 1922. Sir Samuel Hoare, the Secretary of State for Air, saw this as a job more properly done by Imperial Airways as the first stage of the civil air route between London and Calcutta. Consequently an agreement was signed between the Government and Imperial to develop a regular service between Cairo and Karachi; the initial operation, between Cairo and Basra, was scheduled to start in 1926. De Havillands designed the *DH66 Hercules* for this task; five were ordered, each powered by three Bristol Jupiter engines. Sir Samuel decided that he and his wife would make the first journey from London to Karachi. It was something of an event, for not only was it the first flight by a commercial aircraft to India, but this flight together with the return to Egypt covering 10,000 miles had never been done by anyone in any sort of civil machine. That not only a Cabinet Minister but his wife also should attempt it created an enormous stir.

As Ernest did not possess the Post Office's wireless operator's licence that was required, he went off to the RAF Signals School at Flowerdown for a refresher course in November; but vested interests intervened and a professional wireless operator was selected for the flight, leaving Ernest to concentrate on the navigation. The pilot was to be Frank Barnard, "expert and gallant pilot, cheery companion and loyal friend". The story of the flight occupies the next chapter.

In April 1927, after Ernest had accompanied most of the pilots on proving flights between Cairo and Basra, the air mail and passenger service was opened on a commercial basis. Five members of Ernest's class of 'Veteran Air Navigators' were working the route at various times – Frank Barnard, Charles Wolley Dod, Hinchliffe, Dudley Travers and Leslie Walters. In his close association with these men of outstanding character during that spring Ernest found himself increasingly harping on a theme that had been present in his mind ever since the so-called 'Pilots' Strike' at the time of the formation of Imperial Airways. He never altered his opinion that the pilots' affiliation to the TUC and their use of Trades Union methods had been a disaster which had done nothing but detract from their status. By now, the old Pilots' Federation had died, and nothing stood in its stead. Ernest believed passionately that air pilots and navigators should have a professional status at least level with Master Mariners, and argued persuasively that they needed a professional body of unquestionable integrity to safeguard their interests. When Freddy Tymms took over from him the job of Air Ministry Route Superintendent at Heliopolis at the end of May and he returned to Cardington, the mounting delays in the construction of his two airships left him free to continue coaching and examining candidates for the Air Navigators' Licences. He took every opportunity to proselytise. His influence in the world of professional airmen grew all the while.

Soon enough, Ernest found a strong backer for his mission to create a Company of Air Pilots and Navigators. Prior to 1924, Aviation Insurance had been a ruinous business to be in; but in that year the only two survivors of the many firms who had burned their fingers combined to form the British Aviation Insurance Group. This monopoly could well have throttled civil aviation, but the Group appointed a former RFC pilot, Captain A.G. Lamplugh (known universally as 'Lamps') as its principal surveyor; and this great man, who combined scrupulous fairness with great technical knowledge and a shrewd understanding of people, played an immense part, as much among pilots as with designers and engineers and management, in steering civil aviation towards the success that it eventually achieved. 'Lamps' was totally dedicated to the concept of 'professionalism' amongst pilots. Now he gave his enthusiastic backing to Ernest's concept of a Pilots' professional body equivalent to the Company of Master Mariners.

On 5th December 1928 the original 'Veteran Air Navigators' of Imperial Airways held a dinner at Rules Restaurant in Maiden Lane. Its proprietor Tommy Bell had been a colleague and friend of Ernest's at Anglesey in the old airship days. Some of the original 'Veterans' of Ernest's class were, alas, not there. In August the year before, fresh back from Egypt, Frank Barnard, Imperial's brilliant, energetic, sporting Chief Pilot had lost his life while testing the hotted up *Bristol Badminton* for the King's Cup air race. "The contrast between his extraordinary caution as a pilot of passenger machines and his daring, even recklessness as a pilot of single-seaters was remarkable," wrote C.G. Grey. "He had an unusual gift for imparting information in humorous and striking phrases which stuck in one's memory... his ability as an engineer was fully equal to his skill as a pilot". And Colonel Minchin, that much respected man in Imperial Airways, had disappeared without trace in an attempt to fly westwards across the Atlantic in 1927; and in the spring of 1928 the brilliant, erratic genius of Hinchliffe the one-eyed pilot was lost in another Atlantic attempt.

The chief guest at the Veterans' dinner was Sir Sefton. He, having been primed by 'Lamps' (himself an honoured guest), suggested in his after-dinner speech that the time had arrived for pilots who had attained a high professional status as holders of the 'B' licence and the Air Navigator's certificate to form their own Company. The suggestion was received with acclaim, and after dinner a small group gathered around Brancker, 'Lamps' and Ernest to talk about the proposal and see where they might go from there. If Sir Sefton had chosen the moment well, Ernest kept the momentum going. A meeting of all 'B' licence pilots and certified navigators in the United Kingdom, called at Rules the following February, was attended by about fifty enthusiastic people; the proposal to form 'The Company of Air Pilots and Air Navigators of the British Empire' was approved and a committee was set up under the chairmanship of Sir Sefton to work out the details. The other members were Norman McMillan representing the Test Pilots; A.S. Wilcockson representing the Imperial Airways pilots; Lt Colonel G.P. Henderson for the Flying Instructors; V.H. Baker the Club pilots; Wally Hope for the independent airline pilots; Major H.G. Brackley for the administrators in Air Transport; and Ernest for airships. Lawrence Wingfield, a solicitor who as a young RFC pilot had collected a Military Cross and the Distinguished Flying Cross before he was twenty, was brought in as their legal adviser. The drafting Committee did its work well, and departed in two main respects from its initial brief: it advocated the use of the word 'Guild' rather than 'Company' in the title, so as to link the pilots and navigators with the ancient craft associations; and it decided that membership should not be limited to the air transport industry but should encompass all who, holding professional licences, served civil aviation professionally. In April 1929 a second meeting of those in the profession endorsed the work of the Drafting Committee and set up a Foundation Council under Ernest's chairmanship to carry through the formation and registration of the new Guild. Brancker was invited to become the first Master of the Guild, Wingfield its Honorary Clerk. Rules were drawn up in detail and the initial membership of fifty people approved. The Council settled on the composition of the Court, the Guild's governing body, and organised a postal ballot for its election. Ernest drew up a form of ceremony of installation based on the custom of the Master Mariners; this was also adopted. The Council also negotiated the Guild's participation in the 'Tripartite Agreement', a document which defined and acknowledged the functions of the subscribing bodies, at that time the Royal Aeronautical Society, the Society of British Aircraft Constructors and the Royal Aero Club. The Guild's participation resulted in professional pilots and navigators as a body being given defined status alongside the other representative non-governmental organisations in aviation.

Following the postal ballot the first General Meeting of the Guild was held on Saturday 19th October 1929 at the Hotel Cecil. The Chaplain and the Clerk performed the ceremony of installation of Sir Sefton Brancker as Master and of Ernest as Deputy Master and Chairman of the Court. The other members of the Court who had been elected were A.S. Wilcockson, O.P. Jones, A.G. Lamplugh, N. McMillan (Wardens); and F. Tymms, W.L.

Hope, C.R. McMullin, L.A. Walters, F. Dismore, H.D. Davis, G.H. Allison, H.J. Horsey, J.L.B.H. Cordes, N.G. Atherstone, A.E. Jones and C.A. Pike (Assistants).

The inimitable C.G. Grey of *The Aeroplane* commented "When in due course the Company of Air Pilots and Air Navigators has qualified for the prefix 'Honourable', and it has acquired status equal to the other Honourable Companies of this Nation, the name of Squadron Leader E.L. Johnston must always stand as its Founder." And so it happened: twenty-six years after the death of its first Master and Deputy Master in an airship disaster, "The Lord Mayor and Aldermen on the tenth day of April in the year 1956 did grant confirm and ratify unto the good men of the Guild of Air Pilots and Air Navigators of London that they be a Company of the City of London and enjoy a Livery."

During the hiatus between the end of *R33*'s flying programme and the approach to completion of the construction of *R100* and *R101*, Ernest's work at Cardington left time hanging heavily on his hands. The study of climate, weather and winds on the Imperial air routes in conjunction with Maurice Giblett, the chief Meteorologist, and of their effects on the predicted performance of the two airships could only fill so much time. For the rest, he kept tabs on the development of navigation instruments, wrote and lectured on navigation subjects to a wide variety of audiences, coached candidates for the Air Ministry licences and was also called upon to act, somewhat reluctantly, as a relief aerodrome traffic controller at Croydon. Half a century later, the redoubtable Jimmy Jeffs, who had been the Chief Air Traffic Officer, remarked that Johnnie Johnston had never failed to produce a good excuse for not being available for duty at Croydon.

Some of the papers Ernest wrote on navigational subjects during this hiatus make fascinating reading today.

"Aerial navigation may be said to have got its first impetus in September 1911 when M. Lallemand, the French Cartographer, read a paper before the British Association at Southampton entitled *The International Air Map and Aeronautical Marks*. M. Lallemand claimed that it was then time that aviators were given the means of finding their way similar to those which, for a long time, had existed for navigators.

"No definite progress towards the establishment of an International Air Map had been made up to the time of the outbreak of the Great War... In October 1919 a Convention was signed in Paris by some thirty nations and states... It was laid down that there was to be two series of International Air Maps; one series to be known as

'General Aeronautical Air Maps', to be on the Mercator Projection between the limits of 88 degrees North and 88 degrees South on a scale of three centimetres to one degree of longitude at the Equator... the second series to be known as 'Local Aeronautical Maps' to consist of degree sheets on a scale of 1/200,000, no particular projection being laid down.

"The work involved was immense and a considerable portion fell on the shoulders of the British Empire... The question of design of the aeronautical maps had to be seriously considered; it was desirable to lay down a basic scheme which would be logical and applicable to all aerial maps. Terrestrial man has, under normal conditions, a limited view compared with the airman; his view is horizontal and his horizon is usually limited. The aviator is differently situated; he has a large area spread out beneath him, his horizon is extended, he does not require much in the way of names, but he must have the characteristic geographical features and artificial features to stand out clearly. The map being primarily aeronautical, it was obvious that the provision of aeronautical information should be in a conspicuous form, consequently black was chosen to depict aerodromes, seaplane stations, ports of entry, heights of mountains and passes, the position of aerial and marine lights, lightships and wireless stations and any natural or artificial features which are too small to be represented to scale on the map, but which may be of value to airmen. The next most conspicuous colour, red, was chosen for objects upon which the airman places the next greatest value, such as towns and railways... The question of topographical relief was of next importance, and the layer system was adopted for the general map, because more than any other system it enables the navigator, on plotting his position and finding himself in the neighbourhood of an obstacle, to decide rapidly whether to cross the obstacle by climbing without the prospect of getting into trouble on the other side, or to turn to port or starboard with the object of going round it. Moreover, when planning a flight, a navigator can select and plot his proper course with ease on a layered map.

"At the meeting of the British Association in 1921 the action of the Air Ministry in adopting the Mercator Projection raised a storm of criticism, in which the Mercator and anti-Mercator schools became heavily involved. The Mercator school consisted of those primarily concerned in navigation and the anti-Mercator consisted of cartographers.

"If the aviator were always flying over land and the country beneath him was always visible, it is agreed that the question of projection would be of no practical concern; but he does not always fly over land, and he is often in cloud or haze, so that it follows that some means of navigation is required. There are at present at his disposal only three methods of orienting his course, which are the gyroscopic compass, the wireless compass, and the magnetic compass. Navigation by gyrostat is still in its infancy. In an aeroplane it introduces serious practical difficulties entirely absent in a submarine, for instance. Radio goniometry, while being rapidly developed, has not yet reached a stage in which it can be used for the orientation of a course. The magnetic compass remains: at present, and probably throughout the future, its use will continue, for in spite of certain disadvantages it is very far ahead of other methods in simplicity. Other aids will come in time, but it is doubtful if they will ever oust the simple and practical magnetic needle.

"The foregoing remarks are necessary if the question of a projection for flying is to be viewed in its proper light. The first essential in choosing a projection is the consideration of the purpose which the projection is to fulfill. The general purpose in this case was for air navigation, the particular purpose navigation with a certain instrument.

"The profitable function of the gnomonic projection, on which every great circle is shown as a straight line, lies in the fact that, regarded purely as a chart or geographical diagram, a great circle drawn thereon can be transferred with ease to another projection which lacks its valuable feature of rectilinear presentation of the shortest distance. It is thus that it is used by the navigator.

"For navigation by instrument on the aircraft itself, without external assistance, there is no projection so suitable as the Mercator. Here a straight line on a map is a line of constant compass bearing. The projection has very practical qualities and provides a regular graphical method of navigating; everyday problems of navigating are correctly solved with ease on it – and on it alone – by ruler and pencil. It is true that the linear error of the Mercator, especially in high latitudes, is considerable, but this is overcome by simple graphical methods. The great circle is not a straight line – and it is to this defect that opponents of Mercator draw particular attention. But from a gnomonic chart – a mere sheet of lines of meridians and parallels drawn on a scale which will cover a whole ocean – the great circle can be transferred to the Mercator in a few minutes...

"The aviator is entitled to use that projection which is practically the most easily worked, provided always that to such a projection there are not some fatal drawbacks. Since every projection of whatever form has certain disadvantages and is incapable of general applicability, in a sense there cannot be a theoretically best projection, but the Mercator fulfills the main purpose of flying on a compass course; it possesses various incidental advantages and it has no fatal drawback... It does more nearly meet the general requirements of aerial navigation more than any other, and so far from being obsolete or even obsolescent it is being increasingly used in all civilised countries. Having then chosen the Mercator for the solution of the everyday problems of navigation, the aviator is faced with the task of adapting this projection to special needs...

"But the flight of aircraft is neither limited by geographical boundaries nor terrestrial obstacles, and consequently long distance aerial flight of the future will proceed beyond the limits of general navigation. A flight from England to Japan, for instance, will mean crossing the polar cap, outside the limits of the useful purpose served by the Mercator chart. It should be stated at the outset that as navigation is an art, the art of flying in the polar regions must be learnt; there is no royal road by sea no less than by air to a polar landfall. At present there is no chart or map published which is suitable for this particular purpose.

"It is obvious that great circle sailing will be a necessity of air navigation within the polar regions, by which it is understood that great circle sailing is attained by a succession of thumb lines hugging the great circle. The problem of the selection of a suitable projection for great circle sailing has engaged the attention of seamen for many years... The aviator now enters the lists and still can reach no agreement as to the universally best projection to meet this all-important need. As in the past, the controversy still centres round the choice between the stereographic projection and the gnomonic projection. It is claimed that any projection to be of the utmost use to the navigator must be orthomorphic. That claim is rightly justified providing that by retaining that quality some other drawback is not introduced. Clearly the method of navigation should be the simplest and the charts to be used must be constructed to that end...

"The first consideration is, can a projection solve the problems of navigation by methods involving the simplest means of plotting? The navigator is concerned with two principal lines, the rhumb line and the great circle. The projection chosen must delineate these lines in their simplest forms and if by chance the projection is orthomorphic, then all the better. The gnomonic shows the great circle as a straight line but is not orthomorphic, but by graphical means this disadvantage can be overcome; consequently it more nearly meets the requirements of polar navigation than the compromise afforded by the stereographic projection."

The text of part of a lecture given by Ernest to a learned institution offers an interesting insight into his character:

"May I take it upon myself to remind such of you as may be critical, that Meteorology, no more nor no less than the art of navigation, regarded from any point of view, can lay no claims to being an exact science, and from the nature of its belongings it is useless to expect it ever to become so. In actual practice the results of all the various problems in both sciences are but approximate – some, it is true, less so than others – and it is for the navigator guided by knowledge and experience to choose such information as is the most fitting.

"It might not be out of place to remind you that the real metamorphosis of scientific meteorology from the chrysalis of weather lore was in fact due to the wisdom of the navigators of the last century who realised that meteorology was complementary to the art of navigation for the safe conduct of life and property over the seven seas. In making this statement we have only to remember the names of Admiral Fitzroy and Admiral Beaufort amongst scores of other navigators.

"Given the most reliable weather data and a synoptic chart prepared by the finest exponent of the physical processes of the atmosphere, of what value would the information be if the position of the aircraft were not known? The consequences might be to run into the very danger that should have been avoided. To my mind, the Meteorologist will better serve his purpose in the scheme of the progress of aerial transport by reducing his deductions to the simplest form to be interpreted and made use of in the shortest possible time. We are now developing a system of transmitting weather maps by wireless, and when it is perfected the meteorologist will indeed have performed an inestimable boon to aerial transport. As no two men would interpret the same given meteorological data in the same way, I would claim that this method would serve a better purpose than to lose sight of the practical utility of meteorology in the mists of obscure academic theory. Given this unified map and the Meteorologist's observations, all that remains is to make use of the means to avoid any dangers which it would be the Meteorologist's duty to give warning of.

"Another statement which is likely to be very misleading and which is often taken too literally in these days of rapid scientific progress, is that navigation is done by W/T D/F. Without disparaging the almost phenomenal progress and development of the technical and mechanical side of W/T D/F, it is no boast to say that navigation by W/T D/F only starts after the W/T expert has finished. The application of the wireless bearing to the everyday problems of navigation is one of the greatest difficulties which faces the aerial navigator. By this, I do not take into consideration the short stages such as London to Paris where the practice is more that of pilotage than the pure art of navigation which must be used on long-distance flights. The problem of navigation by means of wireless bearings is that the curvature of the earth has to be taken into consideration, and it is a problem which yet requires considerable investigation and development before W/T D/F bearings can be made use of with any degree of reliance. So that really, when the wireless expert comes along after less than a decade of development and claims that he can navigate by simply giving a W/T bearing, he is in fact drawing a long bow until such time as he can give a better explanation for the many unaccountable errors which he dismisses with such vague terms as 'Heaviside Layer', 'Sunrise and Sunset effects' and 'coast interference'. Up to the present day, little success has attended the introduction of W/T D/F into airships. The voltages induced in the metal structure of the airship introduce such quadrantal errors as to make the system of taking bearings from the ship impracticable.

"With regard to pure navigation or the practice of astronomical navigation, the aerial navigator is on the threshold of a great development, and to him belongs the success of long distance air transport, but whatever the future development, the science will have to be built upon the practice of the seafarer. To the aerial navigator the door is open for the development of methods for the facility and simplicity of computation of the everyday problems of navigation. Those who have been brought up to the sea and who have experienced the distaste for long calculations which that kind of life inspires, will not hesitate to admit that the only means of inducing airmen generally to profit by the numerous occasions which offer themselves for finding their position, is extreme simplicity and brevity of computation. It is not, however, merely a concession to indolence that the aerial navigator should find rules and methods which are as easy and simple as possible; the nature of his task demands that every exertion should be made to abridge computation which has often to be conducted in circumstances of danger and anxiety or fatigue, and so to separate the several points that may be referred directly to what concerns his case, to the exclusion of all other matters. Due to the exertions of Major Wimperis, Captain Bygrave and Flight Lieutenant Capon we have in this country made some outstanding developments in instruments to this end."

CHAPTER EIGHT

FLIGHT TO INDIA

The Parliamentary timetable determined the start of Sir Samuel Hoare on Imperial Airways' first flight to India: on Boxing Day 1926. That year's strikes delayed completion of the aircraft; the prototype *Hercules G-EBMW* did not fly until 30th September, and after modifications she was fit enough to be made available to Imperial in November for pilot familiarisation. She was a large (for her day) two-bay biplane with an open cockpit for the pilot and navigator in the nose behind the central engine. The Wireless Operator and seven passengers were accommodated in a spacious cabin, and there was substantial stowage for mail and luggage. The wing span was just over 79 ft with an area of 1547 square ft to carry a maximum all-up weight of 15,600 lb (tare weight 9,060 lb). Her maximum speed was 128 mph; she cruised at 110 mph and her ceiling was 13,000 ft.

The first *Hercules* left Croydon at daybreak on 18th December with Charles Frank Wolley Dod as First Pilot and W.F. Warner as Second Pilot; it was to go as far as Egypt with Brancker and Woods Humphery as passengers. The second *Hercules*, G-EBMX, was not rolled out until a week before the Secretary of State's flight was scheduled, and was being tested and adjusted right up to the day before his departure. The journey from London to Delhi actually lasted thirteen days, stops being made each night and time being spent en route at places of interest to view the sights. The total journey, however, was completed in under sixty-three flying hours. Ernest wrote his own account of the historic flight thus:

"On December 27th 1926, the day of departure, the weather was none too good; a well-defined depression was situated west of Italy and there were strong easterly winds on the Italian coasts. The depression was spreading northward over France which was causing increasing easterly winds. On the first part of the journey and towards the south of France there was risk of snow.

"Some time before dawn in the cold, biting wind of a typical English winter day, after the final adieux had been taken, the giant airliner took the air majestically and set her course away to the East. When the winter sun arose above the horizon the frostbound country was spread beneath in a pretty panorama, and in quick succession at a groundspeed of 100 mph we passed over familiar places in the southeast of England – Biggin Hill, Tonbridge, Cranbrook, Lympne, Dungeness. As the shores of the Old Country receded in the distance, realisation of the magnitude and importance of the task before us drove away our feelings of depression, and with a last glimpse of the cliffs of Dover our course was set across the Channel.

"Very soon we were over the coast of France at Etaples, then, leaving Boulogne and the coast far behind us, we were making moderately good progress, groundspeed 90 mph, against adverse winds across northern France. Our course at first lay over Abbeville and other familiar places on the London-Paris air route such as Poix and Beauvais. Although Paris did not lie directly on our course, we made a slight detour to get a glimpse of this beautiful city which, to those who have seen it from the air for the first time, affords a thrill of amazement.

"Although not landing at Le Bourget we took our departure from this terminal airport of France for our next course, and waved farewell to many of our friends below who we knew would be keenly watching our progress. The rest of the way lay over alternate cultivated fields and forest, and although the weather was decidedly rough the first 373 miles to Dijon were completed in four hours at an average speed of 93 mph. Here the French authorities had arranged a spectacular reception in honour of the Secretary of State. Having refreshed ourselves and refuelled the machine, the journey was continued down the Rhone Valley where the threatened snow was encountered. By flying low, however, the worst of the weather was avoided. Marseilles was reached just before dark at 4 pm, having completed the 268 miles from Dijon in 2 hours and 40 minutes (97 mph).

"The night was spent in Marseilles and an early start made at 7.30 am the next morning in a thick fog. The course lay over the south of France and along the Cote D'Azur, but after climbing above the fog layer the most perfect flying weather was experienced and eventually the fog dispersed. Only a romantic pen can describe the charm and beauty of that journey under a turquoise sky over a placid sea of deepest ultramarine, along a coast of verdant mountains backed by the majestic peaks of the Alpes Maritimes.

"Arriving at Pisa – 3 hours and 10 minutes – having completed another 295 miles of the journey at 93 mph, another hospitable reception awaited us, and after having refuelled and refreshed ourselves the journey was continued without loss of time. Soon the bad weather we were warned of was encountered, and owing to heavy rain and hail squalls the coast of Italy was not seen at its best. The 280 miles to Naples was completed in under three hours (93 mph), and after a brilliant reception we were vastly disappointed by Naples itself: the predominant image that remains in the mind to the exclusion of all else is the impressiveness of Vesuvius. A departure was made the next day at a reasonable hour after refuelling, and we flew over the crater of Vesuvius to obtain an awe-inspiring view of this active volcano as it spurted out jets of steam. Shaping our course out to sea, we next saw Stromboli; and eventually we passed Etna, an active volcano with snow on its crater. It was a remarkable experience to see three active volcanoes in the course of a few hours' journey.

"Three hours after leaving Naples we landed at Catania, 246 miles on, and then made preparations for our first serious sea crossing to Malta. The weather gradually deteriorated, and after leaving Cape Pissaro we experienced a strong cross wind. The sea was lashed up into an angry turmoil, and judging by the fuss the surface craft were making of it, we were thankful to be making the crossing in more comfortable conditions. Flying low under the scudding cloud so as to avoid the worst of the storm, fairly good progress was maintained with a groundspeed of 75 mph, but frequently on account of the terrific rain squalls the engines had to be slowed down to prevent damage to the delicately constructed and balanced airscrews. At last we arrived at Malta. Here we were very much at home amongst our friends of the Royal Air Force, who gave us a rousing welcome.

"During the night the centre of the storm we had experienced the previous day had reached us, and as we were about to depart the trough of the storm passed over bringing torrential rain and a sudden shift of wind. Punctually to schedule, however, the machine made her departure for the next stage of the journey over 230 miles of sea. This was no mean undertaking for a land machine without floats or any means of alighting on the sea, but the engines behaved splendidly and never faltered. The serious business of navigation now commenced in earnest.

"The course was oriented by means of an aperiodic, or dead-beat, compass. In the limited space available in an aeroplane the navigator does not have the luxury of a chart room where he can lay off his course comfortably as in a ship; therefore he must make the best use of the space he has. The maps and charts are kept in a map case which carries a combined parallel ruler and protractor. By a simple manipulation of the protractor the magnetic variation can be set and thus the magnetic course simply determined. The air being a very unstable element, the machine is affected by every change of wind; this affects the speed over the ground and the course to steer in relation to the course to be made good. To determine these data a drift sight is made use of constantly, as a correct knowledge of the drift and the groundspeed is the prime factor in making a successful landfall. When flying over the sea or in fog or over the clouds, the navigator must keep his dead reckoning and check up with astronomical observations. The aerial navigator's sextant is distinctly different in design and operation to the sextant used by the marine navigator, but its purpose is identical. With the sextant altitude, together with the known hour angle of the heavenly body and its declination, a spherical triangle is solved which then gives the necessary data to determine the position of the aircraft. Of course it is impossible to work out this problem by direct methods using tables of logarithmic trigonometric functions because by the time the work was completed the position would be useless owing to the great speed of the aeroplane; therefore the navigator must use a rapid means of solution, and for this purpose he uses a special sliderule which solves the spherical triangle in less than two minutes with a degree of accuracy within two miles.

"As the journey proceeded, the weather gradually improved until at last under truly tropical conditions we sighted Homs, a tiny desert outpost on the African coast. Here, surrounded by the vast Libyan Desert, the Officers of the tiny outpost had prepared a reception second to none in the whole of our journey. A lunch that would have done credit to the best hotel in Europe was served to us, and we were very sorry to leave this hospitable spot. It was here that the native sentry on the lookout tower of the tiny fort reminded us of Jimmy Jeffs, the Officer in the Control Tower at Croydon, and Frank Barnard caused some mirth by referring to him as the Civil Air Traffic Control Officer.

"Next we had a hop of 350 miles over the sea to Benghazi, a small seaport and garrison in Tripoli. Wireless communication over this stretch, as the previous one, was maintained by a patrol of HM Destroyers stationed on the route. We were really glad of their cooperation, but sorry for the discomfort they had to endure, as the destroyers were making heavy weather in the face of a westerly gale. It was certainly very bumpy on the sea, but in the air it was perfect, and although our engines were well throttled down we were at times doing a groundspeed of 135 mph. However, we were not sorry to see Benghazi after such a long sea crossing. We landed 2 hours and 30 minutes after leaving Homs, and spent a very pleasant night with the Officers of the garrison.

"On December 31st our way lay over the Libyan Desert where the few oases are peopled by hostile nomadic tribes whose religious fanaticism is only equalled by their bitter hatred of white people. At Benghazi we heard many hair-raising stories of the torture these people imposed on anyone so unfortunate as to be captured by them, and it was with uncomfortable feelings that we made our preparations for the journey and stowed away emergency rations and water in case of any untoward event that might occasion us to make a forced landing. After saying goodbye to our Italian hosts, who were still full of grave warnings and advice, we set off. As soon as we were in the air, however, our grim forebodings were all dispersed as our engines immediately inspired us with the utmost confidence. We flew over the ancient cities of Ptolemy, Appolonia and Cyrene; then, leaving these relics of an ancient civilisation we traversed the desolate and monotonous Libyan Desert, eventually arriving at the Egyptian frontier post of Sollum to refuel after 3 hours and 24 minutes in flight.

"Beyond Sollum, the way continued over hundreds of miles of still more barren desert until at last the green delta of the mighty Nile gave respite to the eye. We reached Alexandria and landed at Aboukir after three hours flying. Again we had a warm reception and joined in the festivities of the New Year."

At this stage, Captain Barnard handed the aircraft over to Captain Wolley Dod who had brought the first Hercules out to Egypt just before Christmas. Wolley Dod had a unique knowledge of the way ahead, having, together with Colonel Shelmerdine, carried out the detailed ground survey of the Cairo-Karachi sector just over a year before. Major Woods Humphery, the General Manager of Imperial, joined the passengers on this sector to India.

Ernest's narrative continues:

"At midday on 1st January 1927 we set off on the second stage of our flight. Leaving the delta of the Nile behind, our way lay over the arid desert of Philestre; after three hours we landed at Gaza to refuel. From there, our journey lay to the eastward; the land rising rapidly and the machine having steadily climbed we just got a glimpse of Hebron over the brow of a hill. Below us next came the tiny village of Bethlehem which ranks first among the holiest places on earth. Soon we saw a white speck on the hills to the northward: this was Jerusalem. After climbing to 3,500 ft to clear the mountains, we suddenly got our first view of the Dead Sea which conjured up visions of Dante's Inferno.

"A few miles further on, we landed at Ziza, a halt on the Hedjaz railway where an emergency landing ground has been established some fifteen miles from Amman. There is a rest-house here in case it is necessary to stop the night en route, but on account of the complete lack of comfort, the scarcity of water and the terrible loneliness of the place, it is particularly to be avoided. The nights are bitterly cold and it is not infrequently that heavy falls of snow are experienced during the night. The solitude is made gruesome by the hideous howling of the desert jackals.

"The valley of the Jordan and the Dead Sea is separated from the Iraq Plain by a broad elevated tract. At the place where it is crossed by the air mail route this table-land has a width from east to west of about 450 miles and average height of 2,000 ft. Woe betide the unfortunate traveller who gets lost in this region. As we flew over it early in the morning of January 2nd we were thankful for a conviction of the reliability and efficiency of our engines, but we conjured up thoughts of what the terrors of a forced landing in this terrible desert must mean.

"After two and a half hours, having covered another 275 miles (groundspeed 110 mph) we arrived at the outpost fort of Rutbah. This desert fort is maintained by the Iraqi Government for the purpose of affording protection to travellers against raiding tribes, and to guard the water wells, as it is the only place in this desert where permanent water wells exist. The fort is a rest house on the desert motor route which passes close by. This route was surveyed and prepared in 1919 by the indefatigable efforts of one of our passengers, Air Vice-Marshal Sir Geoffrey Salmond, together with Group Captain Fellowes, my present Chief at Cardington, and is a mark in the desert for all time to remind travellers of their indomitable courage and daring. As we landed, a convoy of desert cars arrived en route from Baghdad to

Damascus. The travel-stained and weary passengers flocked into the fort and greetings were exchanged. We heaved a sigh of relief that we had been spared their discomfort and congratulated ourselves that we were doing the journey in as many hours as it took them days. At this place we refuelled the machine and regaled ourselves in the little eating-house inside the fort. I was surprised at the fare served up – even if the camel steak was tough and the lager tepid, one ate and drank with an unusual relish.

"Leaving Rutbah our way lay across still more desert, but the nature of the country changed as we approached the uncompromisingly flat, greyish, dusty plain of Iraq lying between the Euphrates and the Tigris. We arrived at Baghdad in 2 hours 45 minutes after leaving Rutbah, a distance of 250 miles at 110 mph.

"We took off just after 8 am next morning and, after leaving Baghdad, the first place of interest was the site of the city of Ctesiphon. There still remains the ruin of the Great Hall, 148 ft long by 76 ft broad and 85 ft high, spanned by a vaulted roof of which the middle part remains. Diverting from our proper course we passed over the land which is reputed to have been the Garden of Eden, but it is now only a narrow strip of vegetation on either bank of the river, bounded by desert. Eventually we discerned the ruins of the great Palace of Nebuchadnezzar. The site of this palace is an irregular square about 700 yds and masses of burnt brick of considerable height are still standing. It was also just possible to pick up the remains of the Tower of Babylon which stands by itself and is a great mound of unburned brick about 70-75 ft high with sides about 275 yds. The most remarkable site of all, however, was the ancient city of Ur of the Chaldees, the birthplace of Abraham, which we flew over a couple of hours after taking off. Very extensive excavations are at present being carried out. We flew so low here to take photographs that we scared the labourers and incidentally lost our trailing aerial.

"After three crowded hours of interest we eventually landed at Shaibah some ten or eleven miles outside Basra, for refuelling before carrying on with our journey. The heat grew oppressive and even by flying as high as 2,500 ft we found no relief, the sun beating down on us unmercifully. As we approached Bushire the coast became rocky and precipitous, and eventually signs of cultivation were to be seen, and it was a welcome relief to find green fields and pastures when we landed at Bushire after two hours and twenty minutes (groundspeed 108 mph).

"It was here that we met Stack and Leete, the two intrepid sportsmen who had flown from London and were en route to India in their two De Havilland Moth machines with 63 HP Cirrus engines. These two adventurous sportsmen had no navigators or mechanics with them, and had to do everything with their own hands and such tools as they were able to carry, which as far as one could judge was one very meagre toolkit, a twelve inch rule, a pair of dividers and last but not least their now famous banjolele. This meeting was more in the nature of a family affair, and was the occasion of the photographing of a family group – not only ourselves but of the machines, for the two small Moths with their wing span of twenty-nine feet and small engine nestling under the wings of the *Hercules* with its wing span of nearly sixty feet and her three huge Jupiter engines made a striking contrast, illustrating the remarkable talent of their designer Geoffrey De Havilland. The effect was like a mother hen sitting with her chicks.

"It was here in Bushire, our first stop in Persian territory, that we were impressed with the strangeness of this little-known country where we met so many different types, and saw so many strange customs. Communications are almost non-existent, and it is usual for despatches to be carried by relays of messengers from one end of the country to the other. One realises, however, the importance of the situation of Persia and in its present state of unrest it is the weak link in the chain of Empire communications.

"For the rest of the journey down the Persian Gulf, resumed the following morning, the scenery was of the wildest nature imaginable. Great jagged-peaked mountains rose sheer out of the salt-encrusted plain to over 5,000 ft. For miles and miles, fang-like, serrated and terraced ranges reared themselves upward and made a scene suggestive of a nightmare. For miles and miles there is no sign of either life or vegetation. At Lingeh we landed on a coral outcrop covered with sand. As usual, the refuelling operation was hurriedly completed as our course was against the sun, and the distances covered being so great, time was lost each day as we flew further and further eastward; sometimes as much as an hour was lost in a day's flight.

"Leaving Lingeh at 13.24, the track was across the precipitous and inaccessible promontory of Oman rising sheer out of the sea to 5,000 ft. North of Oman the clouds were at 7,000 ft and we climbed a further 1,000 ft to get on top of them. After crossing the Gulf of Oman we landed at Jask, a telegraph station of the Indo-European Telegraph Company. Here we were given a rousing welcome by the few people manning the station, and received every hospitality at their hand. Before we had time to collect our kit, we saw Stack and Leete approaching, and we waited to join in the reception for them.

"We had some distance to go to our quarters, and as Jask is reputed to be the only place in the world which does not possess a Ford car, we had to do the journey by camel. We spent a very jovial night celebrating our reunion, and when we were about to turn in and took a last look at the weather to size up our prospects for the next day's flight, Wolley Dod and I were a little uneasy about the shifting of the wind from northwest to northeast. There was no specialised meteorological information here for us, and not having a local knowledge we could not at first conjecture what this change meant, but, having had good luck so far, we went to bed with what proved to be undue optimism for the next day's chances. As the night wore on, the wind freshened and our sleep was very disturbed. Becoming uneasy, I got up and looked out – imagine my chagrin to find a dust storm was raging and getting more severe every minute. By daylight it was impossible to see 500 yds and the wind was gusting stronger than ever.

"We made all preparations to start, and after consultation with the local weather prophets who assured us that the storm could only be local, and that in any case a dust storm had never been known to persist after 9 am in the living memory of the Oldest Inhabitant, we decided to push on, as we could not afford to lose any time if we intended to complete the next stage of our journey to Karachi. We took off at 0904, but alas it was another of those occasions when the meteorological conditions proved the exception rather than the rule. On climbing we found we could not get out of the storm at 8,000 ft and that the wind was every minute becoming stronger, and although we had gone as far as we had anticipated would be the limit of the storm we could not find a sign of its abatement. The situation called for prompt action – our next landing place was a spot on a featureless desert which would be difficult to find under good conditions, the country to be covered was unknown to us and unsurveyed and our maps were therefore unreliable. The decision was made to retrace our tracks, but owing to the high mountains we were forced to turn out to sea on a heading of 255 degrees and get as far off them as possible so as to avoid any possibility of colliding with them, as we could not see twenty yards by this time. After a while we shaped our course towards land on 315 degrees, and after some anxious moments flying about twenty-five feet over the sea, we flew over Jask and Wolley Dod made a perfect landing to the relief of everyone on the ground who had become very worried about us.

"The visibility was about fifty yards, and so it remained all day. The sand was driven with such force that it opened up newly healed cuts and made them festering sores in a few minutes; and it was even painful to open the eyes. Out of doors the conditions were appalling, indoors they were miserable, and it was a very despondent party that spent the day in enforced inactivity.

"The next morning, although the air was not quite clear, the weather was good enough to proceed, and we set off at 9.19 with the determination to make up for the lost day. The next stage was over treacherous country, mangrove swamp and salt lagoons, to Pasni, a tiny native fishing village on the Makran coast. Arriving there after 3 hours and 39 minutes we just missed the tail end of the storm, and in fact we followed it along for the rest of our journey. In any case we were thankful that we had turned back the previous day because it would have been very difficult to find another place in the world in so desolate and featureless a spot. Imagine our surprise, then, to find a wonderful lunch prepared for us. The food had been brought 250 miles and was supplied by the Khan of Khulat. Liquid refreshment was supplied from glass jugs, and Wolley Dod after slaking his thirst said 'What jolly good whiskey and soda that was'. Tasting the refreshing, cool drink, I replied with derision that it was ginger ale. Such was the state of our palates after having swallowed so much sand during the last twenty-four hours that we were unable to appreciate the bouquet of the vintage Champagne.

"In spite of the magnificent hospitality of the aged Khan we were eager to get on and make up for lost time, for we were timed to arrive at Karachi at 5.25. We took off at 14.25. The rest of the journey was over still more desolate country, where we flew between 5,000 and 7,000 ft for comfort, and then over the sea where we dropped down to 500 ft. At half past five in the afternoon of January 6th we landed at the Royal Air Force Depot, Karachi.

"A general holiday had been proclaimed and a multitude of people witnessed our arrival – the first Air Mail Liner to India. The first span in the chain of Empire communications had been completed to schedule, 5,500 miles in 54 hours 45 minutes flying time. It was a red letter day even in the history of the prosperous City of Karachi, establishing it as the first civil airport in India, where in the very near future the aeroplanes of Imperial Airways will link up with the airship routes completing the journey from England to India in five days and to Australia in another six days.

"The next day we left at 11.20 according to schedule, having made up the time we had lost, and we were in a very contented frame of mind when we undertook to cross the Scind Desert into Rajputana. Here again for nearly 400 miles our journey lay over arid desert – our maps having the terse word 'unsurveyed' printed over a sheet devoid of any features. It is always with a feeling of relief that we approach our objective under these conditions, and it was a pleasant sight at last to see the white city of Jodhpur loom up on the distant horizon. We landed after being in the air for 4 hours 3 minutes, an average speed of 86 mph.

"His Highness the Maharaja of Jodhpur greeted us in person and proclaimed a holiday in honour of our visit. Nowhere before had such a concourse of people turned out to meet us, and our welcome was overwhelming. A State Dinner was held that night and a brilliant company was present. The night was spent at the Palace, and everyone was reluctant to depart from such oriental hospitality and splendour.

"Leaving next day at 09.10 the way lay over less desolate country, and as we approached the fertile valley of the Jumna and Sutlej, we saw on every hand evidence of the vast agricultural wealth of India. At ten minutes before the scheduled time, that is at 12.20 on January 7th 1927, *G-EBMX* arrived at Delhi, the Imperial City of India and the capital of that extraordinary country of magnificence and splendour. Here also a holiday had been declared, and the community turned out en masse. The stream of natives to the aerodrome in every kind of vehicle seemed to be never-ending. The crowd was so great that the police could not hold them back, and their eagerness and excitement were so great that it was difficult to disembark from the machine.

"Thus was the total journey from London to Delhi, a distance of 6,124 miles, completed in 62 hours 30 minutes flying time."

So ended Ernest's account of the flight. On 12th January he and Wolley Dod took the machine up to Amballa where they spent a fortnight while it was overhauled. They returned to Delhi on 30th January to pick up Sir Samuel Hoare's party for the trip back to Cairo, together with the redoubtable Sir Sefton Brancker who, having left England in the first machine on 18th December, had gone on from Cairo to hold further negotiations with the Persian Government at Teheran before coming on to India by boat from Basra. Even at this late stage the Persians were proving to be obstructive. In the event, the Cairo-Karachi service which was scheduled to open in April did not operate for another two years. Even then, the route to India was covered in four stages: by *Argosy* from Croydon to Basle, thence by train to Genoa; by *Calcutta* flying boat from there to Alexandria; and finally onwards to Karachi by Hercules.

When Brancker arrived in India he was delighted with the enthusiastic response of the Indian Government to the Secretary of State's journey, and in characteristic style he decided to strike swiftly while the iron was hot. The Government of India needed a Civil Aviation Department of its own, headed by an expert professional civil aviator; he had an eminently suitable man in Lt. Colonel F.C. Shelmerdine, the Air Ministry Superintendent of the Cairo-Karachi Air Route, residing in Cairo; so, using all his charm, enthusiasm and diplomacy, he rapidly persuaded the Government of India to do what he thought best for it.

G-EBMX left Delhi on 1st February. Sir Samuel decided to break the journey for a whole day at Karachi so that he could inspect the huge airship shed being built there for the Imperial airship programme. Just as the twin sheds at Cardington were the biggest buildings in Britain so this one would be the largest building in all India. He invited Ernest to join him and Brancker. Brancker told Ernest that he was proposing to move Shelmerdine immediately from Cairo to Delhi to become the first Director of Civil Aviation in India, and that he wanted Tymms to come out to Heliopolis to take his place in due course. As an interim measure, he invited Ernest, subject to the agreement of the Director of Airship Development, to act as Air Ministry Superintendent of the Cairo-Basra sector, oversee the inauguration of the Air Mail service, and hold the fort until Tymms arrived. He should be able to fulfill his obligation to Imperials as well, and the arrangements for his wife to come out on the next *Hercules* delivery flight would be unaffected. Ernest accepted the proposal with zest. Brancker characteristically put the wheels in motion within the hour.

The flight back to Egypt passed off with little incident, save that the schedule was altered at the request of Sir Samuel to enable him to fly from Baghdad to Cairo in one day. This was accomplished on 7th February. After a State banquet given by King Faisal at the Royal Palace, attended by his two brothers King Ali and the Emir Abdullah of Transjordania, the *City of Delhi* left Baghdad at 0430 GMT, refuelled at Rutbah Wells and Ziza, and landed in the dark at Cairo at 17.00 GMT, accomplishing a day's journey of 833 miles in 9 hours 42 minutes flying time, then regarded as something of an achievement. Sir Samuel described it thus:

"As far as Beersheba it was still fairly light, but almost the whole way thence to Cairo it was pitch dark without a flicker of a star. For an hour and a half, therefore, we had our second experience of night flying: but once again Captain Wolley Dod and Captain Johnston never left the fairway. Flying entirely by compass they kept to the middle of the course over Ismailia and, if I may continue the golfing metaphor, holed out at Cairo without a mistake. It was a thrilling moment when, after an hour of complete darkness, we caught sight of the lights of Ismailia and a ship or two in the Canal; it was even more thrilling when, after a circle or two over the glare of Cairo, we dropped surely and safely on to the aerodrome at Heliopolis."

At the beginning of February Daisy flew out in the fourth *Hercules*, G-EBMZ, piloted by the legendary one-eyed Captain Hinchliffe, to meet Ernest in Cairo. Her travelling companions were the machine's design Captain, later Sir, Geoffrey de Havilland and his wife. The Johnstons stayed happily in Cairo until Freddy and Millie Tymms arrived by sea. Having completed his work for Imperial Airways and handed over the superintendence of the Cairo Baghdad route to Freddy, Ernest returned to his airships and an early death; but Tymms lived on to do great things for aviation in Africa and India, was twice granted the accolade of knighthood, and eventually became one of the most influential and respected men to have served on the Council of the International Civil Aviation Organisation.

CHAPTER NINE

THE LAUNCH OF R101

On 8th October 1929 the Works formally handed *R101* to her Captain. The flying crew began watchkeeping routine, practising drills, starting and running engines and generally shaking down while they waited for weather suitable for taking her out to the mast. On the 11th the Met Office gave a favourable forecast, and Ernest, together with Lieut Commander 'Grabby' Atherstone and Flg Officer Steff, slept on board prior to rising at 0400 hrs on the 12th to prepare the ship for walking out. There was a feeling of high excitement, for none of her Officers and crew had flown in an airship since *R33*'s final sortie three years before. Indeed, Atherstone had not flown since his tour of duty as First Officer of *R29* in 1919, while Steff, the Second Officer, had no airship experience at all: he was an RAF Balloon Officer who had been in charge of the kite balloons used for working out the detailed mooring drills at the mast and training people in how to operate them. He was an experienced free-balloonist, and because he was so keen and enthusiastic, Scott had taken him on as a trainee airship Officer. Ernest had a dual function in both ships: as Chief Navigation Officer he was responsible to the Captain for all wireless and navigation equipment and for co-ordinating the navigation activity of the other watchkeeping officers as well as controlling the schedule of wireless traffic; and being a certificated airship pilot first class he acted as Officer on Watch when needed. Both Captains also were to act as OOW on longer flights, for reasons partly of economy and partly because Scott wanted to keep his flying staff as small as possible in the early days so that each individual could derive the fullest possible training value from each hour in the air.

So, before dawn on 12th October *R101* was ballasted up slightly heavy in the shed. Scott was in overall control on the ground; Irwin, Atherstone and No 1 Watch were on board; Nos 2 and 3 Watches formed part of the handling party of 400 men; Steff was in charge of the bow handling party (which was first to emerge from the shed) and Ernest the more critical stern. The handling parties in position, Scottie ordered "Ease up the guys – hands off", to make sure that the ship was near enough to equilibrium to be lifted. Promptly at 0545 he ordered "Hold on", then "Lift up the car – Walk ship ahead". As the nose emerged a slight breeze developed, more or less across the axis of the shed, but they held the ship straight; and just three and a half minutes after the evolution began Ernest sang out "All clear aft." There was a loud cheer from a multitude of onlookers. Scott gave orders to manoeuvre her across wind to port to get her downwind of the mast. During the next few minutes the ship became very light aft and Irwin had to valve gas.

When she reached the mooring point, Scott climbed aboard and took control from Irwin; Atherstone in the bows paid out the main wire and the yaw-guy wires which were then shackled on to the equivalent wires already laid out on the ground. R101 was then let go to rise to the full extent of the wires, but about 200 ft above the ground Scott had to drop some two tons of ballast to force her through a strong temperature inversion. When she was steady at 600 ft he gave the order for a white flag to be displayed. The Mooring Officer on the mast, Flying Officer Cook, acknowledged with a similar flag and began to winch the ship towards the tower. From this point onwards, control of the mooring operation passed from the commander of the ship to the Mooring Officer. The ship was hauled on all three wires simultaneously down to within fifty feet of the mooring arm, the function of the yaw-guys, the lead of which was set well aft as well as athwartships, being to prevent the ship's over-riding the mast as well as to prevent the bows' yawing from side to side. At fifty feet the yaw-guy winches were stopped, and the main winch continued to haul at slow speed until the cone on the ship's bow engaged in the cup on the extended mooring arm. This done, the mooring arm was racked vertical and retracted into the tower head. At last Cook reported to the Captain 'Ship Secured'. The bow gangway was then lowered to permit access between ship and masthead; the water main was connected to the ship to provide a supply of ballast to compensate for major variations of the ship's weight and lift; an earthing connection was made, an electrical main supply connected, and also a telephone. The lines for connecting the four ballast weights on the ground along the length of the ship were let down from joints on the main frames.

During the rest of that day and all the following day, tower watchkeeping routine was set up. The routine evolved in R33 was perpetuated in both R100 and R101: the crew, with the watchkeeping Officers, was permanently divided into three watches – Liberty, Standby and Duty. The Duty Watch manned the ship from 0800 hours for the next twenty-four hours, being relieved for meals by the Standby. The Standby also worked normal hours whilst the ship was moored and was next in line to be Duty Watch. In the event of emergency or Storm Routine the Standby Watch was also available to be recalled to the ship to reinforce the Duty Watch. The Liberty Watch was free of all commitments from the time it was released until 0800 the following day, when it became Standby. Each Duty Watch took its turn for the maintenance of the ship, and this routine continued day in and day out, whether the ship was at the mast or in the shed. Normally two watches manned the ship in flight, the third remaining on the ground so as to be able to relieve the flying crew quickly at the end of a trip. It proved to be a taxing routine for the Officers, particularly later with two ships in commission and only six Officers qualified to do it.

Initially for mast routine Irwin decided that until Atherstone and Steff had gained more experience, the Officers should keep watch in pairs – himself with Atherstone, Ernest with Steff. For the whole of the first hectic day at the mast, and the next, the crew (few of whom had ever been in the air before) were hard at work running engines and testing all systems. In the middle of it all, the Chief of Air Staff came on board with Lady Trenchard and their son, as did Brancker later in the day: all were served coffee in the lounge. During the afternoon of the second day, *R101* was let up to the full extent of her mooring wires to test the mast systems and run through the mooring drill.

At 1117 hrs on 14th October *R101* slipped from the mast on her first flight. Scott was in command, with Irwin in the role of Captain under training. 'Mouldy' Booth, the Captain of *R100*, was on board as a supernumerary Officer. The most eminent passenger was Air Vice-Marshal Sir John Higgins, now Air Member for Supply and Research; he was accompanied by most of the senior people at Cardington. The weather was calm, ideal for Ernest's principal task which was to calibrate the compasses and wireless direction finding equipment. During the afternoon the air became moderately bumpy, making the ship occasionally pitch slowly about three degrees nose up and nose down. Ernest and the other three Officers each had a short spell on the rudders and the elevators; the ship answered pleasantly without much effort, and everyone was well pleased with the ship's stability and control. For most of the time only two engines had been operating, so the speed was generally in the mid-30s and did not exceed 45 knots.

Almost before *R101* had landed back at the mast after this first flight, Lord Thomson, who had watched her fly over Whitehall, was dashing off memoranda about his own desire to fly in her as soon as possible, his wish that Sir Samuel Hoare should be given an early opportunity of a flight, and the desirability of planning other public relations flights. As Air Ministry officials began to pester Cardington about organising dates and passenger lists, Scott remonstrated bitterly to Colmore: he had not just one job to do, but three – to test fly a huge ship full of novel design features, to work the bugs out of a prototype mooring system, and to shake down a very green crew. He resented having at the same time to go poodlefaking with every Tom, Dick and Harry who thought he deserved a ride in the new ship. When the Secretary of State himself had been scheduled for the second flight, Colmore minuted his Chief, Sir John Higgins, on the 16th: "I should greatly prefer that no visitors should be carried on the 3rd and 4th flights except airship personnel." He was over-ruled, and nobody had the strength to put a foot down. Sam Hoare and Geoffrey Lloyd headed the passenger list on the third flight. The Mayor and Deputy Mayor of Bedford and thirty-eight senior officials of various Government Departments were scheduled for the fourth; ten Members of Parliament with special aviation interests and twenty-two Air Ministry passengers – including Sefton Brancker – were scheduled for the fifth; and worse was to come: Thomson's answer to growing criticism of R101's shortfall of useful lift in Parliament and Press was to insist that she carry a party of 100 Members of Parliament on her seventh flight. He and his officials in Whitehall obviously had a stronger concern for fatuous propaganda than for the need to give Scott and his Officers a period of undistracted development flying. Irwin, and later in R100 Booth, protested vehemently to Scott about having to pander to a constant stream of joyriders during those vital early flights, instead of proving the limits of the ship's capabilities and training the crew to respond to simulated emergencies: but to no avail.

The second flight, which lasted nine and a half hours, took place on 18th October. Thomson joined the ship at 7.30 in the morning together with Christopher Bullock, his Principal Private Secretary (soon to become Permanent Secretary of the Air Ministry). She slipped at 0812 hrs, Scott in charge, and flew via Birmingham to Nottingham and back. This time all four engines operated at cruising power (the fifth one at this time, owing to the difficulty of designing a reversing mode for those Diesel engines, could only be used for astern power). With half a mind on the safety of his VIP passengers, Scott decided that it would not be prudent to try any of the scheduled speed tests, but some moderate turning trials were carried out at 1,500 ft before the failure of a condenser pump in the steam cooling system caused him to shorten the flight. Nevertheless all the watchkeeping Officers and the Coxswains of the two flying watches had plenty of opportunity to acquire the feel of the ship. Their general impression was that she steered well but was a bit sluggish on the elevators.

As soon as Thomson disembarked he faced a barrage of reporters to whom he made an enthusiastic speech, concluding with the words: "So long as I am in charge no pressure will be brought to bear on the technical staff or anyone else, to undertake any long distance flights until they are ready and all is in order. Subject to this I hope to travel to India during the Parliamentary Recess at Christmas. But whether this is possible or not, the whole policy of the airship programme is 'Safety First' – and 'Safety Second' as well." Ernest and his colleagues greeted reports of this speech with sardonic laughter, and to Colmore and Richmond it was deeply embarrassing, for Richmond and his team were already working hard on schemes to increase her lifting capacity and reduce her weight. While the design staff was scratching for ways to give the ship enough range, Colmore was considering the feasibility of erecting additional mooring masts at intermediate points along the route to India, and Scott was concerned with the immediate problems of training the Officers and crews of two different ships at the same time as proving the basic soundness of one very unorthodox airship in flight. All of them thought Thomson was talking dangerous humbug.

A couple of days after this flight, Maurice Giblett, (one of the most able of the scientific staff of the Meteorological Office, who had been head of the Airship Division since 1925) warned of the approach of widespread bad weather; so Scott decided to take advantage of a calm spell to put the ship back in her shed. He stayed on board for the first part of the operation. Conditions were flat calm and therefore somewhat difficult for accurate manoeuvring; without the help of even a slight breeze to provide either steerage way or dynamic lift, the engines had to be used for movement fore and aft, and the ballasting had to be done very precisely for both vertical movement and trim. The operation took nearly three hours, finally being completed successfully in the dark. For all his apparently casual and often light-hearted approach to his work, Scott was always willing to show the way and never shirked difficult operational decisions.

Useful minor work was done on the ship in the shed. She was ready to come out in the quiet dawn of 1st November, and slipped from the mast a couple of hours later for her third flight. At Thomson's express wish, Sir Samuel Hoare was on board. He greeted Ernest as an old comrade of that earlier pioneer flight to India. Indeed, as far as Colmore, Scott, Richmond and Johnston were concerned, there was a friendly feeling towards Sam Hoare which was entirely lacking in the case of Thomson, whose "Cardington" title they ridiculed, and who, for all his charm and enthusiasm, was always regarded by them with some suspicion, as an outsider who was using airships to further his own not inconsiderable ambitions.

On this and the next three flights the crew settled down to an elaborate schedule of functioning tests covering engine performance, operation of fuel and ballast systems, gas bags and valves, controls, instruments and many other details. Meager, the First Officer of R100, flew on this and the next flight to gain handling experience of so huge a ship, and he confirmed Ernest's view that the elevators were rather sluggish. The flight lasted seven hours. Although Scott was in command, Irwin was given full control of the ship from slipping to mooring. In the light of later events it is significant that Irwin's flight report contains the statement "Gas valved takes an appreciable time to get clear of the ship".

She made her first night flight on 2nd/3rd November, slipping at 2040 hrs and securing to the mast fourteen hours later. In the very early hours of the morning she was put to her speed trials on a triangular course Needles-Durleston Head-Poole-Needles. With four engines at full power she reached 55 knots on the first leg between Needles and Durleston Head, but as she turned towards Poole one of the engines packed up and could not be started again. With three engines at full power she completed the course at 51 knots and everyone was pleased with her steady, stable flight in windy, but not gusty, conditions. While being attached to the mast after this flight she suffered minor damage when the bows fouled the top, but it was repaired satisfactorily during the day. What happened was that during the final stage of hauling down to the mast there was a wind shift; by then, Irwin had handed control over to the Mooring Officer on the mast. When the wind shifted, he stopped hauling so that the yaw-guys could be changed. Scott, judging the ship to be too near the mast-head to do this safely, over-ruled him. On the final haul-in the nose of the ship hit the mast-head and bent one of the nose-tubes. Atherstone, whose station was on the mooring platform in the bows, was extremely critical of Scott, and later voiced his opinion to Ernest, whose job during mooring was to be in the control car to give assistance to the Captain in computing lift and trim. Ernest tactfully suggested to Irwin that at the next suitable occasion Atherstone should be given an opportunity to be in the control car during a mooring in order to get a wider perspective of the whole occasion; for this, Ernest volunteered to take Atherstone's place on the mooring platform.

Scott now felt that sufficient performance data had been gathered to analyse the problems arising from the shortfall of useful lift in relation to the India flight. Richmond had meanwhile produced some proposals for reducing the structure weight by about three tons; and Michael Rope, who had designed the ingenious wiring system by means of which the lift was transferred from the gas bags to the main structure, had estimated that the gross lift could be increased by as much as three tons if the wiring were enlarged so as to permit an expansion of the volume of the bags. Richmond had also worked out that, subject to detailed design and stressing considerations, some further nine tons of gross lift could be provided by inserting an additional bay and gas cell amidships.

Accordingly, for several days after the flight of 2nd/3rd November Ernest was hard at work analysing the various flight plans for the Indian journey in relation to seasonal variations of wind and temperature in the light of the ship's known performance figures. He submitted to Scottie a series of alternative flight times and fuel loads. It was evident from the first that for year-round operation to India the disposable load would have to be increased by twenty tons because of the adverse effect of hot weather on the gross lift; the extra bay would therefore be needed as well as the other measures suggested by Richmond and Rope. What was more difficult to decide was whether, without going to the length of inserting a new bay, the disposable load could be sufficiently improved to permit a cold-weather demonstration flight to India in March. Ernest, the only man at Cardington with experience of flying east of Suez, considered that the ship would not be able to get further than Egypt; Scottie, more optimistically, argued that she should just be able to reach India in March or April given the right conditions, but he conceded that the return flight would be more difficult owing to the adverse conditions between Karachi and Ismailia at that time, as well as the fact that the lift in a hot climate is necessarily lower than that at a cold climate destination. Reggie Colmore coordinated all these complex factors into a report which he sent to AMSR, who put the options concisely and carefully to Thomson on 21st November.

Meanwhile Scott had reviewed the practical problems which had so far been encountered while mooring, and decided to tauten up the yaw-guys substantially. Consequently on 7th November he carried out a series of letting-out and hauling-in experiments with the ship. The tauter guys reduced the tendency of the bows to oscillate and to over-ride the mast, and it was found by trial and error that keeping a steady pull on the main haul-wire without interruption eliminated it altogether, for it was at the point of checking the main haul that the oscillations which had proved so troublesome were set up.

The next day's flight was made solely to meet Whitehall's Public Relations objectives. Unfortunately a night of continuous rain caused the outer cover to absorb something like two tons of water, while a very low barometer resulted in reducing R101's pressure height to 500 ft, above which the gas would be automatically valved from full bags, forcing the Captain either to drop ballast to restore aerostatic equilibrium, or to rely on aerodynamic lift to make up the difference. With forty-four crew and forty passengers on board (including the Mayor of Bedford), two tons of fuel had to be off-loaded before slipping. In a 30 mph wind the conditions for slipping were rather difficult. Having only three engines in commission, the ship lumbered around the local area for a couple of hours before making a faultless return to the mast as a result of the previous day's experimentation. Nearly twenty-six years were to pass before another British aircraft carried so many people in flight. Although Scott was on board in his capacity of Officer in charge of Flying and Training, this was effectively Irwin's first solo as Captain. Neither he nor his Officers were particularly amused by having to make a publicity flight in such circumstances.

The following day Giblett issued another storm warning. This time Scott, with Irwin's full agreement, was confident enough in the ship and her systems to decide that she should ride it out at the mast. Storm routine was ordered: all the Officers and both the Duty and Standby Watches remained on board for what proved to be a very severe test. On 11th November the average wind speed was 55 mph with frequent gusts of more than 70 mph and a recorded peak of 83 mph. During the passage of a cold front the wind swung round through 135 degrees in about a minute, the temperature dropping by 10 degrees Fahrenheit. Throughout the day there was a great deal of precipitation. Thanks to the alertness and skill of Officers and crew, R101 was always under control and came through it comfortably without any violent movement. At the higher windspeeds, however, there was a majestically slow rolling motion reaching a maximum of six degrees during which the Chief Cox'n, Flight Sergeant Hunt, reported considerable movement of the gas bags both longitudinally and laterally, resulting in chafing against the radial frames and several substantial tears. The worst bag affected, No 8, deflated to 60%; they had to gas the ship in the middle of the night and again next day while repairs were under way.

The objects of the sixth flight, which took place on 14th November with a passenger list of thirty-two including Sir Sefton Brancker and ten members of Parliament, were to test modifications which had been made to the engine cooling system and to check that the repairs to the torn gasbags were satisfactory before undertaking the propaganda flight for the 100 MPs. Because of his personal standing among flying men, Brancker was given the freedom of the chartroom and control car, where he spent most of the flight. Ernest was delegated to look after him. Scott and he knew Brancker well, and felt then as always that he was one of the few people in Whitehall whom they could trust and talk freely to.

When Irwin gave the order to slip on this flight, the lift and trim indicator incorporated in the mooring arm indicated that the ship was in trim and the desired quarter ton light. Immediately the coupling was released, the bows shot into the air, leaving the tail down at an angle of twenty degrees or more. Nobody had realised that the gale on the previous Monday had put the indicator badly out. Irwin reacted swiftly, ordering full power on the idling engines to drive the ship upwards clear of the mast, and then bringing her onto an even keel by discharging a ton of emergency water ballast from the stern. Owing to the effect of superheating in the afternoon sun, the gas bags were now full and venting, and despite discharging more ballast the ship had to be flown quite heavy. After a couple of hours cruising in the local area she returned to her base, where Irwin had to drop another eight tons of water to ballast up for landing. This time Ernest operated the lines from the bow platform and Atherstone took his place in the control car. Unfortunately the ground party crossed the yaw-guys, with the result that a small part of the cover at the bows was torn against the top of the mast.

After her performance on that flight, Irwin and his Officers were less happy than ever with the prospect of the overloaded jaunt with 100 Members of Parliament scheduled for the 16th, and it was with very much relief that they received Scott's decision to cancel it because of a forecast of deteriorating weather. Instead, the time was spent in preparing for the first endurance flight. For this, no passengers were to be carried – only half a dozen of the Cardington design and inspection staffs acting as technical observers. The intention was to carry out a flight of at least thirty-six hours, with an extension to forty-eight hours at Scott's discretion. This time, Irwin, although Captain, was scheduled as a watch-keeping Officer; Scott therefore performed the role, which was later to be formalised in both ships, of Officer in overall charge of the flight, rather than in charge of the detailed working of the ship. Irwin as Captain was responsible for carrying out Scott's tactical instructions as to route, height and speed, and the Officers and crew were answerable to Irwin. The two crew watches on board stood turn and turn about (each of four hours except for the two Dog Watches), while Irwin, Ernest and Atherstone each rotated four hours on and eight hours off. In addition to his watchkeeping role, of course, Ernest had a more or less continuous responsibility for navigation, assisted for routine observations by the other two Officers. The unqualified Steff assisted, as a trainee, in Atherstone's watch. 'Mouldy' Booth flew on this trip as a supernumerary Officer.

R101 slipped from the mast shortly after 1030 on 17th November and headed north on what was to prove the longest flight of her career. Weather conditions were fine and settled. During the afternoon she passed over Howden where Meager and his crew were chafing over the delay in getting R100 ready; it was a friendly gesture from one lot of airshipmen to another which was not altogether appreciated by the builders of R100. The flight proceeded very smoothly indeed, but Scott decided to curtail it on the afternoon of the 18th as Giblett (who was part of the flying crew as the ship's Meteorologist) was forecasting thick fog at Cardington during the night and following morning. As it was, she had some difficulty finding the aero-drome – Chief Cox'n Hunt was the first person to satisfy Ernest that he had properly identified a pub close by the aerodrome. Irwin brought her skilfully to the mast in very thick visibility after nearly thirty-one hours in the air. Although no serious snags were observed during the flight, a post-flight inspection revealed that the main bearings of No 3 engine were on the point of failure, while those of the other engines were showing signs of wear.

Officially this was the final flight of R101's acceptance trials in her original form. On the very same day that the endurance flight was terminated, Colmore despatched to Sir John Higgins his formal report on the lift problems of R101 and the measures necessary for making a demonstration flight to India a practical proposition. Higgins put the issues to the Secretary of State. By now, Thomson's political wagon was firmly hitched to the airship programme, and to R101 in particular. As unemploy-ment rose and the economic crisis of 1930 loomed ahead, he perceived the First Imperial Conference, scheduled for October 1930, as the opportunity for a major propaganda coup: his achievement of a return flight to India in his airship before the conference would not only be a substantial triumph for the Government, but would also unlock funds from the Dominion Governments for a grandiose airship programme – and coincidentally would be of some help towards the fulfillment of his own ambition to become Viceroy. From now on, the conduct of the airship programme was to be subordinated increasingly to the accomplishment of a triumphant return of Lord Thomson from an Indian voyage in R101 in time for him to attend the Commonwealth Conference. The evil genius of Burney became a pale shadow beside the ruthless over-confidence of the aspiring Thomson. Nevertheless at the end of November he bowed gracefully to the inevitable, accepting that any attempt to fly to India in the early months of 1930 could result in more harm than good; he agreed to substantial modifications to the ship, including the insertion of an extra bay to increase her gross lift, and that the target should be set for the end of September.

To the dismay of the flying staff at Cardington, the weekend joyride for 100 MPs was rescheduled for Saturday 23rd November. Colmore was on the horns of a dilemma; on the one hand Scott was telling him that to carry 100 passengers was stretching safety to the limit; on the other hand, the terms of his report on R101's incapacity to do the job for which she had been designed would soon become public and draw a great deal of adverse publicity. On top of this, the opprobrium in Parliament, if the long-heralded joyride of 100 of its Members were to be cancelled, might well endanger the extra funds needed for the new modifications. Scott's problem was that the ship would have to fly in changeable winter weather with a barely adequate fuel load and an absolute minimum of water ballast. As there was a reasonable chance that the weather might be too bad for flying anyway, the two men agreed to let things take their course, and Scott gave orders for the ship to be stripped of as much spare gear as was prudent, to be defuelled of all but 5.5 tons and to be gassed up to 97%. In the event, his luck held: the wind rose and the rain fell, and by the time Honourable Members came aboard in the morning he could in all honesty cancel the flight for reasons of bad weather - indeed, he had to bring storm routine into force. The wind rose to a peak of 56 mph while all the guests were enjoying a well-lubricated lunch. R101 rode with such ease and comfort at the mast that many of the passengers left her in total ignorance of having missed a flight. All of them were delighted by the experience.

Storm routine was maintained for most of the week that followed. On the evening of 30th November, however, the wind dropped sufficiently for her to be walked into her shed to make way for R100 at the mast. The next day she was handed over to the Works staff who began deflation on 5th December. Officers and crew alike welcomed the break from almost two months of continual watchkeeping routine.

Apart from her inability to carry sufficient useful load to fly to India or back with just one refuelling stop (or indeed to carry 100 passengers safely on a local flight), R101 had turned out surprisingly well for so advanced a design. What snags had arisen were no worse than any to be expected in an experimental prototype. By the time Irwin handed her over to the Works staff, Colmore had been informed of the S of S's decision to delay the Indian flight until September and let the ship be extensively modified; her Officers were therefore quite confident that she could be further developed to do the job she had been built for.

Ernest, however, had his doubts about the suitability of September, when the southwest monsoon would be breaking up and giving very squally conditions in the northern Arabian Sea. Having taken a close look at the fuel consumption figures worked out from the data observed on the last endurance flight, he saw clearly that favourable winds would be essential to the success of the voyage in either direction. He and Giblett, close friends as well as colleagues, got together and concluded that, outbound, there was at least twice the chance of favourable winds in November; and for the return trip, there was very little likelihood that the winds would be sufficiently favourable to permit the ship to return to England before January. They discussed their findings in detail with Scott, who put the conclusions to Colmore. Unaware of Thomson's reasons for stipulating September, Colmore expressed a strong preference for attempting the flight to India in late November. He was over-ruled. Nevertheless the new timetable still provided for adequate flying trials of the enlarged airship, including a forty-eight hour endurance flight as well as bad-weather and high-speed trials before undertaking the long voyage.

CHAPTER TEN

THE LAUNCH OF R100

The launching of *R100* now awaited absolutely calm conditions at Howden, for the clearance between the top of the ship and the roof of the shed was a bare two feet, while the lateral clearance was no more than ten feet on either side. On 14th December Giblett's department forecast a settled anticyclonic spell, so on the following day Reggie Colmore arrived at Howden with Scottie, Ernest, Steff and Giblett in tow. Booth and Meager, of course, had been there almost continuously since inflation had started in July. Ernest had already been to Howden on a number of occasions to advise and check on the layout and equipment of the navigation and wireless cubicles. All that remained for him to do now was to put his charts on board and give such help in other departments as Booth could make use of. The Officers snatched a brief sleep that night before turning to again at 4 am, when the large contingent of soldiers who were to be the handling party arrived. Ernest took charge of the bow party, the last and most critical to emerge from the shed. At 0720 on the 16th, with Scottie on the ground in overall charge of the operation, *R100* was lifted and walked out onto the landing ground. Then, the engines having already been warmed up in the shed, all that remained was for Scott, Ernest and Steff to climb on board and for the ship to be finally ballasted up for the take-off. At 0753 Scottie, who was in command for this first flight, ordered "Let Go!". She rose gently to a couple of hundred feet, then the engines were rung "slow ahead" and she gradually gathered speed and climbed away.

As it was to be a short flight to the mast at Cardington, watchkeeping routine was not observed: Scottie and Mouldy Booth spent most of the time in the control car conning the ship, observing the effectiveness of the control systems and her general handling characteristics at speeds up to two thirds of available power. Ernest's "office" in *R100* was at the rear of the large control car (unlike her sister ship, where 'Johnnie's cubbyhole' was in the control-room within the hull immediately above her very small control car); he was, as usual on a first flight, mainly concerned with calibrating and correcting compasses. Meager, the First Officer, responsible to the Captain for the functioning of the structure, the lifting system and everything affecting the actual flying of the ship, spent most of the trip clambering into every nook and cranny to inspect the behaviour of the gas bags, the cover, fins, gas valves and controls. It was he who first discovered the somewhat alarming, rigid standing wave formation that developed in the outer cover during flight.

After loitering for a while in the vicinity of Howden getting the feel of things, Scottie ordered course to be set for York. A few minutes later, one of the six engines had to be shut down because of a cracked water-jacket. The flight from York to Bedford took a couple of hours, and after cruising around Bedford and Cardington for some time the mooring wire was dropped just before 1300 hrs. Scottie did the landing himself. R100 did not have the benefit of a dry run like her sister, who was connected up on the ground after she first emerged from the shed. Her crew had been trained on nothing more than a kite balloon, so he quite rightly decided to take his time about it, and went through the motions three times before finally being secured to the mast. Norway, who had never flown in an airship before and was quite ignorant about airship operations, wrote somewhat critically about the length of time it took. The other passengers on board for this flight included Colmore, Rope, Burney and Barnes Wallis.

After the passengers disembarked, Ernest and Steff followed them with No 3 Watch, leaving Booth with No 1 Watch on duty and Meager with No 2 on standby while the ship was being topped up with gas, water, fuel and oil. Scottie and Giblett conferred in the Met Office to decide upon the following day's flying programme.

Had there been a sufficient number of qualified Officers in the airship service, neither the Captain nor the Navigator would have stood watches, since the nature of their duties transcended the bounds of watchkeeping hours. As it was, however, after all the hectic preparations for, and the excitement of the maiden flight, and a bare four hours' sleep in the last thirty-six, it was Booth who spent the night on board, to be relieved by Meager at 0800 in time for final consultations with Scottie, Giblett and Ernest for the day's flight. The three Officers went on board at 0930, and fifteen minutes later Booth gave the order to slip. Ballasted half a ton light, R100 slowly lifted away from the mast; as soon as she was well clear the engines were rung up to half power and she moved slowly forward, still gathering height as aerodynamic lift built up. Once again the weather was perfect, ideal for the speed trials and the demonstration over London which were the main purposes of the flight. Shortly after slipping, however, one of the engines in the rear car stopped, then a minor fabric defect was discovered in the lower vertical fin, so Scottie decided not to attempt full speed and to stay in the vicinity of Cardington. While the ship cruised around at various speeds in the stable air, Ernest calibrated Michael Rope's patent air log and found it remarkably effective. Scottie and Booth observed the ship's controllability at various speeds and were well pleased by the lightness and responsiveness of the rudder and elevator controls. Meager kept close watch on the behaviour of the outer cover, which continued to give cause for concern. After six and a half hours' flying, R100 was secured to the mast again at 1615.

Although it was Meager's Duty Watch, Ernest went aboard at midnight to stand by in the control car so that Meager could get his head down for a few hours' sleep. It was a very cold, calm night, and after the gas had cooled down to ambient temperature the ship floated into perfect stability. During the morning, after conferring with Barnes Wallis, Rope and Norway, Scott decided to take advantage of the continuing calm weather and put R100 into her shed immediately, so as to rectify the fabric damage on the lower fin, to modify the system of wires holding the outer cover in position, and to do sundry minor repairs arising out of the first two flights.

She was brought out again shortly after 0900 on 16th January 1930, and at 0930 the orders "Hands off – ease up the guys – let go!" were given. The objects of this flight were to measure the ship's speed at various engine powers and to do turning trials at various combinations of rudder angles and speeds. As most of the flight was carried out above cloud, Ernest was kept pretty busy. Throughout the day the wind built up to nearly 40 mph from south-south-east, and in the afternoon Cardington reported by wireless that conditions were unsuitable for mooring. At about 6 pm the clouds broke and the lights of a town were seen on the port bow. "It's Spalding," Ernest said nonchalantly. Scottie decided to take a closer look: it was indeed Spalding. Shortly afterwards, Cardington signalled that conditions were now favourable for landing at the mast, and at 2240 the ship was duly secured after a flight of 13 hours and 20 minutes. Although the speed trials had been accomplished, Scottie had decided to abandon the turning trials, partly because it was not practicable to measure turning performance without sight of the ground, and partly because of the unsatisfactory behaviour of the cover (which, in addition to the peculiar 'standing wave' effect at speed, was beginning to show nasty signs of deterioration in certain areas).

The fourth flight was dedicated to investigating the whole problem of the behaviour of the outer cover at speed and the nature of the deformation, and to this end arrangements were made to rendezvous with a photographic aeroplane over the Royal Aircraft Establishment at Farnborough. It was accomplished on 20th January; throughout the flight lasting just over seven and a half hours her outer cover continued to give trouble. During the following week a great deal of effort was expended on inspection and repair of both the cover and its support wiring.

On Scottie's instructions, Ernest planned for the next flight a route down to Spain and on to the Azores, for it was scheduled to be an endurance test coupled with the controllability, stability and turning trials which had been omitted from the third flight. She slipped at 9 am on 27th January with fifty-six people on board and forty-six tons of disposable lift, heading above cloud for Land's End via the Bristol Channel. To everyone's disappointment, however, the first wireless signal to be received was an instruction from Air Ministry restricting the extent of the flight to a line from Fastnet to Ushant and prohibiting entry into foreign air space. Ernest rapidly replanned the flight after discussing the weather situation with Scottie and Mouldy; they decided to fly via Lundy and Plymouth to Alderney, then up the Channel and into the North Sea, then down Channel again and home via the Scillies and the Bristol Channel. At noon, ship and gear having been thoroughly checked, watch-keeping routine was initiated. For this flight, Booth and Meager stood watch and watch about, Steff assisting in Booth's watch and Ernest left free of watch routine. Meager was an enthusiastic and competent navigator, and as so much of the navigation equipment and tables was experimental, Ernest was glad to be able to have the results of Meager's independent observations to confirm his own work, for on this trip he had very little sleep; for one thing, the wireless trials, which were a part of his responsibility, were one of the principal objects of the flight, and for another the greater part of the flight took place in or above cloud with frequent changes of speed and heading as an essential element of the trial objectives.

During the afternoon of Day 1 the ship encountered considerable turbulence while crossing Devon which enabled her to demonstrate how beautifully she handled. In the evening the wind freshened to half a gale from nor'nor'east, against which she plugged all night up Channel enveloped in thick, pitch-dark cloud, the first severe test of instrument flying for her cox'ns. Ernest was up all night navigating by dead reckoning, cross-checking at half hourly intervals against W/T D/F fixes from the ground stations at Croydon, Lympne and Pulham. In daylight about 0800 the ship descended below the cloudbase at 2,000 ft, and shortly afterwards Ernest identified the Newarp Light Vessel, his first visual check on his reckoning since glimpsing the lights of Eastbourne eleven hours before. He then turned in for a nap, leaving Booth on watch to follow the coast to Felixstowe and thence overland to London. Just after 10 am, when they were in sight of Tower Bridge, they ran into thick cloud again which forced them to climb above it into clear sunshine at 3,000 ft. For the next eight hours the only sight of the earth was a glimpse of the Shambles Light Vessel at 1352 when they were descending to explore the level of the cloud base. Ernest reappeared on duty for the noon sun sights. At dusk, off Torbay, it was possible to cruise below the cloudbase at 1,500 ft, so Scottie decided to head for the Eddystone Light and carry out the turning trials around it. These completed, *R100* flew up Channel to Southampton, then back past the Lizard and into Bristol Channel, where she was put through another series of turning trials off Minehead. The flight terminated at the mast at 1630 after 54 hours and 50 minutes in the air.

The following morning, *R100* was hauled down and walked into her shed. A number of important defects, mainly in the power plants, had shown up in this long flight, in which she had encountered, for the first time, serious ice formation. The cover's supporting wiring continued to give trouble, while the cover itself leaked badly, threatening the integrity of the gas bags, which were not designed to withstand wetting. Booth insisted that, before flying again, this be rectified as far as possible by redoping the cover.

The stability and controllability of *R100* in flight had turned out to be excellent. Grabby Atherstone, flying in her as a supernumerary Officer for the first time, was given an opportunity to handle both rudder and elevator controls. He remarked on her sensitivity to small angles of helm and quickness of response. Later, when comparing notes with Ernest, they both agreed that she handled better than *R101* and was much lighter on the controls despite the servo installation in the latter. They thought it might be due to a better distribution of the hull structure about the centre of buoyancy. Wallis' automatic clutch and free-wheel gear on the elevator controls, together with the large diameter of the control-wheel, proved to be a great boon to the height cox'n.

In the speed trials *R100* had achieved a top speed of 80 mph, 10 mph above the design requirement, and her most economical cruising speed worked out at 65 mph. Apart from checking out the rectification of the snags encountered on this flight, her flight trials were virtually over. The thoughts of her Officers were turning towards preparations for the Atlantic flight scheduled for early May. Work in the shed proceeded with enthusiasm. The builders were anxious to hand the ship over to the Air Ministry.

At this stage Scottie was forced to review the performance of his Officers, as he thought it desirable to despatch one of them to Canada in charge of R100's relief watch. It had to be Atherstone, although he was really the lynchpin of R101's crew. In his capacity for hard work and painstaking attention to detail, as well as his thorough knowledge of his ship, he did not differ significantly from his opposite number in R100, Meager, though his flying experience was somewhat less in both amount and breadth. Meager, however, had the advantage that his Captain, Booth, a quiet man and loyal to his Chiefs, was very firm in his dealings with them, and very highly thought of by his crew. He had a steadiness of character which inspired trust in tight corners. Irwin, immaculate, remote, highly strung, was also a superb airship pilot, but he left all the hard work to his subordinate Officers, holding himself aloof from the hurly-burly and tending to opt for peace at any price. The usefulness of Steff, the junior, was limited by his not being a qualified airship pilot, though he was an excellent balloon pilot; but he was learning fast, was an able assistant to the Officer on Watch and, in his own department – the domestic arrangements of the ship – he was very efficient.

The Standing Orders for Airship Crews laid it down that the First Officer was Second-in-Command. At the end of March, however, Scottie caused an interesting amendment to be issued. "If, however, Squadron Leader Johnston is on board as Navigator, this Officer will assume command in the absence of the Captain or if, for any reason, the Captain is unable to perform his duties." Ernest could put his hand to almost anything: his experience of handling both ships was second only to that of Scottie himself, he commanded the professional respect of the Officers and crew of both, and he was an airman whose influence stretched far beyond the airship service. He was an obvious candidate for future Captaincy.

R100 was ready by mid-April, but the weather was not suitable for walking her out of the shed until the 24th when, alas, within a few feet of clearing the shed a small gust of wind caught her laterally; the handling party could not hold her against it; her starboard elevator was damaged by collision with the door of the shed. Scottie decided on the spot to hook her onto the mast in the expectation that the damage could be repaired there. He was over-optimistic: she had to be put back in the shed three days later. Nevertheless he despatched Atherstone and the standby watch by sea to Montreal, determined that the Atlantic flight should be accomplished in May, but although the repairs were completed early in the month it was not until the 21st that the weather allowed *R100* to be walked out. Each day during that period the handling party was ordered for 0300 the following morning; each night at 2130 it was stood down by shining a searchlight from the mast for half an hour; until on the evening of the 20th no light appeared. The crew turned to at 0200. This time, she was out of the shed in a very few minutes without accident, and quickly buttoned to the mast. She was scheduled to slip at 7 pm that evening with Mouldy Booth in sole command for the first time.

The object of this, the sixth flight, was to check out the modifications to the outer cover and give the six new Condor IIIB engines a thorough testing, as well as to measure fuel consumption and to carry out acceptance tests of the W/T equipment, including the Fultograph, a system years ahead of its time for receiving by wireless and reproducing an already drawn weather chart. The flight on 21st/22nd May lasted for more than twenty-two hours. The night was passed off the east coast between the Thames and Flamborough Head, when for the most part the ship was cruising in thick cloud at 2,000 ft with heavy rain from time to time. During the following forenoon, however, the weather improved somewhat and course was set from Hull to Liverpool. Amongst those on board were Sir Denistoun Burney and Squadron Leader Watt. 'Wattie', who had been captain of *R26*, had recently been recalled to the airship service and was designated as Officer in Charge of the tower and shed at Karachi.

Soon after noon when course was set from Liverpool to Bedford, Burney pressed Booth to run all engines at full power for ten minutes; Booth considered that at this stage this was quite unnecessary, but as the ship was still in the Contractor's hands, although he was none too happy, he deferred to Burney's wishes and rang up full power. Speed was increased to 80 mph for a short spell. When the ship eventually reached Cardington, Flying Officer Cook, the mast officer, signalled by radio that the tip of the tail was 'hanging down'. This was a surprise to all on board, who were completely unaware of the consequence of the high-speed run. Booth, ever prudent, decided to terminate the flight despite the very difficult weather conditions prevailing for his first solo landing to the mast. There were frequent heavy thunder showers and squalls which made both ballasting and trimming during the mooring operation very difficult. 'Mouldy's' first attempt, which began at the onset of a heavy rainstorm, had to be abandoned just before the mooring wires were coupled, when the sun suddenly came out, superheated the gas and caused the ship to lift the trail wire off the ground. On the second attempt, he carried the operation through with great deliberation in very gusty conditions, and the ship was safely secured at

1750, exactly an hour after the wires had been coupled.

Although the damage to the tail did not involve the main structure of the ship – a light fairing framework had collapsed in the turbulent wake at speed – she had to be put back in the shed to have it remedied. Four days passed before the weather was calm enough. The flight had also revealed that there were still some problems with the outer cover, particularly in the regions of propeller slipstreams. Ernest was far from happy with the performance of the short wave W/T and the Fultograph. Despite the time lost in rectifying all these matters in the shed, Booth insisted, and Scott and Colmore concurred, that the start of the Atlantic flight should be conditional on the successful conclusion of yet another acceptance flight. A decision had already been made that the outer cover of R100 should be entirely replaced; work was in hand at Howden but it could not be ready before the end of the year. Now, early in June, Squadron Leader Rope reported to Richmond on the result of his investigations into the problems of the outer covers of both ships. His conclusion was that there was no margin of safety for flight in rough atmosphere, and he went on to say "It is for consideration as to whether the risk involved in sending either ship on a long overseas flight is – or is not – greater than is justified by the need to fill public expectation. Is it not conceivable that a public statement could be made which would satisfy the people who matter – to the effect that overseas flights have been postponed for, say, six months on account of improvements which have been shown by test flights to be desirable before long flights could be undertaken with the reliability required of convincing demonstration – etc. etc." This was indeed a dire warning from an outstandingly competent airship design engineer. Richmond's own reputation had been built, however, on the base of airship fabric doping: he decided on 6th June to replace the pre-doped portions of R101's cover with material to be doped in situ. A decision on R100's cover was deferred until after the her next flight.

CHAPTER ELEVEN

R101 PRESENTS PROBLEMS

On 12th June Lord Thomson paid an informal visit to Cardington to acquaint himself at first hand with the progress of several projects in hand – the new tail section for *R100*, the installation of a Rolls Royce Condor engine temporarily in *R101* so that a full speed trial could be done with five engines running ahead, discussions with Burney and Norway about the provision of an additional bay in *R100*, examination of the feasibility of running Condor engines on fuel-gas, the preliminary design study for two even larger airships, and of course the measures to increase the lifting capacity of *R101* sufficiently to fly to India and back. In truth, the Secretary of State was really interested in the last two of these, for he was already thinking in terms of obtaining further financial support through the medium of the Imperial Conference in October. The only record is in Richmond's diary – "Informal visit of the S of S who again stressed the necessity of carrying out the Indian flight, if possible, before October." There were those among the senior wives, however, who afterwards expressed the opinion that this was the day on which Thomson made it clear to Colmore, Richmond and Scott that the future of airships and their jobs were on the line if the Indian flight did not take place before the date on which the Conference was due to discuss air matters. Nothing else could account for the element of almost desperation that entered into some of their judgements thereafter.

On the day before Thomson's visit, the Chief of Air Staff finally decided that *R101* was to fly at the annual Royal Air Force Display due to take place at Hendon on 29th June. This put paid to the installation of the Condor. Thomson had taken the view that it was of great importance that one of the ships should appear before the public. Reggie Colmore's immediate problem was "which ship for public relations at Hendon?". With barely four weeks to go, both were in the sheds, *R100* for repairs and modifications urgently required for the twice deferred flight to Canada, and *R101* undergoing the substantial changes to give her enough lift to make her demonstration flight to India. Burney was pressing him to get the Atlantic out of the way so that he could meet his contractual obligations and hand *R100* over to Cardington without the further loss to his company that providing a whole new outer cover would entail. The Secretary of State's timetable for the Indian flight at the end of September was even more pressing, and after much discussion it was decided that this was the over-riding consideration. Top priority was therefore given to completing the first-phase modifications to *R101* in time for her to fly at Hendon, after which she could be returned to her shed for the larger job of inserting the new bay. The diversion of Cardington's technical manpower away from *R100* during June in order to cope with the amended programme for *R101* meant the postponement of the Atlantic flight until the end of July. Delay was now beginning to pile on delay, for the minimum modifications to *R101* necessary if a March flight to India had been decided upon were still not completed at the beginning of June; the insertion of the additional bay, originally scheduled to be completed at the end of July to permit plenty of time for adequate flight trials before the departure to India at the end of September, was now being held back solely for the purpose of the Hendon Display flight. The pressure on Colmore and his staff was beginning to build up. And the events following the emergence of *R101* from her shed early on the morning of 23rd June 1930 were not propitious.

Soon after she had been attached to the mast, Meager, standing outside *R100*'s shed, noticed the whole of the outer cover of *R101*, particularly along the top, start rippling from bow to stern. The wind was light, but the atmosphere was very humid. Quite suddenly, a 140 foot long split appeared on the upper starboard side of the ship. As the forecast weather conditions precluded her being taken back into the shed without prejudicing the chances of flying at Hendon, repairs were begun immediately in situ, and were finished by the early evening despite the gusty winds and heavy rain which developed during the day. Next day a similar but shorter split occurred on the topmost part of the cover; this, too, was repaired at the mast. Altogether Flight Sergeant Hunt, the Chief Cox'n, and his team of riggers put up a splendid show. In the knowledge that she would get a new cover when she returned to her shed, Colmore and Scott decided to accept the risk of flying her at Hendon. Before doing so, however, it was essential to carry out a test flight to clear the first-phase modifications made during the past six months. The main structure, the passenger and crew accommodation, the power plants and systems had been lightened by nearly three and a half tons. The gas bag wiring had been let out to increase the volume of hydrogen, resulting in just over three tons more lift being generated at a penalty of a couple of hundredweight of extended wiring and reinforced cover. All this added up to a net increase of five and a half tons of useful lift, equivalent to another 650 nautical miles still air range at maximum cruising speed.

The test flight, lasting four and a half hours, took place on 26th June. As 'Grabby' Atherstone had not yet returned from Canada, Ernest acted as First Officer for the short local flight. The ship left the mast superheated on a hot, sunny afternoon, and on ballasting up for landing late in the evening had to jettison two tons of fuel. Irwin thought at the time that this was in compensation for the loss of superheat lift. Flying with the control servo gear removed, Ernest noted that the controls were powerful and fully adequate. Irwin's after-flight report indicated that the ship behaved well.

The next day *R101* took part in the rehearsal for the RAF Display during a twelve and a half hour flight. This time Mouldy Booth acted as First Officer. Ernest took the forenoon watch as soon as the ship left the mast at 8 am. As the day developed, conditions became rather bumpy, and Irwin, anxious about the outer cover, kept the speed below about 42 knots. She wallowed noticeably, and Ernest observed that the height cox'n was using almost full angles of elevator to control the ship in level flight. Booth, who took over from Ernest as Officer on Watch at noon, remarked that, good as she was on rudders, she seemed to be very unstable on her elevators. He thought that it might be due to the low speed. During the afternoon the height cox'n reported that he was having considerable difficulty keeping her at the ordered height of 1,000 to 1,200 ft, and when ordered to bring her lower over the aerodrome at Hendon, he let her fall into a rather steeper dive than had been intended. The ship appeared to get progressively heavier, and during the flight about nine tons of ballast was dropped in addition to the consumption of a couple of tons of fuel. When Booth drew his attention to the general heaviness of the ship, Irwin expressed the opinion that the gas valves were giving trouble, probably chattering as a result of the slackness of the outer cover.

Ernest and Mouldy subsequently discussed the difference in handling between the two ships, and agreed that it was quite remarkable. They both understood that the deep, triangular planes of *R101*, set right aft, were supposed to be more efficient than the low aspect ratio fins of *R100*, and could only conclude that perhaps *R101* had not attained the speed necessary to make them fully effective. *R101* was not only unstable in pitch in the bumps, but also seemed to hunt a lot when over-controlled. Booth reckoned that Chief Cox'n Hunt, despite his great experience, was generally inclined to use too much elevator. Ernest agreed that R100 was always more or less on an even keel compared with R101, which seemed to be up and down all the time.

On 28th June the pattern of the previous day was repeated. This time it was Meager who acted as First Officer. The weather was similar – bright sunshine, a build-up of fair-weather cumulus, and bumpy. Ernest again took the forenoon watch. Gerrish, the shed Manager, was invited into the control car for a while and discussed with him how he thought the large elevator movements might be reduced by using a larger hand-wheel with different gearing. Irwin relieved Ernest at noon and the ship duly saluted King George V and Queen Mary at Hendon punctually at 1550. Meager, who took the Dog Watch, began to get worried by the way the ship kept falling into a short, sharp dive from which she only slowly recovered. Oughton, the height cox'n of the watch, confessed that it was all he could manage to hold her up. Meager immediately let go a ton of ballast: Oughton thought it made height control easier. Meager remarked to Ernest that, although he was not familiar with R101's idiosyncrasies, he would expect her to be quite light if his experience of his own ship was anything to go by, and more likely to have to valve gas than discharge water after ten hours cruising. Ernest agreed with him, and told him about the previous day's heaviness. When Irwin relieved him at 1800, Meager reported his concern about the heaviness and Oughton's height-keeping difficulty, and suggested making a landing straight away. Ernest was surprised by the force with which Meager expressed himself. Irwin, however, took a somewhat haughty line and was rather acid about the release of water, which he would have preferred to keep for landing ballast, affirming to Meager that the ship's behaviour was entirely the result of atmospheric turbulence. He rejected the idea of landing as he thought conditions were still too bumpy. Nevertheless, prior to landing to the mast at 2050 something like ten tons of fuel and water ballast had to be dropped before R101 was in static equilibrium.

She was taken into the shed next day. Meager was sufficiently concerned after this flight to make representations to Booth, his immediate superior, about the seriousness of R101's heaviness. Indeed, Irwin was concerned himself. The three June flights had provided, for the first time, somewhat rough flying conditions (though insignificant in comparison with what could be expected on the route to India); the in-flight heaviness was a new phenomenon, and he did not believe it could be entirely due to leaks caused by the chafing of gas bags which had been expanded as part of the scheme to increase lift. Richmond, however, after causing some calculations to be made, expressed himself as being somewhat startled by the magnitude of the loss of lift that could be induced by small chafe-holes, and asked Scottie to collect details of the location and size of all holes found by the crew in future. The problem of holes in the gas bags was not entirely novel, for a tendency to chafe had been noticed while *R101* was riding out the November gale at the mast, and after she had been put back into the shed a most careful investigation of the holing of the bags was made. Each bag was taken out of the ship in turn, and checked. Every bag except one was found to be holed. Since it was obvious that the enlargement of the bags would reduce the clearances between them and the surrounding structure, thereby increasing the risk of chafing, no fewer than 4,000 anti-chafing pads were manufactured.

Following these flights there was a great deal of concern at Cardington, and in the Air Ministry's Aeronautical Inspection Directorate, about both the validity of the policy of padding so extensively and the efficacy of the padding itself. Mr F. McWade, the AID Inspector-in-Charge at Cardington, whose own Director said of him that he was "a most exceptionally experienced airship Inspector", argued boldly and cogently against both the policy and its efficacy. Scottie called him "a bit of an Old Woman", but it was not the job of an Inspector to take risks, and McWade had been in lighter-than-air almost continually since joining the Royal Engineers' School of Ballooning in 1895. Often a thorn in Richmond's flesh, he was not a man whose well-found opinions could be dismissed lightly. In a strong letter to his Director about the problem, dated 3rd July, he concluded "I am fully aware that to remedy the faults complained of is in the nature of a large undertaking and it may be necessary to remove the bags from the ship. Until this matter is seriously taken in hand and remedied I cannot recommend to you the extension of the present Permit to Fly or the issue of any further Permit or Certificate." Coming on top of Rope's plea to consider deferring the overseas flights because of the poor margin of safety in the outer cover, and Meager's expression of profound concern, McWade's letter ought to have caused Colmore to cry halt, for a re-think of the development programme. Instead, under Richmond's strong influence, he argued flatly that the policy of padding could not be abandoned if *R101* was ever to fly to India, and persuaded McWade's own Director to over-rule him without reference to higher authority. There can rarely have been a greater abrogation of its responsibility by the Directorate of Aeronautical Inspection. McWade was summarily told that it was his job to see that every point in the hull which might lead to damaging the bags was padded in a proper manner, while Irwin was instructed to carry out a minute inspection of the bags to record the position of every single hole and to apply preventive padding wherever it was necessary. Richmond never faltered from his opinion that padding was an adequate cure for this source of loss of lift.

As for Irwin's concern about loss of gas through the valves, it was established by Richmond's people that before the ship had been taken out of the shed for the June flights there had been no time for functioning tests on the valves after they had been attached to the bags. The sensitivity of the valves, when they were tested before being installed, was such that gas was likely to escape in any weather conditions which caused the ship to roll more than four or five degrees from the vertical. It was decided, therefore, to carry out thorough checks in situ before the next flight.

As Captain of R101 Irwin tended to hold himself remote from the nuts and bolts and hard graft; for this, he depended entirely on his First Officer. During these three flights of the significantly modified R101, Atherstone was absent. As a consequence, whilst a great deal of attention was paid to the technical problems of preventing the serious losses of lift which were evident, the associated problems of stability and controllability were entirely overlooked. Booth was too courteous to comment adversely on the other man's ship, while Irwin ascribed Meager's views to his unfamiliarity with R101. It was not until nearly a year later that, on the initiative of another Secretary of State, the RAW was asked to look at the behaviour of R101 during the two Hendon flights. Booth, now filling Scott's shoes, wrote: "I am of the opinion that the pitching movement of R101 was far greater than the pitching movement of R100 under similar conditions, and that this difference was due to some design factor and in no way attributable to any difference in the skills of the respective height coxswains. It might be suggested that this instability was due to the ship being flown too heavy. This, however, does not agree with the National Physical Laboratory, who maintain that a heavy ship in trim does not tend to nose dive but rather to assume steep angles up by the bow, which have to be corrected by carrying down-elevator. The evidence of the Display flights would indicate that difficulty was experienced in keeping the bow of the ship up; in fact, the general tendency was for the bow to drop. This, in my opinion, was again due to some design factor and not manipulation error, as R100 has never shown similar symptoms. As regards previous experience, the height coxswains of R101 were more fully trained than those of R100."

R100 was ready on 2nd July 1930 to take the air for what everyone expected to be the final test flight before setting out for Canada, but it was not until the 25th of that month that the weather was calm enough to bring her out of her shed. There was a proposal to defer the installation of the new bay in *R101* so that she could stand by in reserve for the Canadian trip, should *R100* not perform her test flight satisfactorily; but on 21st July the Secretary of State, who had earlier confirmed his insistence on the programme for the Indian flight being adhered to, firmly refused his consent to using *R101* as a standby. He ruled that the Atlantic flight must, if necessary, be put off until *R100* was proved fit for it. Would that he had been so positive about *R101* in respect of the Indian flight! At Cardington there was some surprise at this ruling, for all the flying staff felt that the Atlantic flight was of greater significance for airships than the Indian flight – after all, the right place for operating airships was over the sea, and the real future of airships now lay in developing the transatlantic route which was far beyond the capacity of any aeroplane. It was three and a half years since Ernest had pioneered the first commercial aeroplane flight to India, and he certainly did not relish the prospects of the trans-Europe and the Cairo-Karachi portions of the eastern flight in *R101* without intermediate mooring facilities.

At the same time, the Secretary of State accepted a revised programme which Colmore had put up, setting 22nd September as the date for completion of *R101* with her new bay. This allowed for one fully successful trial flight of what was virtually a new Mark of the ship, before leaving for India at the end of September (always supposing they could get her out of the shed in time). Irwin told Atherstone that he hoped they would have a flight of at least thirty-six hours and preferably forty-eight hours at a reasonable cruising speed in bad weather in order to test out the ship thoroughly. Atherstone thought that she ought to fly at full speed continuously for four hours. Both were concerned to test thoroughly the efficacy of padding and the integrity of the outer cover, and both thought that the ship ought to go into the shed for a complete inspection afterwards.

In the light of experience with both ships to date, Colmore was certainly cutting things very fine, and Sir John Higgins, the Air Member for Supply and Research, wrote to Lord Thomson "This date does not leave any margin for unforeseen circumstances". It did not even leave any margin for what ought to have been foreseen – the inevitable wait for conditions sufficiently calm to bring *R101* out of the shed. To Higgins, Thomson replied airily "I am sure everything possible will be done and am not unduly pessimistic."

R101 was cut in two within a few days of *R100*'s emergence from her shed; the work of enlargement, with a vast range of consequential adjustments, went on at high pressure and without intermission until 25th

September. The power system was modified so that all five engines could provide forward thrust and two of them be reversible, but it was not possible to introduce certain major measures planned to reduce their weight.

CHAPTER TWELVE

R100 FLIES TO CANADA & BACK

On 25th July the crew and handling party assembled at 2 am to take *R100* out of the shed and put her on the mast; operations, however, had to be postponed until 10 am because of a crosswind. For the rest of the day everybody was hard at work preparing to slip at 8 pm. Examining the behaviour of the outer cover was again the principal objective of the flight. *R100* slipped on time and carried out a circuit of southern England, flying for the most part in rain underneath or in heavy cloud, the wind rising to 40 mph. For the first time in flight the three-watch routine intended for the Atlantic flight was instituted, No 3 watch being Officered by Ernest and Steff together. Apart from the navigation and watchkeeping, Ernest's main concern was the calibration of the Wireless Direction finding installation and the Fultograph. Although the D/F installation operated satisfactorily, he was far from impressed by its accuracy. The Fultograph, moreover, although it had produced excellent teleprints of weather maps on the bench at Cardington, continued to be disappointing in the air.

The ship moored up in the evening of 26th July after being in the air for just over twenty-four hours, and Scottie, who had been in charge of the trials, immediately called a conference of the Officers. At its conclusion, he decided that he was satisfied with *R100*'s all-round performance and that instead of being returned to the shed she should remain at the mast while preparations were made for the Atlantic flight. The outer cover was still not up to the condition that Mouldy Booth wanted for regular overseas flights, despite the various compromise measures which had been taken to inhibit the tendency to flap, and to make it more water-resistant so as to protect the vulnerable gas bags, but after a detailed inspection on 27th July under the eagle eyes of himself and Meager, he declared that he would accept it for the one flight to Canada, which was to be the final flight before Air Ministry took the ship over from the Contractors. Scottie thereupon proposed, and

Colmore agreed, to fix the start of the Canadian flight for early on 29th July.

The 28th was, consequently, a very busy day for everyone. Ernest, with the assistance of Keeley, the Chief Wireless Operator, removed the Fultograph and the Direction Finding equipment from the ship, as their performance did not warrant their extra weight. Then he brought his charts and navigation gear on board, including the special volume of sight reduction tables that he had prepared for the trip by cutting out a number of selected tables from various books. His, perhaps, was the first inkling of the need for special air navigation tables designed for rapid sight reduction. During the afternoon he spent much time with Giblett in the Met Office studying the forecast charts and assessing the routing options likely to be available to them. Meager was fully occupied all day until midnight superintending the gassing, fuelling and ballasting. Steff oversaw the commissariat. Booth attended a number of conferences with Colmore and Scott to assess the weather reports and to report to them on the state of readiness of the ship.

There was never any doubt that Scottie would participate actively in the first Canadian flight. Colmore was nevertheless concerned to avoid a possible confusion between the responsibilities of the Assistant Director (Flying) and the Captain. It had already become standard practice that Scott gave no orders to the crew, but dealt only with the Captain, and now in the final conference with AMSR before setting the departure date, Colmore sought Sir John Higgins' views. Sir John said that he wished the two Captains henceforth to have full responsibility for their ships. "Major Scott's position on board should now be that of an Admiral, not Captain of a ship... He should give advice to the Captain, but the Captain was not bound to take it." The position as subsequently codified at Cardington was that Scott was the authority for deciding on the course to be taken, the flying height and speed. The Captain was entirely responsible for the preparation, airworthiness, flying organisation and handling of the ship and the discipline of her crew.

Only thirteen aircraft, three of them airships, had successfully flown non-stop across the Atlantic when R100 set out on 29th July. Alcock and Brown made their historic hop of 1,700 miles downwind in the summer of 1919, and less than a month later R34, commanded by Scottie, made the very first two-way flight of more than 3,000 nautical miles non-stop to New York and 3,000 back. In 1924, four years before any aeroplane made the crossing from east to west, the German Zeppelin ZR3 was delivered to the United States Navy as the *Los Angeles* by Dr Hugo Eckener. In 1928 the *Graf Zeppelin*, commanded by the redoubtable Eckener, made the second recorded double crossing as the precursor of several others. All crossings by heavier-than-air machines had been made with the prevailing winds from west to east save only two: Hermann Kohl's *Junkers W.33* in April 1928 from Ireland to Labrador, and Charles Kingsford-Smith's flight from Ireland to Newfoundland in June 1930 in a *Fokker*. Cardington was therefore awash with confident excitement.

Most of the supernumeraries – including Burney, Norway, Squadron Leader Archie Wann (who had been Captain of *R38*) and McWade – went on board in the early evening; the full complement came on at midnight. Each of the Officers managed to snatch a couple of hours' sleep before 0200, when the final preparations began.

R100 slipped at 0248 GMT after dropping two tons of water ballast. With fuel for eighty-five hours of cruising flight she carried a payload of seven passengers and their baggage, 0.61 tons altogether. Booth took what was left of the Middle Watch as soon as Meager and Steff stood down and turned in after supervising the crutching of the gasbags. Ernest shared this Watch with Booth, to see the ship settled on her way to Liverpool Bay. When Meager took over at 0400 he turned in so as to be relatively fresh for his first watch-keeping trick with Steff at 0800. The Officers continued to rotate watches after this pattern throughout the voyage, while the crew rotated on a two-watch basis.

The last manuscript written by Ernest before his death in *R101* was an account of *R100*'s Canadian flight:

"As the result of a considerable amount of investigation over a period of some months prior to the flight to Canada, six alternative routes were selected for the England-Canada flight. The choice of any of these alternative routes obviously depended upon weather conditions prevailing at the time of departure and also any deviation from the selected route would depend on the weather encountered en route.

"The weather report received on the day of departure indicated the selection of the route either via Greenland and Belle Isle (2,937 nm) or via Malin Head direct to Belle Isle (2,831 nm). By following a route north of the Hebrides depression, some assistance from the winds could be expected once the airship reached the north of Ireland. The general tendency on the western side of the Atlantic was for a southwesterly drift, although gradients appeared as though the winds would be on the light side. The low pressure over Hudson's Bay was likely to give thundery storms in Eastern Canada within two or three days' time. It is to the credit of the Meteorological Office to note that the latter 'long shot' forecast did eventually prove exact, and we did actually experience these thunderstorms on our arrival in Canada.

"We were weighed in and ordered aboard at midnight, 28/29th July, and set about the final look round to see that everything was on the top line. At 0248 hrs GMT on 29th the airship was slipped from the mooring tower, and after climbing to pressure height (1,400 ft) course was set for Malin Head cruising on four engines, which gave her a speed of 47 knots (54 mph). The wind was rather gusty but the visibility was good and the base of what low cloud there was was at about 2,000 ft. The watches were set immediately on leaving, the Captain taking the first watch, and everything was soon shipshape and Bristol fashion.

> "The principal navigation equipment consisted of:
> Dead-beat compass (Hughes),
> Turn Indicator (Schilovsky-Cooke),
> Periscopic drift sight (Hughes),
> Seamarkers for instrument setting (Aluminium dust by
> day, calcium phosphide flares by night),
> Mark VII bubble sextant,
> Air log Marine chronometer and deck watch,
> Goodwin's *Alpha, Beta and Gamma Tables*.

"The method of navigation was as follows. The course was set and the track maintained by observations of the drift whenever the surface was visible. At two-hourly periods, or more frequently when necessary, double-drift sights were taken on sea markers to determine the wind direction and speed, and the ground speed. At hourly periods, or whenever the engine speeds were altered, the airspeed was checked on the air log, and whenever the ship's shadow was in a suitable position the groundspeed was checked by timing it over a point. Astronomical sights were taken on the prime vertical for longitude, which were a valuable check on the speed made good; ex-meridians for latitude were a check on the northerly or southerly drift; and whenever possible position lines were determined to fix a position. Very reliable checks were obtained from D/F W/T bearings from merchant ships, and one cannot speak in high enough terms of praise for the whole-hearted cooperation of the Merchant Navy. It is a happy augury for the future to feel that there is a very great bond of brotherhood between the seaman and the airman.

"On the outward and homeward flights there were long periods when the surface was not visible, and course had to be altered from positions determined by astronomical observations, and it is of particular interest to note that although at times the intercept was as much as seventy-nine miles from the DR position, the ultimate landfalls confirmed the accuracy of the observations. In the vicinity of the Isle of Man and the Mull of Galloway it was overcast with rain, but as we reached the north side of the depression the cloud broke up and the wind became more northerly.

"In the vicinity of Inishtrahull the ship was over low cloud, the top of which was about 1,000 ft. The wind was now 030 degrees true, 18 mph, and it was decided to set course true west so as to bring the wind on the starboard quarter and take full advantage of the fair wind by making good a track south of west. The wind, however, soon backed to the north, and by keeping the same course and making a southerly drift a good groundspeed was maintained. Sights for a position line were taken at our departure point off Oversay, which was the last land sighted.

"We had now really started the great adventure, but we were a well-found ship, had thirty-four tons of fuel on board which was good for ninety-two hours at our present rate of consumption, and everyone was full of interest and confidence. The domestic department were working like Trojans and our gravest fears were the prospects of the results of over-eating.

"Communications were working excellently. The route was divided into four sections for the purpose of wireless communications. The first stage was from Cardington for a distance of some 600 miles, when routine was commenced with Rugby and carried on to longitude 35 degrees west. West of that meridian we worked with Louisburg until we picked up St Hubert, and then we worked direct with that station. The return journey worked in the reverse order.

"In the afternoon watch sights were taken for position line, and later, in the dog watch, sights were taken on the prime vertical for longitude. The sky was about 5/10ths covered with cumulus at about 1,800 ft, the visibility was good, but there were very heavy clouds to the westward at sunset. About midnight we spoke to the *Winchester Exporter* and got bearings which worked in well with our position. On the whole, the Mark VII sextant gave very satisfactory results, and a degree of accuracy of the very highest order. On occasions when only a single sight could be shot on account of cloud, the ultimate landfall confirmed the accuracy of the observations. This naturally gives a considerable amount of confidence in astronomical navigation.

"In the early morning of the 30th the wind, after having decreased, began to veer and increase, and eventually got away round to the south east, reaching 32 mph. The *Arabic* reported the barometer falling, and our altimeter correction was 372 ft to add. We were now making a considerable amount of northing and eventually reached a groundspeed of 73 knots. The sky was 10/10ths stratus, and it was raining fairly heavily. Sights were out of the question, so we were glad to get bearings from the *Caledonia* and the *Montclair*. At daylight we were over a dense layer of stratus at 1,200 ft. Soon afterwards we ran into a clear patch, and to our extreme pleasure sighted the *Ausonia* westward bound, about five miles away. This was the first sight of anything we had had since leaving Oversay, and there was great excitement both among the forty-five on board the airship and the crowd on board the steamer. Greetings were exchanged, flags hoisted, and from the white crest of steam from her whistle we guessed that her Master was determined to wake the sluggards amongst his passengers who had not yet appeared on deck to greet us.

"Our Meteorologist, Giblett, who had all this time been working hard but unobtrusively, gave warning of the approach of another depression, so we decided to keep making our northing so as to get to the north side of the centre. After flying at about 1,000 ft over a layer of stratus lying at 500 ft and through a lot of drizzle, we found a good following wind, and we ran into quite a good patch with good visibility at 1,500 ft. We now increased speed and got going on six engines at 1,400 rpm and had every prospect of creating a new record.

"In the dog watch we got busy taking sights and from our reckoning estimated sighting Belle Isle at 9 pm local time. Unfortunately, Belle Isle was shrouded in fog, but we sighted Cape Bauld at 8.45 pm, and at 9.15 pm we were actually over Belle Isle, just being able to see it through a hole in the fog.

"The compass behaved splendidly all the way across, and at no time was there any evidence of loss of directive force. The maximum deviation observed at any time was less than two degrees, and most of this was probably due to personal error. At first one is inclined to be over-awed by the large amount of change in magnetic variation on an Atlantic crossing, the maximum amount being in the order of 35 degrees west. The big change is, however, in a way of considerable advantage as it changes in such a manner that only a very small alteration in the magnetic course is necessary to follow the great circle track. One is of the opinion that this fact has not been fully appreciated by aeroplane pilots when undertaking the Atlantic crossing. The result is that much greater alterations of course are necessary to follow the Mercator track.

"The Belle Isle Strait was full of fog up to 1,500 ft and as the coasts are badly mapped and we had to avoid any high ground it was necessary to keep well in the middle of the strait. It was a pitch black night and the visibility was nil. Consequently on the morning of the 31st we ran down the strait on a tail bearing from Belle Isle D/F station until daylight, when we ran into fine clear weather. From there on it was just a matter of going from point to point. Enthusiasm ran high; sweeps on the day's run gave place to bets on the time of arrival. There was every prospect of a wonderful record and we anticipated getting to Montreal that night by about 7 pm. But Man proposes, God disposes: at about half past two in the afternoon when just off the Saguenay River the airship was struck by a sudden white squall which made her roll badly, and on inspection it was found that the fin covers had been badly damaged. The ship was slowed down and repair work was commenced with all available hands, riggers and engineers alike, who worked like demons to make good the damage. Booth and Meager soon had the situation in hand, and by their complete sang froid inspired everyone with complete confidence.

"Our dreams of a record were now dashed to the ground. Giblett, moreover, was beginning to worry about the thunderstorms he had predicted three days ago, of which we were now getting warning in the weather reports. The weather was not anything too good, and there was a stiff headwind, and consequently every inch of ground covered and change of wind had to be jealously watched. It was now that we really felt the benefit of our periscopic drift sight as we were able to get results of the highest order of accuracy. By the double-drift method we could determine our groundspeed without making use of the very doubtful measure of altimeter height. Every little alteration of drift could be followed, and a resultant wind point determined which gave us the wind direction and velocity to a measure of extreme accuracy. The use of this instrument also entirely eliminated the use of the standard course and distance calculator.

"By the time we had passed Quebec at about 6 pm, temporary repairs had been effected, and the engines were speeded up. At 8 pm, in the vicinity of Three Rivers, the airship ran into another violent

R101 being hauled to the mast, Cardington 1929.

Above: R100 at the mast at St Hubert, Montreal, Canada, August 1930.

Johnston taking a sun-sight from the top of *R100* over the Atlantic, August 1930.

Lord Thomson greets *R100*'s crew at the foot of the mast on their arrival back from Canada. *Left to right:* Steff (hat under arm); Johnston shaking Thomson's hand, Colmore in light overcoat between them; Scott; Booth and Meager.

Below: R101 engine car.

Overleaf: R101 split at frame 8, immediately aft of the passenger accommodation, for the insertion of a new bay.

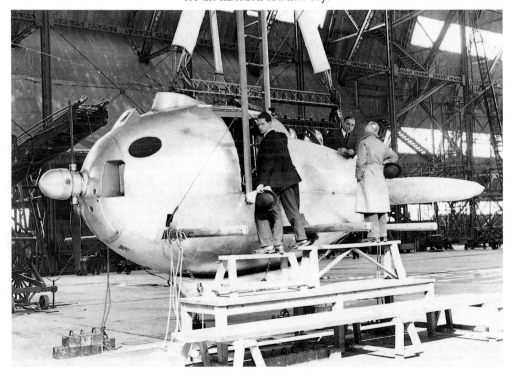

The passenger lounge of *R101*, looking towards one of the two promenade decks.

Below: Final embarkation - Johnston, Sir Sefton Brancker, the Secretary of State's Private Secretary Major Louis Reynolds, Lord Thomson and Richmond.

Opposite: First Officer Steff on *R101*'s entrance ramp checks the manifest as crewmen on the mast-head load passengers' baggage.

R101 in her full glory.

squall which developed so rapidly that we were not able to avoid it. As the front of the squall approached, the ship got a violent up-bump which took us from 1,200 ft to 4,000 ft. There have been various estimates of the times which the ship took to rise this amount and the angle at which she took the bump, none of which might be called conservative estimates. The fact remains, however, that whatever the effect on the ship was, it was accentuated a hundredfold by the clatter and confusion from the galley and saloon and the store-room. It just happened that the tables were laid for supper and the cook had his pots and pans on the stove ready to serve up. One must admit that we were so accustomed to being on an even keel that everyone alike was neglectful of securing loose material. The result was, as the ship's head was put down to check the up-bump, pots and pans and plates took charge and for a moment it seemed as if chaos reigned. In the debacle a bucket of water upset in the crew space and drained into the control car and over the instrument light batteries. This caused an earth in the instrument light circuit. The result was that we were unable to see the instruments, either to note the rate of rise by the climb meter or to note the exact time it took the ship to take the bump. Any estimate of these happenings was purely conjectural, and differed in proportion to the state of one's imagination. My own impression was that the bump lasted some four and a half minutes which, after all, was not serious. It happened also that the clatter in the galley was mostly due to empty pans rattling as supper was served up at the scheduled time, and it was not noticeable that any food had been lost. However, the experience had one good result, in as much as it made us all a bit more careful in securing loose gear, which after all is only a wise precaution.

"At the rear of the squall we experienced the expected down bump, but this was not quite so violent as the first one. It was an education to watch Scott handle the ship under these conditions. He appeared to know the very phases of the squall and anticipated their arrival and manoeuvred the ship to met them. It was like watching a patient horseman humouring a frightened thoroughbred.

"This squall was the fore-runner of the anticipated thunder-storms of which we were now getting constant warning and advice. We could see these storms to the southwestward, right in our track, so it was decided to 'lay to' and wait. Consequently we hove to with the wind on our starboard bow, and took careful visual bearings of the most concentrated part of the lightning and by this means found how the storms were moving, and eventually worked in behind them and arrived over Montreal at 1 am in the morning of 1st August. We hung around until dawn broke before making a landing, and eventually secured to the mooring tower at 4.30 am (the altimeter correction was 227 ft to add).

"We had completed the journey of 3,364 nautical miles in 78 hours and 49 minutes at an average speed of 42 knots, and had five tons of fuel remaining, which was enough for another 14 hours at our average rate of consumption. It has been criticised that this reserve was inadequate for a journey of this nature, but those critics have overlooked the fact that we had deliberately hung around for some considerable time to make a daylight landing, and the amount of fuel used in that time should justly be credited to the final reserve."

Ernest's account of the damage to the outer cover which resulted from the encounter with the squall over the mouth of the Saguenay River was typically laconic. During the early afternoon the ship had received a wireless message from Montreal wishing to know the time of arrival so that they could deal with the crowds. Under pressure from Burney, Scott had agreed to try to land before dark, and prevailed upon Booth, against the latter's better judgement and inclination, to increase speed to 70 knots. About an hour later, out of a practically clear blue sky, the ship was hit broadside on by a severe gust which caused her to roll through nearly twenty degrees. Meager described it as the most severe roll he had ever experienced in an airship, and all the old hands were agreed that it was no ordinary performance. Booth immediately slowed down, and on checking over the ship Meager discovered that the covering on the underside of the port fin had disintegrated over an area of roughly fifteen feet by twelve feet. There were two minor tears on the bottom fin and a longitudinal split of about twelve feet on the outboard edge of the starboard fin. All of this needed immediate attention if the whole coverings of the fins were not to disintegrate. All the riggers on board were assigned to working parties and repairs were completed in about an hour under Meager's direction. The cover of the starboard fin suffered further and more extensive damage during the later encounter with the thunderstorm. Permanent repairs had to be undertaken at Montreal, where the Canadian Vickers Company were able to produce suitable fabric panels.

There is little to add to Ernest's own account except, perhaps, Norway's vignette written at 0230 Zone Time on 31st July when *R100* was running up the St Lawrence River: "Johnston is asleep in a chair in the saloon, in Teddy (flying suit) and uniform cap. He is a splendid navigator and works like a horse; I believe he had only two hours' sleep last night."

The damage to the fins occasioned by the white squall over the Saguenay River was made light of and forgotten in the euphoria of the tremendous welcome which the Canadians gave the ship on her arrival at Montreal. Hundreds of thousands of people visited the airport to look at her; the streets of Montreal were placarded with welcome signs and there was even a popular song about *R100* with Booth's portrait on the sheet music. Scottie, however, was somewhat upset because the Press Notes issued in Canada made it seem to the public that he had been superseded by Booth as the ship's Captain, and indeed on more than one occasion he was introduced at one of the innumerable functions which swamped her Officers, as Booth's second-in-command.

As for the thunderstorm, some people have criticised Scott's judgement for pressing on through it. Meager was OOW when the line-squall appeared on the horizon ahead of them, and Ernest was at his chart-table throughout. Booth was called down for consultation, and Scott went with him. The storm lay across the horizon and appeared to be difficult to avoid, but Meager thought it could be done, or should at least be attempted. Scott decided otherwise, and instructed Booth to continue flying up the river for, as Ernest pointed out, the ground on either side was quite hilly and any vertical disturbance might have been worse. "Anyway," Booth remarked later, "It wasn't a fatal decision."

On 3rd August a split was discovered at the top of No 7 gas bag, caused by chafing consequent upon the protective cord netting around the exhaust trunk having carried away. The repair was completed simply enough, but it meant that the whole of the next day had to be spent checking all gas bags and cord netting for similar trouble.

As soon as repairs to the fins had been completed, the ship was passed fit for the Canadian demonstration flight, a twenty-four hour tour of major Canadian cities with representatives of the Canadian armed forces and the press on board. *R100* slipped the tower at St Hubert at 1818 local time on 10th August, and in the course of her 800 mile flight showed herself over Ottawa, Toronto, Niagara Falls, Hamilton, Kingston and Cornwall. When she arrived back over Montreal, thunderstorm activity delayed her landing for a couple of hours or so, and whilst she was loitering in the vicinity the reduction gear of the forward starboard engine disintegrated, damaging the propeller and part of the base boom joint of one of the ship's main frames. She secured to the tower at 2015 on the 11th. Under Norway's direction the next day, the crew was able to repair the damage to the boom. Wing Commander Colmore, the Director of Airship Development, accepted

Scott's recommendation that, with the prevailing winds helping the ship on her way, the return flight should be planned without the use of the defective engine.

Ernest's account continued:

"At half past eight on the night of August 13th (ominous date) we cast off from the tower for the return flight with thirty-two tons of fuel. There was the promise of fair weather in the Atlantic and everyone was in good spirits. We got away from Montreal with a good following wind with four engines at cruising speed and doing about 70 knots until daylight, when the wind became light and indefinite and was of little help to us. For the remainder of the day the weather was fine and clear, no low cloud, good visibility. At 10.45 am we passed Greeley Island where Kohl and Fitzmaurice landed last year – what a place! At noon we were five miles south of Belle Isle South Point lighthouse. Course was set to make good a track east true, and with a light following wind we set off at about 60 knots groundspeed. The sea was like a sheet of glass and the sky was cloudless. Position line sights were taken for carrying on later. There were innumerable icebergs of all sizes to be seen, and it is not difficult to realise what a menace they must be to shipping when the treacherous fogs are prevailing on the Banks. The air temperatures were fairly high, the mean being of the order of 55°F, and there was no evidence to show that the bergs affect the temperature at 1,500 ft more than about one degree Fahrenheit. In fact, this slight drop might have been due to some other cause.

"About an hour before sunset we ran under a wedge-shaped pall of cloud, the point of which was to the northward. This cloud was associated with an occlusion; the wind was light and indefinite and the sky looked very dull to the eastward. A little later we ran into light rain and began to recover water for ballast. We altered course to make northing to a point in 55 north and 35 west where we hoped to pick up a fair wind; but about 10 pm the wind changed to ENE about 5 mph and the rain increased. There was now evidence that we had run into the north side of a depression, and by midnight it was entirely overcast, visibility nil, and the wind was backing and freshening. Our groundspeed was now down to 35 knots. It was raining with almost tropical intensity and we recovered seven tons of ballast in the downpour.

"By daylight on the 15th it was blowing a moderate gale, the sea was a whipped-up fury, and we altered course to the southeast to get on the south side of the depression so as to get to the westerly winds. Never were we so glad of having a good drift sight as we were now, anxiously watching every little shift of wind and jealously keeping every inch of groundspeed we could. At last about 8.30 pm there was a distinct rise in temperature (from 48°F to 63°F) and for a few minutes the air was very disturbed, so it was obvious we had passed into the warm sector of the depression. At 9 am the clouds had lifted considerably and broken up somewhat. The wind had backed to SSW and was still freshening. By noon we were doing 82 knots and had once more resumed our course to make good a track of east true. The sea was still a turmoil of tumbling water and we were very thankful we were not being tossed about in a ship.

"Meals seemed to follow one another so quickly, owing to clocks being put ahead frequently as we changed from one time zone to another, that there seemed every likelihood of our all becoming dyspeptic. By 4 pm the weather had moderated considerably, and after passing over a layer of dense stratus we passed into a clear patch and were able to get sights. At 6.30 we passed over the *Beaver Brae* in latitude 55-22 north, longitude 19-51 west, which verified the sights we had obtained. We were now on course for Fastnet, which we expected to sight at 2 am, and doing 60 knots. Except for some low cloud the weather was quite good. At 1.25 am on the 16th we sighted Bull Rock on the port bow, and at 1.46 sighted the Fastnet light ahead.

"We were now on the last lap; at 5 am we shifted the clock forward for the last time, and at 6 am boosted up our speed. It was a beautiful morning, clear sky, and old England looked at its best as we came up the Bristol Channel. We arrived over Bedford at 9.50 am, and after ballasting up secured to the mast at 11.06 am, completing the return trip of 2,955 nautical miles in 57 hours 36 minutes with 11.5 tons of fuel in reserve. And who can say that the prophecy is not to be fulfilled?

For I dipt into the future, as far as human eye could see,
Saw the vision of the world, and all the wonder that would be:
Saw the heavens fill with commerce, argosies of magic sails..."

On this flight, because of the lighter load of fuel needed, some additional passengers were carried, most of them representatives of the leading newspapers on both sides of the Atlantic. The proper demands of news correspondents to file their stories through the single W/T channel of communication with the outside world could not but clash with the demands of routine operational communications, including the regular receipt of the large quantities of meteorological data which Giblett needed for drawing up the synoptic charts. It was left to Ernest, who was in charge of communications, to sort this out. The encounter with the depression on the night of the 14th/15th was not forecast, so, when the electrical circuits serving the galley stove and the heating in the passenger lounge were put permanently out of action as a result of penetration by the heavy rain, Giblett came in for some ragging. As every meal thereafter had to be served cold and the air temperature dropped well below 50 degrees, the error of his ways was not quickly forgotten. Giblett, normally the mildest and most kindly of men, vehemently swore that it was Johnnie's fault for letting the Press so clutter up the W/T channel that a vital synoptic report which would have given him warning of the swift development of the depression had been missed.

As soon as R100 was secured to the mast at Cardington, Lt Commander Atherstone, the First Officer of R101, came aboard with a duty watch made up of R101 personnel, so as to let the flight crew go home promptly to rest before mustering early next morning to take her into the shed. There was a small welcoming crowd of friends, relatives and staff from the Royal Airship Works at the foot of the mast, led by Lord Thomson of Cardington, the Secretary of State for Air. Quickly, after the congratulatory words and the poses for the Press photographers, the travellers dispersed to their various homes.

R100 never flew again.

The weather being calm, very early next morning her Officers and crew assembled to bring her down from the mooring tower and walk her into her shed. Booth and Meager took up their stations on board while Johnston and Steff took their usual places in charge of the ground handling parties of a couple of hundred men at each end of the ship. Three of the relief crew from R101 who had spent the night on board were found lying drunk in the crew's quarters, having rifled several of the Officers' quarters where some presentation bottles of spirits had been left. The Chief Steward reported to the Captain the loss of his liquor stores which had been locked in his cabin before he went ashore. Shortly after the relief crew went on board, some of them had been seen drinking rum in the crew space. Squadron Leader Booth mustered the relief crew as soon as R100 was in the shed and, after questioning them, ordered a search of the ship. Ernest, who had performed his usual duty in charge of a handling party on the ground, went on board about this time and was cursed by three of the relief crew who objected to the search. Discovering that his cabin on the top passenger deck had been broken open and various articles stolen, he went down to report the loss to Sqn Leader Booth. The three men, still at the head of the ladder leading to the control car, were again abusive. They followed him down, overheard him reporting his losses to Sqn Ldr Booth, and in abusive tones asked if he accused them of being thieves. An altercation followed in which the three men adopted an insulting and threatening attitude towards the two Officers. Ernest knocked one of them down with his fist for the purpose of breaking up the disorderly assembly. "Very Merchant Service but rather unnecessary, especially ashore," was the stiff comment of Atherstone, very much the retired regular Officer of the Royal Navy. The party broke up and made off. The men were suspended by Scott as being unfit for duty, but it was an angry Ernest who then gave Scottie a lift in his car back to the mast.

If in the very early years *R100* had seemed a bit of a joke to some of the senior people at Cardington, the very success of her Canadian flight tended from now on to condition their minds to sending *R101* to India without fully digesting the lessons which were there for all to see. The fragile outer covers were very vulnerable to the severe aerodynamic loads which some sorts of overland weather conditions could induce. Rope might have said "I told you so", were he not so modest a man. Whilst Colmore grasped the desirability of providing a mooring mast at the entrance to the St Lawrence so as to avoid having to fly overland to Montreal – the mail could be handed over to an existing aeroplane service connecting Montreal to the East coast – at the same time he seemed remarkably blind to the hazards of the overland portions of the route to India.

CHAPTER THIRTEEN

THE PRESSURE MOUNTS

After the euphoria of Canada and the low-key return to Cardington, Colmore found himself within minutes of disembarking immersed not only in the problems of *R101*, but also in the future airship programme and its politics. Lord Thomson shook hands with all and sundry at the foot of the mast, and was then away with Richmond to look at *R101* in the shed, and later to discuss the forward programme with Colmore. Ever since March, when a Future Projects Office headed by Squadron Leader Rope had been set up under Richmond, work had been directed towards shaping the programme for the next four years which the Secretary of State wanted to present to the forthcoming Imperial Conference, with a view to obtaining financial support from the Dominion Governments. The first problem had been to define, in the light of what had been learned from *R100* and *R101*, the specification of an airship actually capable of doing what they had originally been intended for. The preliminary study indicated that an airship of nearly twice their volume was needed – nine and a half million cu ft.

Early in August AMSR had held a meeting to review the situation, and two important decisions were made: first, that design work should be started immediately on two "stretched" versions of *R101* at seven and a half million cu ft, to be designated *R102* and *R103*; and second, that a full review of the forward four-year programme, now in draft, should be made after the flight of *R101* to India. Consequently, by the time Colmore returned from Canada, Richmond and Rope were well advanced on producing a costed programme for the years 1931-1935, covering the operation of *R101* and an enlarged *R100*, the design, building and operation of *R102* and *R103*, the enlargement of the existing sheds, the building of a new double-ship shed and the erection of a second mooring mast at Cardington. After Colmore had put the final touches to it, this 'Programme of Airship Development' was sent off to the Air Ministry in London on 23rd August. It involved some 15,000 flying hours for the four airships and was costed at £2,750,000 spread over four years.

When Colmore, in the middle of July, had pointed out that the timetable for lengthening R101 left no allowance for unforeseen hold-ups, Thomson had insisted that the India schedule be adhered to as he had made his plans accordingly. He intended to leave during the weekend of 26th September and be back in London by 16th October. In the days following their return from Canada, Colmore and Scott reviewed progress with Richmond, and found that, although it looked as if work on the new bay would be completed by 22nd September, there was some doubt whether the reversing engines and airscrews could be installed and working until the 28th. Time had then to be allowed for taking her out of the shed (which was contingent on calm conditions), carrying out a twenty-four hour trial flight and any consequential rectifications, and preparing her for India. Thomson, conceding that further delay was unavoidable, undertook to have the Air Agenda of the Imperial Conference moved back to after 20th October, if necessary, and directed Colmore to do his utmost to start the flight to India on 4th October.

At a meeting on 29th August Thomson considered the new Four Year Programme. He felt that it was "quite a reasonable programme to put to his colleagues in the Cabinet and then to the Imperial Conference". It was decided, however, not to include this programme in the formal Paper for the Conference, but rather to formulate the Conference Paper in such a way "as would lead logically into a decision by the Conference to go forward with a programme on these lines": and Lord Thomson would fill the Conference in on the details after his triumphant return from India. On 6th September a formal Air Ministry submission was made for Treasury approval of the proposed Four Year Plan, including the placing of orders for new materials for R102 and R103 in the summer of 1931. This submission pointed out, inter alia, that the Imperial Conference provided a natural opportunity, which would not recur during the development period of the airships, for framing an agreed scheme in which all parties had a financial interest, and that the opportunity, if lost, might well prove expensive in the end. The Treasury agreed to make funds available but also made a proviso of fundamental importance: the programme was to be subject to endorsement by the Imperial Conference on Lord Thomson's return from India. This decision filtered down to Cardington, where it was taken to mean clearly that the whole future of airships now depended on R101's leaving for India on 4th October.

There now took place two significant changes of personnel at the Air Ministry in Whitehall; Sir Christopher Bullock became Permanent Secretary and Air Vice-Marshal Dowding succeeded Sir John Higgins as AMSR. Bullock expressed his views very firmly to Dowding: the building of R102 and R103 should be postponed and "we should concentrate – as the next stage – on the real crux of the matter, the demonstration of the practicability of regular operation with the enlarged R100 and R101." He thought that the Four Year Programme which his Secretary of State was now embracing so enthusiastically was a sheer gamble. It was a view that the cautious Dowding, an aeroplane man pure and unalloyed who knew nothing about airships, expressed on his first visit to Cardington on 18th September, to the consternation of Colmore and Richmond. With their own immediate Chief seeming to be opposed to the Four Year Programme, and the Treasury requiring a flight to India as well as endorsement by the Imperial Conference as a condition of providing further funds, they felt that the heat was being turned up. R100 was still the Contractor's ship, and even to Scottie, Ernest and Steff, who were as much concerned with flying her as R101, she was always 'the other ship'; while R101 was the Cardington ship, designed, erected and flown by their own tight community. In the eyes of everybody but her own crew, R100's successful flight to Canada was something of a sideshow compared with the crowning importance – and greater difficulty – of flying the Secretary of State to India and back in time to persuade the Imperial Conference to approve the Four Year Programme. They remembered, too, Thomson's grim warning in June that failure to meet the Indian deadline could mean severe curtailment of the whole airship programme as well as the loss of his political support.

The man at the very centre was now Scottie, for, by the end of August Richmond had put his technical reputation on the line by asserting his absolute confidence that R101 would be in good order for the Indian voyage; despite the major structural alterations now embodied, there should be no reason for the Air Ministry to hold back the issuing of the Certificate of Airworthiness. It remained only for Scottie, as the man in charge of flying operations, to satisfy himself that she was adequately flight-tested and operationally fit to undertake an exceptionally arduous flight with distinguished passengers on board.

At Cardington, however, Scott was somewhat isolated from his subordinate Officers. Now in his early forties and still an airshipman with an international reputation, and without question the most experienced airship pilot in the country, a man of courage, always willing to accept responsibility in the air, he nevertheless seems to have failed in the last few years to acquire the maturity which his position of Assistant Director of Airship Development demanded. Like many a brilliant man, he was careless about detail; like many a fine aviator he did not take kindly to paperwork. He was a civilian, and he set his own pace – and his unpunctuality was a byword. He continued to live in the young aviator's tradition of wine, women and song.

His two Captains, both regular Air Force Officers, were men of greatly different temper. Booth had steadily grown in stature following his brilliant handling of R33 when she broke away from the mast at Pulham. His diffident, almost shy manner, his superbly ironic sense of humour and quiet charm, which were the source of his nickname 'Mouldy', concealed a man of strong will and first class professional competence. He knew his ship and her men, and what they could do, from A to Z. His crew held him in the highest respect; and the support that he gave to his Chief, Scott, was the fearless support of a confident junior commander who knew his job. R100 succeeded, he said, because they all had plenty of time to think; but perhaps it was rather because Mouldy Booth insisted that the lessons of each new phase were learned properly before the next was allowed to begin.

By contrast, Irwin seemed rather aloof from the totally dedicated airship community, almost as though he were standing on his dignity as an Air Force Officer and perhaps resentful that his proper Service career was being prejudiced by his secondment to a civilian airship programme. Although he had worked out an excellent and detailed trials programme for R101, he seems to have lacked the personal authority to insist on its being carried through. During 1930, moreover, he suffered a domestic tragedy and was also preoccupied with his studies for impending promotion examinations. Although a fine airship pilot he was outshone technically by his No 2, Atherstone, who probably knew more about the details of R101 than any other single person. Unlike Booth, Irwin appeared to be unable to give his subordinates the support they needed in getting things done to the ship by the technical staff, whilst his aloofness failed to provide the checks and balances that Scott's somewhat casual approach sometimes needed. It was doubly unfortunate that Atherstone had not taken part in the June flights. By the time he returned from Canada the minor panic which had swept through Cardington over the loss of lift had calmed down, and Richmond and Rope were satisfied with the preventive measures in hand. It was Atherstone's job to see that padding was carried out to his Captain's satisfaction. The controllability problems experienced during the June flights were never really explained, and Irwin perhaps dismissed too easily what, oversensitively, he took to be jealous criticism of "his" ship by Booth and Meager. Atherstone was the sort of man who would have dug his heels in until he had found a satisfactory answer; but he returned to operations too late and to a programme perhaps too crowded for him to assess the full significance of what had happened in his absence.

In the race against time to beat Lord Thomson's deadline, therefore, too much was allowed to hang upon Scottie's impulsive "press on spirit". It is probable that by now the idea was forming in his head that the best solution was to avoid having to make a decision that would be odious: "let the Minister have a run for his money: start for India on schedule, and if the ship couldn't make Egypt or was held up over France, or an engine packed up, well they could always turn back for home, and no skin off anyone's nose." The possibility of disaster was simply never entertained at any level. Airships had a tradition of safety in peace and war. All the lessons of the R38 disaster had been learned and painstakingly put into effect, it was thought. This was why the Secretary of State flew on the second flight of R101, and why on every subsequent trial flight the serious experimental purpose was hampered by the presence of joy-riders of all shapes and sizes. Booth, on his first solo flight as Captain of R100, which lasted for nearly twenty-three hours, had to contend with the distractions of looking after an Under Secretary of State, a whole RAF Specialist Navigation class, the inevitable Press people and a whole host of minor VIPs. The acceptance by everybody from the top downwards of the thesis that an airship designed to carry passengers should always carry passengers, even on her proving trials before having earned her Certificate of Airworthiness, does much to explain why Thomson was not opposed more strongly.

There was, too, the ever present example of the German airship *Graf Zeppelin* which visited Cardington that summer. She was a three and three-quarter million cubic foot ship designed and built expressly to operate a mail, freight and passenger service between Germany and Brazil. Completed in the summer of 1928 she had, after half a dozen trial flights over Germany and the North Sea, carried out a return flight between Friedrichshaven and New York carrying twenty-five passengers in October of that year. During the next few months she carried out, inter alia, two cruises in the Mediterranean as far east as Palestine and Egypt. In May 1929, after leaving with eighteen passengers on her second voyage for USA, four of her five engines broke down and she carried out successfully a very difficult and dangerous forced landing in the Mistral near Toulon. In August she flew round the world with twenty passengers – not, be it admitted, without some highly adventurous experiences. By May 1930 she was able to inaugurate what she had been designed for, the steady, unspectacular routine of a regular summer service to South America.

As soon as Ernest had caught up on some sleep after the Atlantic flight, removed all his gear from R100 and written up his reports, he plunged into preparations for the voyage to India. Early in September he produced a detailed timetable for the double journey based on a provisional starting date of 4th October. Then, when the news of the Treasury's decision on the four-year programme was given to Cardington, Scott told him that he was in line to command one of the new ships.

That September was nothing if not a hectic month. Although the problem of providing some reverse thrust had been cracked in principle in March by Major George Forsyth of the Air Ministry, who suggested a way of modifying the camshaft of the Tornado engine so as to enable the crankshaft to rotate in either direction, the detailed engineering took some time, with the result that even as late as mid-August there were doubts as to whether the date for the Indian flight could be met. The gantry test of the first reversing Tornado was not run until 12th September, and it was then discovered that the newly designed airscrew for it would not absorb full power at 900 rpm ahead. When the engine was running in reverse, moreover, and the airscrew was rotating the 'wrong' way, its effective thrust was reduced by half. The delivery of an unexpected second reversing engine was promised for 17th September, and Scottie was so insistent on the desirability of fitting it that Colmore and Richmond agreed to forego the usual gantry test, install it and give it its proving run on the ship before she left the shed.

The issue by Air Ministry of a 'Permit to Fly' was contingent on the receipt of a report from Professors Bairstow and Pippard, who had been invited by the Air Council in June to undertake a detailed investigation of the effect of the new bay on the ship's airworthiness. These two gentlemen had been concerned with the original airworthiness investigations in 1929, and on the basis of their detailed, voluminous report, as well as the results of periodic inspections by the Air Ministry's Aeronautical Inspectorate, the various trial flights had been authorised by temporary 'Permits to Fly'. The procedure in relation to the lengthening of R101 was somewhat less deliberate, so urgent was the Minister's programme. Sir Sefton Brancker's Directorate of Civil Aviation had the statutory responsibility for the issue of the Permits to Fly needed for the trial flights, and the Certificate of Airworthiness required for the forthcoming international flight. Brancker was confident in the ability of his officials to deal properly with these matters, but as a professional aviator of very great experience he was a little bit uneasy about the wider considerations of rushing a virtually new airship, as the rebuilt *R101* was, into so gruelling a venture as the flight to India. He did not share Thomson's view of the overriding importance of flying to India before the Imperial Conference; but he himself had no responsibility in the matter apart from the purely technical one of issuing the Certificate of Airworthiness. Nevertheless he thought it desirable to visit Cardington on 22nd September to get the feel of things. Despite the confident attitude of Colmore, Richmond and Scott, it did not escape his professional eye that with barely twelve days to go to the scheduled departure, *R101* was empty of gas, installation of the second and untested reversing engine was not yet complete (and indeed they could not even start the engine designed for starting up the Tornado itself); and Richmond was still heavily involved in stress calculations to satisfy the Airworthiness Panel. They reassured him that if *R101* left the shed as scheduled on 28th September, there would be time for one trial flight of at least twenty-four hours. Brancker left Cardington knowing that they would have liked a longer trial flight and more time for post-flight inspection, but were willing, if all went well, to stick to Lord Thomson's schedule because so much appeared to depend on it. With a more sophisticated understanding of the political scene, however, he was less convinced than they were of setting out so precipitately. He resolved to take the earliest opportunity to make his views known privately to Thomson.

Two days later there was another panic at Cardington when McWade discovered that the rubber solution which had been used to apply various patches to the original cover at the bow of the ship had interacted with the dope and substantially reduced the strength of the fabric. The outer cover between frames 1 and 3 in the bows and frames 12 and 13 aft had not been renewed, as they were parts of the original cover which had not been pre-doped. There was no time to do anything else but stick down reinforcing strips of cotton with red dope, all along the lines of rubber solution on those parts of the outer cover, and trust that any further weakness would be shown up by the trial flight to come. "A patched shoe is never as good as a new one," Scottie commented.

On Friday 26th September *R101* was gassed up and became airborne in the shed. Her crew took her over next day; watchkeeping routine was resumed, and lift and trim trials were done immediately. The disposable lift worked out at 49.36 tons, an improvement of nearly 14.5 tons over the original ship. Nearly nine tons of this was attributable to the new bay. All was ready for her to leave the shed on the target date of 28th, but inevitably the wind kept her immobilised until the morning of 1st October. Shed watchkeeping routine was augmented by keeping the Liberty Watch and the ground handling party at standby daily. Finally, the new *R101* emerged at 0630 on 1st October and was secured to the mast after slight problems with the main downhaul wire. Scottie, Ernest and Steff then took the ground handling party to No 2 shed, whence they brought out *R100* and walked her into No 1 shed where she was going to have her new bay installed. That was the last the outside world saw of her.

Meanwhile, on 26th September the Air Ministry had obtained by telephone Professor Bairstow's sanction for a Permit to Fly to be issued, and requested him to submit his full report (which was then in an unfinished draft stage) in time for the issue of the Certificate of Airworthiness needed before the ship could fly to India. Bairstow pointed out that, whilst he was satisfied that *R101* in her new form complied with the specific requirements of the Airworthiness of Airships Panel, he and Pippard had been surprised by the magnitude of the differences of loading of *R101* now submitted, as compared with the original design. "A good deal of general thinking and comparison on limited information has been required in reaching our conclusion", he wrote, "and we have not had time since receiving essential information from the RAW to prepare a sufficiently considered final report." It was on this basis that Air Ministry issued a Permit to Fly on 1st October for the trial flight.

After hectic preparations, *R101* slipped from the mast at 4.30 pm that afternoon. Already, however, Colmore had sought and obtained AMSR's agreement to curtail the duration of the flight to less than twenty-four hours "if the ship behaved well and Major Scott was satisfied." So the stipulation made by AMSR in December that the issue of a Certificate of Airworthiness would be contingent upon a trial flight of forty-eight hours was not only thrown out of the window, but the whole responsibility was thrown by Air Ministry down to Scottie with a vengeance. To Dowding's one query Colmore replied that his only reason for cutting the duration of the flight was to make Thursday as well as Friday available for work that would be necessary to prepare the ship for departure on Friday evening. Dowding himself was aboard for this flight; it was the first time he had flown in an airship. During the flight he talked to Colmore, Scottie, Irwin and Ernest, and remarked afterwards that "the atmosphere was quite serene". Richmond also was on board: he recorded "Trial flight. Impossible to carry out full speed test owing to early failure of oil cooler in forward starboard engine. The conditions were very perfect, and under these conditions, all other items in the ship behaved perfectly." As there was no time afterwards for anyone to make the usual written reports (except, oddly enough, Ernest's report on the wireless installation), and all of those of consequence were killed three days later, little is known about the flight. Atherstone's diary recorded that the trial was "very successful"; the ship appeared to be much better in the air than before and the cover was very good. After flying over London and down the Thames, she spent the night cruising off the east coast and landed back at the mast at 0920 on Thursday 2nd October, having been in the air just over seventeen hours in absolutely smooth flying conditions.

G.D. Raisbeck, one of McWade's Inspectors, flew on the trial to make a special in-flight inspection of the ship for the issue of a Certificate of Airworthiness. By agreement with Irwin, he paid special attention to those items which he thought were important in flight, including outer cover, gas bags, gas valves and controls. In the very smooth flying conditions he noted practically no movement of the outer cover; all sealing strips appeared to be secure; no leaks were observed at the gas valves; the movement of the gas bags was so slight as to be barely perceptible; and the padding was secure. All other items were found to be in good order and functioning satisfactorily. He reported that Irwin was satisfied with his (Raisbeck's) independent inspection, which tallied with the reports he had received from his crew.

On the previous day, Professor Bairstow had written to the Air Ministry confirming the view of Pippard and himself that the ship now complied with the airworthiness requirements, and that the first draft of the Bairstow-Pippard report was being put in its final form. Bairstow was still working on his report when he heard of the disaster. On Thursday, therefore, without having seen this report, the Deputy Director of Civil Aviation signed the Certificate of Airworthiness and forwarded it to McWade at Cardington for issue to Irwin after a satisfactory pre-flight inspection.

There can be little doubt that at the conference which Colmore held in his office that Thursday morning, everyone – Richmond for the technical side, Scott for the flying side and Irwin for the ship – must have expressed satisfaction with the trial flight as far as it went. But it is not improbable that Irwin advanced the view that he had always held, that a lengthy flight in adverse weather conditions, including at least six hours at high speed in bumpy air, was essential before embarking on so imponderable a venture as the Indian flight. This was certainly Ernest's view.

There were strong reasons for further trials. First: R101 as enlarged and modified was virtually a new airship with different stability and handling characteristics; logically, therefore, she should have undergone a full series of handling trials, including manoeuvring in different trim conditions at various speeds up to maximum power, just as the original ship did (though she never reached maximum cruising speed, let alone full speed). Second, on the June flights, she had displayed undesirable handling characteristics which needed to be investigated in depth. Third, the efficacy of the padding needed to be tested in rough air. Fourth, the integrity of those portions of the outer cover at the bows and stern, which had not been replaced and which had shown signs of weakness, needed much more severe testing than the easy conditions of this flight had provided. Fifth, the two reversing Tornados had had less running than would normally be required for flight clearance, and indeed one of them had had to be shut down early in the flight. Booth in similar circumstances might have insisted on further flying. Indeed, when asked the question at the subsequent Court of Inquiry whether, had he been responsible, he thought the last trial was adequate, he replied: "I think that the Officers concerned who had more experience of the ship than I had (and of course Major Scott who had more experience of airships than anyone) were quite satisfied with the ship. They were confident in the ship and in their crew, but, at the same time, I feel that their decision to leave, or their agreement to leave, at that time was biassed by the fact of the Imperial Conference coming off, and the psychological moment in airships when they could carry the Secretary of State for Air to India, and bring him back to time. It biassed their judgement in agreeing to fly. If that Imperial Conference had not been coming off, I feel confident that they would have insisted on more trials, as was done in the case of R100 before she left for Canada." Ironically, there was one more reason that was never even considered: were Irwin and Atherstone and their crew sufficiently experienced in long-range airship operations to undertake this voyage so soon? The question was never asked in their life-time; but no sooner were they all dead than some of the leading technical people at Cardington, as well as some of the politicians and top civil servants in Whitehall, were not only asking it but answering it in the negative.

Wing Commander Cave-Brown-Cave, who was responsible under Richmond for the installation and testing of the power plants and associated equipment, brought up the risks of leaving without a full-speed test or, alternatively, of doing the test after departure for India with the Secretary of State and a full load of passengers and fuel on board. Colmore replied that there was no time for another test flight: he had been told quite definitely that "if the ship does not succeed in getting the Secretary of State to India in time for him to arrive home for the Imperial Conference, no further money would be available for airship development and none would be asked for." Because of the risk of some sort of failure, Colmore was not prepared to authorise a full-speed trial on the way to India.

It is unlikely that Colmore ever calculated the risks on that Thursday morning, for he was being swept along by an inexorable stream of events. He, Richmond and Scott were united in their determination to overcome all the obstacles and get the Secretary of State on his way to India as planned. The possibility of disaster was simply not considered. At worst, if they found the ship could not make Egypt she could always get back to England somehow; beyond Egypt it was not yet possible to look. Even if the voyage to India was a total success, the climatic statistics made it seem probable that she would have to stay there for many weeks before she could safely fly home; and should she arrive at Karachi distressed, there was a shed to put her in, even though it would present a long, slow supply-line for remedial action.

Later on Thursday Lord Thomson pressed Colmore for a departure on Friday evening, then Saturday morning; but in the end he yielded to planning a start on Saturday evening, 4th October, because Richmond wanted time for some remedial work on the power plant installation, Scott wanted a flight plan that terminated in Egypt after dusk, and Irwin wanted time not only to prepare the ship but also to give his crew some rest. Having pushed hard for nearly a year to accomplish his objective, Thomson could now afford to appear magnanimous: "You mustn't allow my natural impatience or anxiety to start to influence you in any way. You must use your considered judgement."

CHAPTER FOURTEEN

THE END OF R101

At Cardington Irwin, Atherstone, Steff and Ernest together with the crew were hard at work, combining normal watchkeeping routine with detailed post-flight inspection and rectification, followed by flight planning, gassing, fuelling, ballasting and provisioning. It was a tight and hectic schedule carried through with efficiency and a quiet, courageous confidence. On the trial flight Ernest had been testing a sonic altimeter, but although it worked fairly well it was among many items of experimental equipment removed to lighten the ship as much as possible. At the same time, ironically, the lounge and the long entrance passage from the bow hatch were carpeted, at a weight penalty of over 1,000 lbs, in order to demonstrate the luxury of airship travel to the guests at the State Dinner Party planned to be held on board during the night's stopover at Ismailia.

At noon on Friday Colmore conferred with Scott, who had spent much of the morning with Irwin, Ernest and Giblett studying weather prospects, and decided to set the departure time between 6 pm and 8 pm the next day. The forecast conditions looked fine. That evening Atherstone wrote the last lines in his private diary: "Everybody is rather keyed up now as we all feel that the future of airships largely depends on what sort of show we put up. There are very many unknown factors, and I think that that thing called 'luck' will figure rather conspicuously in our flight. Let's hope for good luck and do our best."

This dogged airshipman of proven courage and skill, who did not suffer fools gladly, spoke for them all. He, perhaps, knew more about the detail of the ship than anyone else, and he was not concerned with the politics of it: he would have protested most vigorously to Irwin if he was not satisfied with the corrective measures that had been taken. And Irwin knew, beyond all doubt, that as Captain of the ship he was entirely responsible that she was airworthy and well-found in all respects before the flight commenced, for only that morning he had sought clarification as to his position vis-a-vis Scott. This arose partly as a result of Scott's objection to the terms of an Air Ministry press release which indicated that he was flying merely as a passenger. On the day before *R101* set out for India, therefore, a fresh statement was drafted to satisfy both Scott and Irwin: "The Assistant Director (Flying) would discuss with the Captain or the Navigator and the Meteorological Officer the general weather conditions and as a result would decide on the courses to be taken, the flying height and the speed of the airship. He would also advise on the amount of fuel and water ballast to be carried. The Captain of the airship is entirely responsible for the preparation of the ship for flight and that it was airworthy and well found in all respects before flight commenced. He was responsible for maintaining the ship in correct flying trim throughout the flight and carrying out general orders in regard to height, course, engine speeds etc. as laid down by the Assistant Director (Flying). He was entirely responsible for the flying organisation of the ship and the discipline of the crew." Booth, who was also present when this was drafted, remarked that it was the only practicable arrangement in view of the fact that the Captain was also a watchkeeping Officer.

Four basic routes had been selected as options for the journey to Ismailia: the longest, 2,440 nautical miles, via Brest, Pamplona, Barcelona and Malta; the shortest, 2,075 miles, via Lyons and the Rhone Valley to Marseilles, thence direct to Ismailia; the Rhone Valley route and thence via Malta; and the route via Toulouse, Narbonne and Malta. From Ismailia there were three options: the shortest, about 2,125 nm, was to fly eastwards across the desert direct to Baghdad and thence coastwise through the Persian Gulf; the longest, some 2,860 nm, was the Red Sea route to Aden and then direct across the northern Indian Ocean to Karachi; and the third, to fly northeast to Aleppo and then down the Euphrates to Baghdad and on through the Persian Gulf. The flight time England to Egypt was of the same order as that between Egypt and India, forty-eight to fifty hours.

On Friday morning Scott provisionally selected the route through the Toulouse-Narbonne gap for the first leg of the flight. On the basis of Giblett's forecast winds, Irwin and Ernest worked out a fuel requirement of twenty-two tons at maximum cruising power, and Irwin decided to take on a fuel reserve for another three hours at reduced power, about three and a half tons. Although other tanks were empty, the weight that the ship could carry was the limiting factor. The quantity of water ballast had to be reduced below what Irwin would have liked to take, but in emergency several tons of fuel could be jettisoned simultaneously. The payload – passengers and baggage – amounted to just over one ton.

Irwin and his Officers were concerned primarily with the problem of demonstrating that R101 could fly to India in favourable conditions, and even return. With so firm a deadline forced upon them they were beginning to realise, while they did their lift, load and flight plan calculations, how much more difficult the additional commitment due to the presence of the Secretary of State and his entourage – in terms of both responsibility and weight – was going to make the attainment of their object. There was nothing they could do, however, but get on with the job calmly and efficiently. If any of them had thoughts about the folly of rushing things, they kept them to themselves. In London, however, they had, without knowing it, a champion who understood their dilemma: Brancker. His part in the unfolding events is best told in a letter written privately by one of his senior Staff Officers, Major Oliver Villiers, to Sir John Simon during the subsequent Inquiry into the destruction of the ship.

"On Friday October 3rd 1930 there was another lunch at the Army and Navy Club at which Bertram, the Deputy Director of Civil Aviation, Shelmerdine, the Director of Civil Aviation in India, Brancker and [Villiers] were present. Bertram and Shelmerdine were late, and [Villiers] took the opportunity of telling Brancker that Colmore desired to have further mooring masts, and that he and Colmore both thought that Document 16 should be re-edited and the necessity of these masts should be brought home to the public. Brancker said that at 3pm that afternoon he was going to see the Secretary of State about the National Flying Services and their finances, and that he was going to tell 'T' again that the whole policy of this trip was all nonsense: that he had told 'T' and would tell him again that the airship should stay in England for the duration of the Conference, and that that would give the Delegates the opportunity of flying, eating and sleeping if necessary in the old ship. He said that he had told Lord Thomson that if he did go to India it would not convince any of the Dominion Premiers; that although Lord Thomson could say he had had a marvellous journey, or that the engines ran smoothly, it was not going to be the same thing as though they themselves had gone up in the ship and seen for themselves. At this point Bertram and Shelmerdine arrived...

"On Saturday October 4th [Villiers] saw Brancker for a moment or two in the hall at Air Ministry in order to identify Brancker's luggage which [Villiers] was taking down by car. Brancker then went off to

Stag Lane where he flew to Ipswich to christen an aeroplane piloted by Miss Spooner, and Miss Spooner flew him back in her plane to Henlow where [Villiers] picked him up in the afternoon to take him to Cardington. Brancker sat alongside [Villiers] in the front seat... During the drive to Cardington [Villiers] asked Brancker what had happened the previous day. 'I got rapped over the knuckles and I got no change, he repeated all his old arguments over and over again.' Brancker then said Lord Thomson had said 'I have told them that I am going to be back in time for the Conference. We have already done the first flight to Canada, we must do the first flight to India. So that when we approach the Dominions for further cooperation in the scheme I can say we have done Canada, we have done India, and now you can see what airships can do.'"

On the morning of Saturday 4th Scott held a weather conference with Irwin, Ernest and Giblett; it seemed that the weather in the evening promised fair to cloudy over northern France with moderate southwesterly winds. Two further forecasts issued to the ship during the day indicated some deterioration in the weather at Cardington during the evening and over northern France during the night, without any significant increase in the wind strength – forecasts which, if not good, were not bad enough to force Scott to contemplate postponing departure. He was nevertheless sufficiently anxious to issue instructions to hurry his distinguished passengers aboard in order to leave as early as possible. Richmond and a very tired Ernest shepherded Lord Thomson and Brancker for a final round of press and newsreel photographs before ushering them into the lift, and all went on board.

At 1824 GMT on 4th October *R101* slipped from the mast in fine rain and darkness. Formal watchkeeping began at 7 pm GMT, Atherstone taking the first watch. Flying just below the cloud base at 1,500 ft, she was pitching and rolling rather heavily. Just after 8 pm, when she was over London, the ship received a weather forecast which showed a serious deterioration along her route over northern France, not only in terms of low cloud and rain, but also of an increase in wind speed to about 40 or 50 mph, a velocity which no British airship had encountered over land before. Scottie, Irwin and Ernest probably discussed it at length round Ernest's chart table in the control room. Already the decision had been taken, and confirmed by wireless, to proceed by Paris, Tours, Bordeaux and the Narbonne gap. The increased wind speed, hauling around more southerly, would slow the ship down; but Irwin would be most concerned about the effects of turbulence in gusts on the handling of the ship close to the ground. Normally a cox'n would expect to control her within 250 to 300 ft either side of the desired cruising height in bumpy conditions; in really bad conditions this hunting might extend to 400 or 500 ft either way at the very worst. The risks were considerable, but the flight had only just begun, and it is consonant with Scottie's character that the decision was probably made to press on at least as far as Paris to see how things might turn out. A request was made to Cardington for a fresh forecast for the Rhone Valley route, with special reference to wind and cloud. With the knowledge that the dice were beginning to look loaded there must have been some tightening of faces when the decision was made to press on.

The Rhone Valley forecast was received as R101 passed over Hastings at 9.35 pm, and during the couple of hours it took to cross the Channel Ernest was regularly making drift observations on calcium flares dropped into the sea. Atherstone went off watch at 11 pm. It is impossible to be certain about the order of watchkeeping. Irwin is known to have been discussing the engines with the Chief Engineer, Mr Gent, and the Foreman Engineer Mr Leech, in the smoking room at about 1 am, which suggests that he might have been off watch at the time, as the Officer of the Watch (OOW) would not be expected to leave the control car. Ernest was receiving Wireless bearings at about 0145.

The crash occurred between five and ten minutes past two. Within seconds of striking the ground the hydrogen gas ignited: R101 became a holocaust.

The Report of the R101 Inquiry [Cmd 3825], while it is somewhat imprecise about the actual cause of the crash, listed a number of facts which it said "may be regarded as definitely established". In substance they were:

(a) When the watch was changed at 2am, there was no cause for immediate alarm known to those in charge of the navigation of the ship. The vessel must have been at least 1,000 ft above the ground.

(b) At 2 am the elevator wheel would be handed over to another height coxswain.

(c) The weather was exceedingly bad... the wind was not steady but was blowing in fierce gusts which would cause the nose of the vessel to move through a considerable angle above and below her horizontal line of flight. The height cox'n would seek to limit or counteract this movement by use of the elevator.

(d) The ship on her trials had lost gas at an abnormal rate, certainly by the wearing of holes in her gasbags, and perhaps through her valves when she rolled.

(e) On the Indian journey she had rolled more than ever before, and had failed to keep height as the officer of the watch intended at an earlier period.

(f) If she was becoming increasingly heavy, this could be counteracted by suitable use of the elevator, but in very bumpy weather it would be more difficult to detect the rate and extent of the change.

(g) All the engines had been running satisfactorily at cruising speed for a considerable time right down to 2 am.

(h) In these circumstances, at about five minutes past two, her nose dropped and she continued in this position for about 30 seconds, descending rapidly during that period of time. Her pitch downwards was sufficiently severe to wake up a man who was asleep in his bunk, and to cause things to slide to the lower end of the smoke-room.

(i) The height cox'n, by putting his elevator up, succeeded at length in bringing the ship again to about an even keel, but she remained in this position for only a few seconds.

(j) At about the time when it appeared that she was not further responding to up-elevator so as to recover height, the officer of the watch gave orders through the engine-room telegraph to reduce speed.

(k) About this moment the vessel got into a second steep dive, which lasted for only a few seconds before she struck the earth. The impact was not severe.

(l) The slowing down of the engines combined with the warning given by Chief Coxswain Hunt to Disley and the crew, is only consistent with the view having been taken that the vessel could not recover.

(m) Apart from reducing speed, the only other action that could be instantly taken to lighten the impact would be to drop such ballast as could be released from the control car. Releasing ballast in the nose of the ship which could not be automatically controlled was a further and slower operation, and yet orders were given to Church to do this.

(n) The fire did not break out till after the ship struck the ground.

In moving towards its conclusions as to the cause of the crash, the Court had the benefit of taking the views not only of the three most experienced surviving British airship Captains – Sqn Ldr Booth, Sqn Ldr Wann and Capt. Meager – but also those of the world's greatest and most experienced airship pilot and operator, Dr Hugo Eckener. It was Eckener who first advanced the hypothesis, slightly modified by the other three, which the Court finally accepted as the most likely explanation of the crash. The Court was also able to enlist the services of the National Physical Laboratory to make a series of calculations, based on wind tunnel data, for the purpose of ascertaining what would be the theoretic movement of *R101* on various assumptions as to loss of gas, angle of elevator, buffets of wind and so forth. The wind tunnel work was carried out by Dr R. Jones and Mr A.H. Bell; the complex and exceedingly laborious calculations were carried out by Messrs D.H. Williams and A.R. Collar. On the basis of assumptions postulated by the Court they were able to demonstrate that the airship would in fact go through a series of movements which closely approximated to those which actually occurred. There are limitations to the validity of this theoretical work; nevertheless the correspondence between its conclusions and the explanation of the accident presented by the operational experts is very significant.

Since many serious writers have criticised the findings of the Court, it is worth quoting in full from the *Report*, published early in 1931, its conclusion as to the cause of the disaster:

"The clearest way in which to explain the theory of the accident which the Court adopts, is to regard the final movements of the *R101* as consisting of three phases. In the first phase she drops her nose and descends, at a noticeably steep angle, for half a minute or thereabouts before, by use of up-elevator, she is brought back to an approximately horizontal position. The second phase then begins and continues for a short time during which, in spite of her utmost efforts, she does not succeed in getting her nose appreciably up but continues horizontal until she suddenly passes into a third phase, when she dives again and strikes the ground almost at once at an angle of at least 15 degrees.

"In seeking the explanation of these successive movements, it is best first to direct attention to the second phase. Notwithstanding that the vessel had lost much height during the first phase, if she had been in a normal condition there seems no reason why she should not have pointed her nose up again and regained altitude. From the fact that she failed to do so, it may be argued most conclusively that she was by then crippled beyond recovery, and the inference is that, though momentarily on an even keel, she was descending rapidly to earth. The action of Chief Coxswain Hunt in leaving the control room to warn the crew indicates that, in spite of his great experience, his assistance there was no longer of any use and that those in charge knew there was nothing they could do which would prevent the ship from stranding. And the explanation of this would be provided if she had lost sufficient gas in the fore part of the ship. All that remained was to minimise the impact, and accordingly orders were given to stop the engines and release ballast. If this was the course of events the ship would proceed to put her nose down again, enter upon her second dive and crash.

"Now, working back to the first phase, the question is what was the course of events which brought the ship down from say, 1,200 ft, into the first long dive? Inasmuch as the reasoning above set out suggests, and, indeed, practically requires, that at the end of the first dive the vessel had lost a quantity of gas forward, it is natural to assume that this loss of gas had begun before the first phase was entered upon, though it became greater as the vessel descended. If the fore part of the cover had become torn and the wind entered the envelope, serious damage to gasbags would be most likely to occur with startling suddenness.

"The reconstruction of the first phase would therefore be some-what as follows: Assume that the vessel had become somewhat heavy and was being buffeted in the wind so that her nose was sometimes above and sometimes below the line of horizontal flight. If she had been raised by a buffet, the elevator would be put down by the cox'n who had just come on duty to check and counteract the movement. The cox'n, not yet having got the 'feel' of the ship thoroughly, might put his elevator rather more down than was necessary, or keep it down longer than was exactly right. The vessel's nose would drop. If when her nose is inclined downwards she gets a strong buffet of wind above her nose it will push her nose further down. If she was already heavy from loss of gas – especially if a rent had occurred in a gasbag which involved progressively rapid deflation – the descent is emphasised. The ship is now on her downward track in the first phase. The cox'n will begin to put his elevator up, and in order to get the ship out of her first dive has to put it up harder. None the less, she does not come out of her first dive as rapidly as she should because she is losing more gas all the time. The slowness of her recovery would give significant warning of the crisis.

"This gives the explanation of the course of events which is most consistent with the evidence, and at certain points is the only expla-nation which readily presents itself in accordance with the facts. At other points it is no doubt possible to assume certain variations in the data. For example, the final dive might have been assisted by another buffet of wind, and the exact relation between the angle of the elevator and the amount of gas lost can never be ascertained by any process of reconstruction.

"How the vessel began to lose gas can never be definitely ascertained. The weather was exceptionally bad; the gasbags were hard up against padded projections, some of which may have begun to wear the fabric; the bumpiness of the wind and the pitching of the ship would intensify the strain; and earlier flights had indicated the possibility of leakage through chafing, or, if the vessel rolled through an unusually large angle, through intermittent opening of the gas valves. But it seems very probable that the more serious and sudden loss of gas which followed was connected with a specific misfortune such as the ripping of the fore part of the envelope. Something of this sort had happened on a previous occasion and no amount of care could secure that it would never happen again. If a rip had begun in the fore part of the envelope it would tend to develop into a larger tear which would both check the speed of the *R101* through the air and expose the gasbags to additional strain. This seems the most probable explanation of a further loss of gas in increasing quantity and suddenness. But whatever the precise circumstances may have been, the explanation that the disaster was caused by a substantial loss of gas in very bumpy weather holds the field. This is the unanimous view of all three members of the Court of Inquiry."

AN AIRSHIP ORPHAN'S JUDGEMENT

My Mother, Daisy Janita, bore me at North West Castle, Stranraer, while my Father Major Ernest Livingston Johnston AFC RAF was in command of the airship station at Luce Bay. I cannot recollect any period of my early life when it was not taken for granted by me and by everyone else that I would follow my Father into the skies. When my Mother died less than two years after him, two *R101* widows, Jess Scott and Eve Atherstone, offered to take me into their families. I was not consulted and do not know why Jess was selected for this onerous task, but as she lived only five minutes' walk away from my School boarding house it was obviously a convenient solution. For me it was an immense privilege to become one of her family – "my half-son" as she introduced me to all and sundry – and it was the direct cause of my meeting, on the annual summer holiday on Garelochside, the girl who was to become my wife. Jess blessed me throughout the next five critical years with undemonstrative love and understanding without which my life might have been bleak indeed.

From Cranwell, after various post-graduate courses, I was assigned to a Flying Boat Squadron operating Saro Londons. We went to our War Station in the Shetlands in the summer of 1939, and shortly after hostilities broke out I was made a Flying Boat Captain and found myself doing at 75 knots precisely what my Father had been doing at 35 knots in his Coastal airships – Convoy Escorts and Anti-U-Boat patrols over the North Sea. Later, I was selected to attend the Specialist Navigation Course at the School of Air Navigation, and for the next three years I was employed as a Navigation Instructor. When at last I managed to break out of the rut, I was lucky to be posted to Coastal Command's crack Leigh Light Liberator Squadron as Flight Commander and aircraft Captain. Now I was techno-logically a step or two ahead of my Father, pursuing U-Boats at night with radar, sonar and acoustic torpedoes. Thereafter the RAF continued to give me a most interesting career including heading the Air Ministry section responsible for formulating the RAF's long-term requirements for navigation and blind bombing equipment; Command of the Armament and Instrument Experimental Establishment in the Ministry of Supply; and a couple of years on exchange duties in the Operational Requirements Directorate of the US Air Force in the Pentagon. These appointments gave me a close insight into the tensions between politicians, finance branches and the people managing aeronautical research and development, while my spell in command of A.I.E.U. showed me something of the pressures that various sorts of deadline can impose on the men in charge of experimental flying programmes. During my career I flew a wide range of aircraft, some of them between UK and North America as well as along the route to India, which gave me practical insight into the operating problems which the Imperial Airship Programme must have faced.

When Nevil Shute Norway published his bitterly unbalanced story of *R100* in his book *Sliderule* early in the 1950s I was sufficiently disturbed by what seemed to me to be a number of serious distortions, to get in touch again with Wing Commander Ralph Booth. He lent me his copy of the transcript of the *R101* Public Inquiry, and we had an interesting correspondence, but he was a very discreet man. I also discussed Norway's account at some length with Lieut Cdr Atherstone's widow, my very dear friend Eve Waley Cohen, but formed the view that she had a somewhat jaundiced view of Major Scott's part in the tragedy. After that, airships dropped out of my mind for thirty years or so, until my attention was brought to Sir Peter Masefield's book about the airship story, *To Ride The Storm*, while I was recuperating from an illness in my mid-sixties.

Masefield's evaluation of the causes of the disaster, written with all the enormous authority which he commanded in aviation circles, not only had to be taken seriously, but seemed to me to be flawed. I entered on a long and most rewarding correspondence with him which forced me to dig deeply into my memory and my archives and to apply my own judgement, based on a not insignificant range of knowledge and experience in aviation matters at many levels, to all the evidence available. As we were unable to reconcile our differences I decided to examine the whole recorded evidence de novo, going back to original sources, most of them available in the Public Record Office.

My first object was to try to determine who was in control of the airship when it crashed. I sought first to establish what could be learned from the reports of those who observed the crash, those who recovered the bodies, and those competent people who examined the wreckage. I then examined minutely the evidence of those of the crew who survived and made statements, preferring, where there were contradictions, that which was given under examination in Court. I analysed very carefully the plan made by the Gendarmerie which is the only authentic data about where the bodies were found. By the time any British personnel arrived on the scene all the bodies had been removed from the wreck. The Air Attache reported "We feel that it is important to record that in no instance were features recognizable, all bodies being terribly incinerated." I analysed T.S.D. Collins' original notes of the state of various bodies which he saw in their coffins and of the associated bits of clothing and belongings by means of which identifications were made. I read the note of the RAF Officer who had charge of the bodies and attended the inquest: it was evident that the Coroner made no individual identifications, and that once the decision was made to bury the dead in a common grave, identification was treated somewhat perfunctorily. There is absolutely no evidence, however, that either Irwin or Atherstone had retired to rest and was in pyjamas, as Sir Peter Masefield has asserted. Irwin's body, identified by a signet ring, was almost clear of the port side of the lower passenger deck. The body officially identified as Atherstone appears to have been in the area of the control car, but there is considerable doubt in my mind as to the validity of the identification. Taking due consideration of the condition of the wreckage following the fire, the very approximate nature of the Gendarmerie's plan, and the tenuous nature of some of the evidence of identification, it is not possible to determine from the evidence at the scene of the crash who was in control of the ship at the time.

Irwin, Atherstone and Johnston were all in possession of current Airship Pilot's Licences, First Class, and were qualified to take charge of watches. Steff, on the other hand, was neither licensed nor qualified, although he had gained a measure of experience as a watchkeeping Officer under supervision on all the flights of R100 and R101; his official status was 'trainee'. In the flight orders, Irwin, Atherstone and Steff were listed as watchkeeping Officers, while Johnston, as Navigator, was designated to stand duty as and when required. The flight orders specify three-hourly watches for the crew between 2000 and 0800 hrs, but are ambiguous as to whether the officers were to keep similar watches or their customary four-hourly tricks. I could find no record of any instruction specifying who should take which watch. Sir Peter Masefield conjectures that Steff was in charge of the watch when the ship crashed; it seems far-fetched that, with so many VIPs on board, an unqualified, unlicensed trainee would be left in charge at night in the worst weather ever flown in by a British ship. I found nothing to gainsay the evidence given to, and accepted by the Court, that it was not possible to determine who was in control of the airship at the time of the crash. Since the Captain's cabin, however, was closely adjacent to the Control Room, it is not unreasonable to suppose that in emergency he could have been present very quickly. So could Major Scott.

The circumstances of the crash are related in the evidence of the six survivors. They made statements to the Air Ministry Investigation team while they were in hospital and they also made separate statements to the Attorney General which were presented as evidence to the Court of Inquiry. There are some important differences of both detail and emphasis between the two sets, so that in general I deemed it desirable to accept as definitive the evidence taken in Court, since it was on this that they were cross-questioned.

At about 0200 hrs Foreman Engineer Leech was relaxing in the smoking room. He described how he, together with tables and loose articles, slipped towards the forward bulkhead, and a soda water siphon and some glasses fell onto the floor. His first estimate of the duration of the first dive was forty-five seconds, but on reconsideration he thought it might have been only fifteen or twenty seconds before the ship began to straighten out again. His initial statement was that the angle of the second dive was about the same as the first; in Court, however, he concluded that the second was slightly less steep.

Engineer Bell said that shortly after he had taken over his watch at 0200 hrs the ship suddenly took up a nose-down angle of 45 degrees, which was quickly rectified; he estimated that it did not last longer than about thirty seconds. His companion in the after car, Binks, agreed. Bell thought that both dives were at about the same angle

Electrician Disley was asleep in the switchroom adjacent to the control room. He appears to have wakened only in the last stage of recovery from the first dive. Engineers Cook and Savory simply did not notice the first dive.

As for the duration of the level phase, Leech first thought that it was one minute or possibly less, but he later revised this drastically downwards. The fact remains that he was able to pick glasses and a soda siphon off the floor and put them back on the table while the attitude of the ship was substantially level. This suggests a time of fifteen to twenty seconds. Bell thought not more than five seconds, Binks not more than ten. Disley thought that after recovery from the first dive the ship climbed again; then Chief Cox'n Hunt came into the switchroom as the ship reached the crest after the dip, and as he went off again the next dive began. Nobody else commented. Leech put the duration of the second dive at ten to fifteen seconds, and heard the engine room telegraphs ringing about two seconds before impact. Binks puts the dive at ten seconds. Bell is perhaps more authoritative - "at the next moment the nose went down again to about the same angle as before. I then received an order over the engine room telegraph to go to 'slow' and while I was taking action the crash came". Questioned "How long was it after the ship got into the second dive before it struck the ground?", he replied "I had time to answer the telegraph and get my engine to slow. I should say that was about twenty seconds." Cook noticed nothing untoward until after receiving the telegraph order to slow and "was actually reducing engine speed when the ship took up a diving attitude". Savory said that the dip was sharp enough to throw him off balance, but that he received no signal on the telegraph. The beginning of the second dive also threw Disley off balance, back onto the bed that he had just got out of. He then heard the telegraphs (this was after Hunt had left). The crash came shortly after, but not before he had reached the field switch panel.

The evidence of the wreckage and the marks on the ground indicate that impact occurred at a nosedown angle of slightly more than 20 degrees. The three who noticed both dives are agreed that they were of similar steepness. The most likely duration of the first dive is thirty seconds; the level phase, five to twenty seconds, but bearing in mind Leech's actions, most probably fifteen seconds; and the second dive, ten to twenty seconds. The absolute values must be questionable, but it is probable that the relative values of 30:15:15 are valid.

In addition to Rigger Church who survived the crash, six bodies were found forward of frame 6, and we do not know where the other surviving rigger, Radcliffe, escaped from: he made no statement before he died. Two of the six bodies were identified as riggers – Rudd and Richardson – and three were engineers. The presence of the three riggers forward of frame 6 suggests that those in charge knew that something was amiss forward.

Rigger Church probably went on watch at 0200 as the rigger of the watch in the fore part of the ship, carried out his routine inspection as he went forward, and reached the area of frame 0 between 0205 and 0206 when he would have reported into the control room on voice pipe. Shortly afterwards the ship went into a steep dive. His evidence, as recorded when he was in extremis by Sqn Ldr Cooper, reads: "I was walking back when the ship took a sudden steep diving attitude. At this moment I received an order to release half a ton of emergency forward ballast. But before I could get to it the crash came." Sqn Ldr Cooper, cross-examined in Court, said (a) "I am not sure that much reliance can be placed on the statement which I did obtain from him"; (b) "He gave me the impression that he started to go aft because of the acute angle of the ship. He thought he had better get back. I think those were his words." (c) "He did not reply directly to the questions I asked." The crisp, precise statement which is quoted from the Court's report was Cooper's interpretation of poor Church's semi-incoherent words and not a verbatim record. I therefore concluded that I was justified in making a free, if not actually different interpretation of these words. I concluded that shortly after the first dive began Church, alone in the darkness and confusion, not really knowing what was happening, became alarmed by the steepness of the dive and started to walk aft. I had to accept, because he repeated it three times, that he had been instructed to drop half a ton of ballast, but I knew that there was one ton available at frame 0, and I could not conceive that the Captain, in the circumstances, would hang onto any of it; hence my supposition that Church was intercepted by another rigger who, knowing the urgency of the Captain's orders, went with him to speed up the release of the two half-ton bags.

The only direct evidence relating to actions of the control room personnel comes from the chief Wireless Operator, Mr Disley. He told the Court that as the ship levelled out from the first dive, the Chief Cox'n came to the switchboard and remarked "We are down, lads." Cross-examined, Disley said "He certainly did not seem excited, but anyone in the vicinity would have heard him had they been awake." Hunt then left the switchroom and went aft in the direction of the crew-space, and at that moment the ship began her final dive and Disley heard the engine room telegraphs ringing.

Flight Sergeant Hunt was a man of strong character and immense experience, having been in flight crews of airships continuously since joining the non-rigid *Beta* in 1913. After service in *SS* and *Coastal* non-rigids, he had become Second Cox'n of *No 9*, then Chief Cox'n of *R29* and *R33*; he had been aboard the latter when she broke away from the mast and survived despite severe damage to her nose and the loss of the two forward gasbags. As Chief Cox'n he was not a watchkeeper, but was responsible for the general supervision of the Assistant Cox'ns and watchkeeping riggers. The hull, cover, gasbags, gasbag wiring, ballast and flight controls all fell within his sphere of responsibility. He must have gone into the switchroom from the control room and it has to be concluded that his statement to Disley could only have been formal notification of a command decision. As Chief Cox'n his place in an emergency would be in either the control room or the control car giving such assistance to the Officer in charge as might be required, and it is not in his character to have deserted his station. One must therefore deduce that towards the bottom of the first dive Hunt had been ordered to notify crew and passengers that the ship was about to be forced down, and that those in charge were preparing for an emergency landing.

The Court of Inquiry paid scant attention to the evidence of observers in Beauvais, Allonne and the vicinity of the crash. Mr W. Newman Alcock, a retired naval architect who made a deep study of the causes of the failure of the British airship programme and won the *R38 Memorial Award* for 1955, carried out a painstaking analysis of this evidence in an attempt to define the flightpath of *R101* between 0204 and 0209 hours. The vertical profile which he established showed the ship alternately climbing and diving about a mean height of about 1,000 feet above the ground. At 0204 she was level at a high peak. She then descended as she overflew the western edge of Allonne village, flew level for about thirty seconds and began to climb again at about 0206. She peaked shortly after 0207 before beginning her final descent to the ground from about 1000 feet. Speaking of her final descent M. Rabouille, who was very close to the point of impact, averred "it did not travel horizontally at all" and stated that when it nose-dived at the end, "there came a tempest from the west." On the basis of topographical lines of site, Alcock deduces that this final dive began from about 200 feet and that it was induced by the "tempest from the west", causing high hull moment but low empennage moment. He also deduces that during the last minute or so the ship yawed from a heading of 190 degrees true to 225 degrees and back to 205 degrees just before impact.

From an examination of the survey drawings of the wreckage submitted to the Court of Inquiry it is clear that:

(1) The initial impact of the ship was at a nose-down angle of 18 degrees below the horizon, against an upward slope of the ground of five degrees, and the downward velocity of the ship was almost wholly absorbed by the deformation of frames 1 and 2 and the consequent compression of lower longitudinal girders to frame 3.

(2) The deformation of frame 1 and the bow structure ahead of it was such as to dig the mooring cone on the nose into the ground and mark the point of first impact.

(3) With the weight of the bow structure and frames 1 and 2 borne on the ground, there was sufficient excess buoyancy in the hull aft of frame 3 to destroy the downward momentum of the centre of gravity (approximately at frame 8A), and for the tail to lift slightly, just enough to lift the distorted bottom of frame 2 clear of the ground, but

not before the extreme bow structure was compressed further.

(4) The damage to the bow structure would probably have released the one ton of water ballast still left in the two canvas bags at frame 0, giving the ship slight positive buoyancy overall.

(5) The whole structure lifted slightly off the ground in substantially the same nose-down attitude and was carried by its own decaying momentum (at least one engine was still running at cruising power) some 90 feet along an upward slope of slightly over 2 degrees. Because of the compression of the bow structure, however, the nose-cone moved only 61 feet from its initial mark on the ground.

(6) The net rotation of the longitudinal axis of the ship between the first and second impacts was probably no more than 4 degrees in a tail-down sense: this can be deduced from the locus of the tip of the propeller disc of the starboard fore engine which did not hit the ground until the second impact, when it left clear marks.

(7) On the basis of the amount of deformation of the bows, it can be estimated that the vertical deceleration on impact was about 0.5g and that the time between first and second impact was about eleven seconds. The horizontal deceleration would therefore be about 0.05g. In comparison, the airborne deceleration during the final eighteen seconds before impact was about 0.02g.

(8) The ship must have been heading almost straight into the wind, having no drift.

(9) In the second impact, the first point of contact was the tip of the propeller of the starboard fore engine, and it is evident on the drawings that the brunt of the second impact, as the wind bore the ship down, was taken by the two engine cars on frame 4. The starboard engine car rotated horizontally through some 180 degrees and must have been forced up into the longitudinal reefing girders.

(10) The ship stopped dead, her tail still up in the air at an angle of about 15 degrees to the horizontal and 20 degrees to the general slope of the land. The bottom of the control car at this juncture must have been about 25 feet above the ground.

Immediately after the second impact there was an explosion and fire broke out in the fore part of the ship. From the drawings it is clear that as the fire destroyed the ship's buoyancy, the hull rotated about the point of the bows, due allowance being made for a substantial compression between frames 8 and 8A (probably caused by the high power which continued to be delivered from the starboard engine at frame 9 up to and after impact). The key evidence about the initiation of the fire, as recorded in the transcript of the Proceedings of the Court of Inquiry, was:

(1) Engineer Cook (port mid car): "I was looking out when the ship struck. After the first impact the ship seemed to rebound and then crashed again and, immediately after this, became enveloped in flames. My car sank to the ground quite an appreciable time after the ship struck. In fact, I had time to stop the engine." Under examination he said "...a matter of seconds between first and second striking of the ground"; the second bump and the explosion "were simultaneous"; "I stopped my engine on the first impact... and it was just one continual noise and then a sort of extra loud crash in the second bump, and then the explosion"; it seemed to him as if his car fell away from the ship "but not from any great height and the bump to the ground was a very slight bump".

(2) Engineer Binks (after car): "A crash. Engine is stopped immediately... Explosion and fire." After some time he got clear and observed "It was raining heavily and half a gale blowing diagonally across the ship from the starboard bow and bringing to us thick smoke and flame from the accommodation part of the ship..."

(3) Engineer Bell (after car): "We got clear... by that time the passenger accommodation was blazing but the bow and the stern of the ship only showed patches of fire."

(4) Electrician Disley (switch-room, just above and to port of the control car): "I would say the crash was a crunch rather than a violent or sudden impact. I have a faint impression of tripping one of the electrical field switches before the crash came. The first explosion came immediately after the crash and was very violent. The two which followed were far less violent."

(5) Foreman Engineer Leech (off duty in smoking room, above and immediately aft of the control car): "Simultaneously with the impact the lights went out and within perhaps a second there was a flash of flame – not a violent explosion but just a 'woof'... there was no concussion with it... the smoking room door swung open and it appeared to originate from over the control car, but of course I could not say whether the flame had drifted down from the forward part of the ship or not... It was very white, and not at all like a hydrogen flame... At the moment of the flash I jumped off the settee but because the upper deck had shut down on top of this settee I could only more

or less rise about 4 feet... No flame at all in the smoking room, only thick, choking smoke."

(6) M. Rabouille (who was just over 200 metres from the ship's nose when it hit): "Its forepart crashed in to the northwest edge of the Bois des Coutumes. There was at once a tremendous explosion, which knocked me down." Also "the whole ship took fire at once, sheaf of red flame forward rather than aft." He picked himself up from the ground, hearing two further and lesser explosions.

A tree, ten to twelve feet high, stood undamaged on the centreline of the ship between frames 8 and 8A.

The investigation carried out by the French Aviation authorities reported that:

(1) The starboard fore engine car seemed to have cut the ground violently with the engine still running. It was turned back to front.

(2) The port fore car was split open by an explosion.

(3) The starboard midship car was badly damaged and its propeller broken.

(4) The port midship engine was almost intact, the propeller nearly vertical, the engine evidently stopped before it hit the ground.

(5) No. 5 car very little damaged.

On the assumption that there had been an explosive mixture of hydrogen and oxygen in the ring space between the outer cover and the gas bags, the following causes of fire were examined on behalf of the Court of Inquiry:

(1) The starboard fore engine, while still running, forced up into the hull on the second impact. The engine exhaust was not a likely cause unless the engine was still running at high power.

(2) Ignition of petrol carried in a power car for the starter-motor.

(3) Breakage of a main electric cable between forward generator and switchboard. Although Disley thought he had probably tripped only one of two field switches, it must be presumed that the circuits were protected against major shorts by means of efficient circuit overload trips.

(4) Sparks caused by the breakup of the nose structure.

(5) Ignition of calcium flares in contact with water after the impact. These flares were carried in boxes, and it was thought that they would have to be immersed in water, rather than merely to come into

superficial contact with a wet surface, before igniting.

The clearest description of the origin of the fire seems to have been given by Engineer Cook, who was actually looking out of the window of his engine car while the impacts occurred. The sequence which he describes is corroborated by Electrician Disley. Poacher Rabouille's evidence was somewhat confused, but he had no doubts about the severity of the first explosion and that it was followed by two smaller ones after he had stood up again. The evidence of Bell and Binks, while less clear, does not contradict this sequence. The inescapable conclusion from the evidence thus far is that the initial explosion and fire occurred while the control car was still several feet above the ground. This rules out the calcium flares as the origin of the fire.

Only Foreman Engineer Leech's evidence appears to be inconsistent with the foregoing. Accepting the "Cook" evidence, it would seem that Leech only heard the "whoof" of the passage of the hydrogen fire as it traversed the ship after the initial explosion, and that much of his evidence relates to later stages of the fire. The upper deck would not have collapsed before the major structure of the ship fell to the ground as the hydrogen fire destroyed its buoyancy; the white flame which he indicated as happening coincidentally with this collapse might well have come from the ignition of the calcium flares by either the prime fire or burning fuel; while the thick, choking smoke could have come from either the flares or fuel. If it can be accepted that Leech's evidence does relate to later stages of the conflagration of the ship, then it becomes quite compatible with the "Cook" thesis and tallies with what Binks and Bell saw.

It seems incontrovertible, therefore, that *R101* was destroyed by a fire having its origin in an explosion in the fore part of the hull as she made her second impact at an angle of about 20 degrees to the slope of the land. It seems very likely that the explosion was caused by the hot exhaust of one of the fore engines, still running, igniting an explosive hydrogen/air mix in the ring-space between gasbag No.4 and the outer cover as the hull was driven down by the wind onto the engine-car. From the site wreckage, the starboard fore engine appears the more likely in that it was found lying on top of a piece of the hull structure; on the other hand, the French authorities wrote of the port engine car that it had been split open by an explosion. The later explosions were probably caused by the ignition of groups of fuel tanks as the hydrogen fire swept along the length of the ship. The calcium flares would have been ignited by the general conflagration.

The Report of the Court of Inquiry deals at some length with the history of the chafing of gasbag fabric and the specious dismissal of McWade's representations. It is, however, surprisingly perfunctory about the very serious deficiencies in the ship's outer cover, and implies erroneously that a whole new cover was fitted before the ship left for India. Rope's memorandum to his Chief, Lt Colonel Richmond, drawing his attention to the inadequate margins of safety of the outer covers of the two ships, was not among the papers submitted to the Inquiry. Despite the confidence of both Richmond and the head of his fabric department, J.W.W. Dyer, the conclusion has to be drawn that, after seven and a half hours' flight through rain and rough air at fast cruising power, the portion of the old cover between frames 1 and 3 (which bore the brunt of the aerodynamic forces) must have been very susceptible to failure. In my view, the Court in its findings underestimated the probability of failure.

Following our long correspondence arising from his controversial hypothesis about the causes of the loss of R101 advanced in *To Ride the Storm*, Sir Peter Masefield was moved to influence students and staff in the Department of Aeronautical Engineering at Bristol University to study the behaviour of the airship. Aerodynamic data were derived from wind-tunnel measurements on a model. A computer was programmed to solve the fundamental equations of motion of the airship, given the observed aerodynamic data and a number of other variable inputs such as elevator movements, the dropping of fuel and water ballast from various stations, the loss of lift from leaking gas bags, changes of engine power, the variation of wind with height and the effect of random gusts. In effect the original work carried out for the Court of Inquiry by D.H. Williams and A.R. Collar (R&M 1401, 1931) was brought up to date and enlarged in scope. Undergraduate work by Messrs M.F. Auckland and C.J. Light confirmed a number of important conclusions which Williams and Collar had discovered half a century before, and was able to quantify for the first time the significant increases in drag and pitching moments which would result from a tear in the outer cover of the nose.

Towards the end of 1985 Professor Alan Simpson, the Head of the Department, invited me to help to specify, more precisely than had been possible hitherto, many of the operational assumptions and inputs for a further computer study of the behaviour of R101 during the last few minutes of flight. Over the next couple of years he fed several hundred cases through his computer, not only applying the fundamental equations of motion of an airship used by Williams and Collar, but refining them to deal with the behaviour of a large body moving through a wind-shear. He concluded that he now had the most sophisticated elementary model of unsteady longitudinal motion of an airship that was possible without experimental determination of indicial aerodynamic forces associated with gust penetration.

In order to reproduce the flight profile described by the surviving crew members, and to satisfy both the initial conditions of safe cruise and the final conditions as deduced from the wreckage on the ground, the variable inputs had to be fed into the computer in a correct sequence. The crew control actions were assumed to conform to what would be expected of a skilled and competent crew in the light of the options likely to be perceived by them at the time. These cases were progressively refined by trial and error until a final series was run, having the designation of *Case R101 NEW/Nov 87*, which not only reproduced a flight path as nearly matching the known facts as might reasonably be possible, but also seemed to provide the most rational explanation of the final minutes of the last flight of *R101*. Professor Simpson demonstrated beyond doubt that a substantial gust, which need not have a large vertical component, was an essential requirement for inducing a suitably steep first dive. He also concluded that large drag increases, engendered perhaps by atmospheric turbulence as well as by envelope damage, were an essential ingredient in the catastrophe.

His final case starts from the generally accepted basis that at 0200 hrs the airship was flying at a mean height of 1,500 feet above sea level (1,200 feet above the ground), but oscillating about 250 feet above and below the mean. The change of watch occurred at this time and by 0204 the stand-down watch would be retiring to rest stations, leaving in the control car the Officer of the Watch (OOW), the new Height Cox'n on elevators and a Rigger on the rudders. The Chief Cox'n was probably in the control room above, together with the Rigger whose duty was to act as a messenger. There was one Rigger on roving patrol in the forward section of the hull, and a second aft. The engineers were in the five power cars. . The engines were running at fast cruising power, which would normally give an airspeed of about 54 knots, and an analysis of the observed wind and the known progress of the flight broadly confirmed that this must have been her actual airspeed. This sets a limit on the likely static heaviness of the ship, for if her hull had had to carry a great deal of aerodynamic lift her airspeed would have been noticeably reduced. She had consumed about 2.5 tons of fuel. Expert evidence indicated that her cover would have absorbed about four tons of rainwater. Loss of gas through the valves, as the result of rolling in the turbulent air, and through holes in the gasbags due to chafing, amounting to some 2.5 tons loss of buoyancy compared with the fully inflated condition on departure, would be in accord with past experience.

A continuing loss of gas at this rate would prejudice the possibility of reaching Egypt, and would therefore require a Command decision in due course, but in itself it did not constitute any sort of emergency at 0200. That there was such a loss of gas accounts, perhaps, for the presence of Sqn Leader Rope, observed just after 0200 hours by Engineer Binks in the vicinity of frame 8A, presumably even at this late hour keeping a designer's eye on the behaviour of the gas valves and gasbag wiring as the ship rolled and pitched in the turbulent air.

During the June flights when flying with considerable negative buoyancy, *R101* had shown a marked tendency to go into short, steep dives from which she recovered slowly. In attempting to reproduce this characteristic, which had occurred at airspeeds around 42 knots, Prof. Simpson's computer study showed that at such low speeds, if the ship was trimmed nose heavy, the effect of a small nose-down pitching moment was in fact very much greater than that of a similar nose-up moment, and in certain circumstances the rate of fall of the nose could be, for a short period, more than the rate at which corrective elevator action could be applied. It was therefore assumed that at 0200 hrs on the last flight, the 2.5 tons loss of buoyancy had all occurred in the gasbags forward of the centre of buoyancy.

At 54 knots the power of the elevators of *R101* was very considerable; they would have had no difficulty in holding up the nose even after the complete deflation of two forward gasbags. For the 'first dive' to be induced with adequate severity, the power of her elevators had to be reduced by flying at a considerably slower speed; and to bring this about a substantial split was predicated in the fabric of the top of the outer cover of the airship between frames 2 and 3. Trial and error placed this event at 0204 hrs, which was then taken as the datum t=0 seconds for the computer runs. This split would not be known to the crew. The Officer of the Watch and the height coxswain would only gradually perceive its effects through a slow climb of about 150 feet, caused by the resultant nose-up pitching moment (which the height cox'n would counteract by winding on down-elevator), and by a fall-off of the airspeed caused by the increased drag. Both effects could have been to some extent masked or confused by the normal wallowing in the turbulent air, but after about a minute the speed would have stabilised at about 40 knots while corrective elevator action held her in level flight.

The clear indication of a 26% loss of airspeed without any change of engine power, plus the need to carry an additional eight degrees of down elevator, would suggest to the OOW a classic case of a general and substantial loss of buoyancy, and it was assumed that at this stage the OOW must have called the Captain in accordance with standing instructions, and ordered Flight Sergeant Hunt to alert the stand-down watch of riggers. The Captain, deducing that the ship had suddenly become heavy due to some sort of damage, would take immediate steps to lighten her, with a view to slowing down and effecting repairs. The computer showed conclusively that the aerodynamic effect of lightening her in the condition that she must actually have been in would have been to pitch her nose down steeply. A gust was then fed into the computer just as the airflow began to impinge on the upper part of the nose where the outer cover was torn, causing damage to the two forward gasbags and consequently a very rapid deflation. The prolonged dive therefore became too steep for the elevators to cope, and four tons of fuel had to be jettisoned from forward tanks before the ship virtually levelled out while still falling.

The general conclusion reached by the study was that the observed conditions of the first impact and the evidence of the survivors could only be satisfied on the assumption that those in command attempted, towards the end of the first dive, to drop further fuel and ballast and reduce power in such a way as to soften an inevitable grounding. In Professor Simpson's final case, the ship was about one ton heavy on impact, and one ton of water ballast remained at frame 0.

The optimum example of Professor Simpson's cases is described in detail in the Appendix.

Professor Simpson then investigated by means of a series of computer runs whether, by application of full power, *R101* might have been able to climb away. The details are also in the Appendix. It has to be concluded that after the deflation of the gasbags in the first dive *R101* was in a very critical condition, and if the decision to apply full power was to be made it had to be made within a time-window of probably no more than fifteen seconds to succeed. Moreover, recovery thereafter would have been totally dependent on Rigger Church's success in reaching the ballast at frame 0 in the nose and releasing all of it not more than twenty seconds after the time the ship actually crashed. Even on the computer it looked as if it would have been a close scrape. Correct control of ballast was vital. The ballast dropping programme for climbing away at full power would have been totally different from that needed for either establishing static buoyancy or attempting a soft nose-down landing. And the point has to be made that at the crucial 'window' time (t=240 sec) there would have been no need apparent to the Captain for applying full power, since he had sufficient ballast available to achieve slight positive buoyancy even with gasbags 1, 2 and 3 fully deflated. It was only when it proved impossible to drop the ballast at frame 0 that the additional nose-up pitching moment which full power would have provided became essential.

Clearly the problem of a full power recovery is a very delicate one. It is important to realise that Professor Inglis told the Court of Inquiry that a pull-out with gasbags 1, 2, and 3 fully deflated would not have been possible: this represented contemporary knowledge which would have influenced the Captain's judgement. What made any pull-out possible in the computer runs was the additional nose-up moment caused by the torn envelope, only now quantifiable, and certainly unbeknown to the ship's Officers. In all the circumstances of the dark, turbulent conditions, and of the risks involved, the fact that a full power recovery was not attempted cannot be a matter for blame. Even if it had been attempted, a great deal of luck would have been needed for it to succeed. Had another gasbag begun to deflate, it would have been impossible to stay in the air.

The computer study not only gives credence to the hypothesis that R101 crashed as the result of a massive deflation of gasbags 1, 2 and 3 following a tear in the top part of the outer cover between frames 2 and 3, but also indicates that the ship's Officers handled the unprecedented emergency with competence. The impact with the ground was not a heavy one, the attitude of the ship was about right for an emergency landing: had the airship not caught fire, few lives, if any, would have been lost.

Wider questions, nevertheless, remain to be answered: was the ship really airworthy for such an arduous flight? should she have been tested more severely before embarking on it? should she have embarked upon it in the expected weather conditions? Once under way, should measures have been taken to reduce the stresses? And if the answers to these questions indicate that errors of judgement were made, where does responsibility lie? The Court of Inquiry Report contains no clear conclusion as to the airworthiness of R101 in the full operational sense of the word. Indeed, Major Phillip Teed, a former airshipman who, as a practising Barrister, represented the family of the Captain of R101 throughout the proceedings, wrote afterwards "There is no proof that the airship was airworthy in the operational sense when she left for India, while as regards gasbags and wiring, gas valves and vertical control there is evidence that she was defective. The distribution and method of release of water ballast was unsatisfactory." Mr McWade, the A.I.D. Inspector-in-Charge at Cardington who had been over-ruled by his own Director, reaffirmed in Court that 'padding' to the extent employed in R101 was not acceptable to him and asserted that if it had been left to him the airship would not have been granted a Certificate of Airworthiness.

For her final trial flight before leaving for India, R101 was granted a temporary 'Permit to Fly' and the Court went at considerable length into the investigation into her structural strength and what it called "the rather hurried circumstances" in which this Permit was secured. For her international flight she required by law a Certificate of Airworthiness, for the issue of which the statutory authority was the Director of Civil Aviation. There were three stages which had to be completed before the Certificate could be issued: the Airworthiness Authority had to clear the design strength of the alterations; the test flight had to prove the modifications to the satisfaction of the Captain and the Technical Staff; and the ship had to pass a final inspection by the AID Inspector, in this case Mr Raisbeck, McWade's Chief Examiner. After the ship had been inspected formally, McWade made what he later termed a "friendly visit" and passed his "most exceptionally experienced" – (his own Director's description of him) – eye over her. The Certificate was issued on 2nd October, to be handed over to the ship as soon as the AID were satisfied; it was issued on the recommendation of AMSR, based on a short letter from the designated Airworthiness Authority which said that, although they had not had time to draft a proper report and their calculations were based on very limited data, they were satisfied that R101 as lengthened complied with the special requirements of the Airworthiness of Airships Panel. It is quite clear that there was immense pressure on everyone concerned to cut corners to meet the deadline for departure. And it was purely for this reason that authority was granted to curtail the duration of the crucial test flight. So, one after another, all the checks and balances were eroded and there was no-one of independent standing to cry "halt and think a while" except for Brancker's informal submission to Lord Thomson: and that was brushed aside too.

The Report of the Court of Inquiry states: "It is impossible to avoid the conclusion that R101 would not have started for India on the evening of 4th October if it had not been that reasons of public policy were considered as making it highly desirable for her to do so if she could." Those reasons of public policy were enshrined in the Secretary of State's will. If the airshipmen made hasty or even faulty judgements, their actions have to be measured against the demands put upon them by Lord Thomson.

In a politically-inspired compromise Thomson had originally decided that the Government would embark on its own airship construction programme at the same time as giving Burney and Vickers a contract for designing and building one airship of their own to the same Government specification. This had the calamitous result of spreading the country's meagre design, construction, and indeed operational, resources far too thinly. The number of available people who could honestly be called airship experts could be counted on the fingers of two hands. Nevertheless the programme was not only set in train by Thomson, but was endorsed by his successor, Sir Samuel Hoare. For the next five years, as Hoare (later Lord Templewood) recorded, "there was scarcely a day on which awkward problems connected with the double programme did not arise. Throughout these months of controversy I greatly missed the guidance of some expert and experienced mind."

The spring 1929 General Election brought the Labour Party back into office with Thomson once again as Secretary of State for Air. A minor political figure whose power-base rested narrowly on his personal friendship with the Prime Minister, Ramsay Macdonald, and a romantic at heart, he hitched his wagon to the old concept of the Imperial airship service. The achievement of the India flight at the earliest possible opportunity became an obsession with him. He proceeded to devote a great part of his energy to pushing ahead and, although it was nearly two years behind schedule, expanding the programme. When the Treasury agreed in principle to the expenditure subject to endorsement of the programme by the Imperial Conference after his return from flying to India in *R101*, his Permanent Secretary, Sir Christopher Bullock, urged caution; he felt that the programme was being rushed, and that *R100* and *R101* should demonstrate the practicability of regular operations before so ambitious a new programme was initiated. "My primary objective," he wrote, "has been to ensure that, if the Secretary of State insists on a gamble, he does so with his eyes open and realises that he is making a radical departure from the wisely cautious policy he has hitherto pursued."

Nevertheless Thomson pressed ahead with his plans. The situation was aptly summarised by Col. Moore-Brabazon (later Lord Brabazon), one of the two Assessors on the Court of Inquiry, in a minute addressed to the President on the subject of blame for the accident:

"1. Subordination of technical problems to political pressure.

2. Consequent starting during unfavourable weather which was largely a contributory cause to the accident.

3. Introduction of many new devices which necessitated extensive trials to try them out. Trials were shortened, nor were 'contract trials', so to speak, such as *R100* had gone through, ever performed before she was hustled off to India.

4. The organization of the Air Ministry shows no over-riding power of veto on the airship colony at Cardington. Higgins and Dowding... were quite unable to take a strong line on airship policy,

and the whole of Cardington found themselves practically forced to take the bidding of the Secretary of State. There would seem need for somebody on the Air Council strong and independent enough to put a veto on any project, however desirable from the political point of view, not ready from the technical side."

The senior professional airshipman was Reginald Colmore, a serving Wing Commander in the Royal Air Force, who, having been connected with the programme from its inception, was appointed Director of Airship Development in the summer of 1929. There were two crucial meetings between the Secretary of State and Colmore, one on 29th August which began with a review of the prospects of R101's projected flight to India in the light of the status of the major modifications which she was then undergoing. Neither Higgins nor his successor Dowding was at this meeting; Colmore was the only professional officer present. The second, on the evening of 2nd October, immediately after the final trial flight, was called by the Secretary of State to determine whether and when the Indian flight should take place. As Dowding said to Colmore before they went into the Secretary of State's room at the Air Ministry, Colmore was his advisor and he would back him up whatever line he took. But, from the line Dowding had taken on his first visit to Cardington, he was suspected, as the 'new boy', of being too much under the influence of the cautious Permanent Secretary Bullock. Colmore was an honest, decent Officer; he was also a peacemaker. He chose to continue committing himself to Thomson's bandwagon.

Richmond, the head of the design and construction teams, had emerged as the dominant personality at Cardington by virtue of his outstanding managerial ability and his sound grip of the technical programme. He was not a man who accepted criticism easily, as he demonstrated in the way that he caused the Director of Aeronautical Inspection to over-rule his own most exceptionally experienced Inspector in the matter of padding. His acceptance of the problems raised by the expansion of the gasbag-wiring, his failure to renew the outer cover forward of frame 3, and his failure to insist on rigorous flight-testing of the ship after the major modification programme, amount to a considerable sum of technical misjudgements. There is reason to deduce, however, that on the occasion of his visit to Cardington in June 1930 Thomson had been very emphatic that everything must be subordinated to the importance of demonstrating R101's capabilities to the Imperial Conference. Whatever technical decisions were made after that visit have to be judged in the light of Thomson's persuasiveness. Richmond can be said to have done his best in the time available to him. Equally it can be said that when the Treasury conditionally approved his ambitious plans for *R102* and *R103*, he was less and less prepared to accept opposition, however legitimate, as the deadline approached.

There cannot be the slightest doubt that, following the long history of troubles with the outer cover and with the gasbag leaks during the summer flights, the remedies provided by the technical staff were insufficiently flight-tested. Bearing in mind, moreover, the very substantial enlargement of the ship and the installation of two newly designed reversing Tornado engines, it is beyond doubt that much more flight-testing was necessary to establish the operational airworthiness of *R101*, as opposed to the technical airworthiness for legal purposes. Colmore nevertheless chose to seek the authority of AMSR to curtail the final test flight if all went well and Major Scott was satisfied with the ship.

Although there was much in his life-style that was erratic, Scott was a courageous and experienced airship operator who was always ready to face risky ventures with quiet humour. He understood as well as anyone the ship's limitations and the risks that were being taken; but if Richmond and the technical staffs assured him that they had put the ship into the best physical condition possible, Scott would see it as his duty to get her to India on schedule: it was for others to decide whether the schedule was a necessary one. Colmore put the onus squarely on Scott to decide whether the final test flight was an adequate one, and it was not in Scott's nature to take a negative attitude to any challenge.

The final decision to leave on the evening of 4th October in the face of an unpleasant weather forecast was also Scott's. Some two hours before departure, the forecast offered winds between 20 and 30 mph in northern France, lighter to the south, between west and southwest, cloudy with local rain. Though not an ideal forecast, there was nothing in it which would have justified a postponement of the flight in the circumstances. An hour and a half after she slipped from the tower, however, she received a very different forecast as she flew over the northern suburbs of London; it warned of winds over northern France between 40 and 50 mph from west-southwest, becoming 30 to 40 mph over central France, with much low cloud and rain. Conditions had deteriorated so rapidly that the Meteorological Office was now forecasting winds of a strength beyond anything which any British airship had experienced over land before. Now, if ever, was the time for Scott, who was in charge of the flight, to consider whether they should loiter in comparative safety over the sea until the storm blew over. With no knowledge of the circumstances in which the decision was made to press on, no judgement can be made of the validity of that decision. Even the options for reducing the ship's cruising speed en route were limited, for the June flights had demonstrated the ship's stability problems in rough air at 42 knots; and at her current 54 knots the headwind component was likely to give her barely 20 knots speed over the ground.

The first flight to India would have been a formidable operation even for a well-proven *R101*, so marginal was her performance, without having to demonstrate additionally the concept of carrying a Cabinet Minister in luxury, even to the extent of providing a State Banquet on board at an intermediate stop. Colmore's decision, and his Officers' agreement to carry out the programme when they did, was an example of high corporate courage, even if some of their judgements were questionable. As for Lord Thomson himself, it was well written of him by an American historian, Professor Henry Cord Meyer, "When he saw circumstances closing in upon him, he did with quiet resolution and a kind of self-certain innocence what he thought was required of him as a leader to see the project through."

If one has to make a final judgement, it is this: that *R101* came to earth as a direct result of the failure of her outer cover and was destroyed by a hydrogen fire after grounding; that the cover failed because a crucial part of it had not been renewed; that its weakness would probably have been disclosed had the ship undergone adequate flight testing; that the disposition of, and arrangements for dropping ballast were inadequate for dealing with a major emergency; that the ship was not operationally airworthy and the departure for India was therefore wholly premature.

Wing Commander Colmore must be held responsible for these technical and operational misjudgements, but it is evident that too heavy a burden was placed on this comparatively junior Director of Airship Development at a crucial stage in the programme. The Secretary of State, wholly underestimating the technical and operational problems with which the people at Cardington were faced, in the end allowed his amateur enthusiasm, his political ambition and his amour propre to bear too heavily on the course of events. Lord Thomson's minute to Sir John Higgins in the middle of July – "I must insist on the programme for the Indian flight being adhered to as I have made my plans accordingly" – cannot be swept lightly aside. The President of the Court of Inquiry himself asked Higgins whether this minute had influenced the course of events; he replied he then realised that the Secretary of State was quite determined to have the ship ready to go to India at the end of September if possible, and every effort was made to speed up the work. "I was somewhat surprised", he told the Court, "that Lord Thomson insisted so strongly on doing nothing which might cause any delay in getting *R101* ready to fly to India." It is in the light of this determination and insistence on the part of their ministerial Chief that the subsequent decisions of Colmore, Richmond and Scott at Cardington must be judged.

So much for an airman's professional assessment, derived from a calm consideration of evidence recorded in original sources. Many years ago, however, I wrote a more intuitive personal conclusion based on many conversations with the widows, Jess Scott, Florence Richmond and Eve Atherstone (later Waley Cohen) and Wing Commander Ralph Booth. I see no reason to alter one word of it – it is still the final judgement of an airship orphan:

"Whatever the technical or operational causes of the disaster, Colmore, Richmond, Scott, Irwin, Atherstone, Johnston, Rope and all their colleagues died in the same instant as Thomson because, in the end, they had not been strong enough to stand up against the ruthless determination of that ambitious politician who had hitched his political reputation to the performance of 'his' ship. Thomson too had courage, for he must have had an inkling that the dice were loaded against the successful accomplishment of the Indian voyage; yet, having laid his timetable on the line, he was too proud and obstinate to listen to those who counselled caution. Only Brancker, who died with him, that outstanding pioneer of both military aviation and the civil air routes to India and through Africa to the Cape, a man of proven accomplishment and personal bravery in the air, had the strength of character to argue against him, suggesting postponement right up to the day before the ship left. But Brancker had no authority over the airship development programme; he could only speak as an airman of judgement and experience, admired and trusted by the whole aviation community, a leader who knew how to listen to what was said by the people who flew."

THE OPTIMUM COMPUTER CASE

The fuel tanks and water ballast tanks or bags of R101 were carried on the ship's main load-bearing frames, numbered from 0 in the bows to 16 in the stern, including 8A which was the frame introduced to provide the additional bay. The contents of some of the fuel tanks were jettisonable; this action could be initiated remotely from the control car. Similarly some of the water ballast tanks could be operated remotely from the control car, but the emergency water ballast bags had to be released locally. According to the evidence submitted to the Court of Inquiry, the likely disposition of jettisonable fuel and water at the change of watch at 0200 hrs was:

Frame 0:	1 ton water (local control)
Frame 3:	2 tons fuel (remote control)
Frame 5:	2 tons fuel (remote control)
Frame 6:	1 ton water (remote control)
Frame 8A:	4 tons fuel (remote control)
Frame 10:	2 tons fuel (remote control)
Frame 11:	1.75 tons water (local control)
Frame 12:	1 ton water (local control)
Frame 14:	0.5 ton water (local)

The gasbags were numbered 1 to 16 from bow to stern. Nos 1 and 2 were interconnected. They were all of different sizes and therefore of different maximum gross lift. The smallest was No 1, 0.595 tons, and the largest No 8A, 15.737 tons. The ones at the core of the emergency were No 1 (0.595 tons), No 2 (3.519 tons) and No 3 (9.395 tons); and the one next most likely to have been at risk was No 4 (12.728 tons).

At t=0 sec (0204 hrs) Professor Simpson's final computer case, *R101 NEW/Nov 87*, starts with the occurrence of a tear in the fabric of the top outer

R101

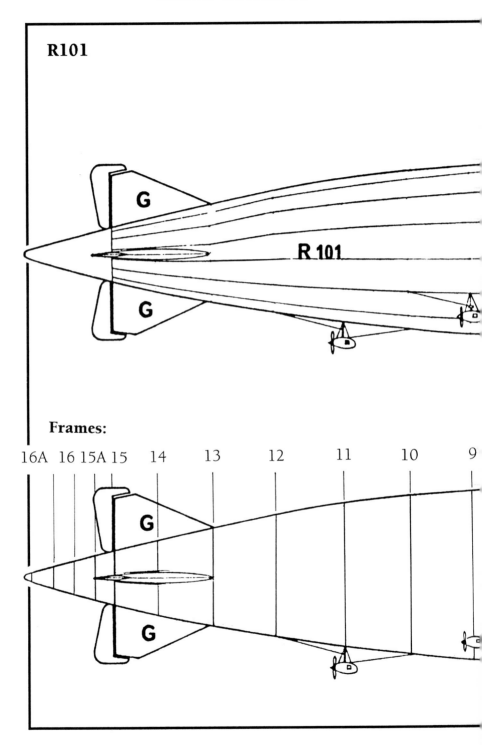

R 101

Frames:

16A 16 15A 15   14   13   12   11   10   9

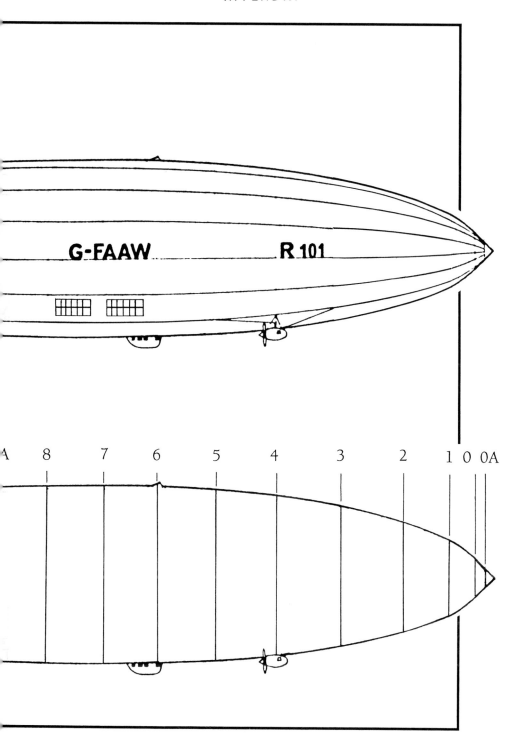

cover between frames 2 and 3 while *R101* is cruising at 54 knots and oscillating about 250 ft on either side of a mean height of 1,500 ft above sea level (1,200 ft above ground): the presumed height at t=0 was 1,400 ft. The ship was 1.5 tons generally heavy (due to accumulated rainwater less fuel consumed) and 2.5 tons nose-heavy (due to loss of gas in forward bags). In order to provide 4 tons of compensating dynamic lift the ship was pitched up 3 degrees, and 3 degrees of down-elevator was carried to balance her.

By t=60 sec the airspeed had apparently stabilized at about 40 knots, the ship's attitude was level, and she was in level flight as the result of the height cox'n having applied 8.5 degrees of 'down' elevator to keep her steady. The clear indication of a 26% loss of airspeed at unaltered power settings, plus the need to carry an additional five and a half degrees of down-elevator, would suggest to the OOW a classic case of general loss of buoyancy. At this stage, therefore, it was assumed that the OOW must have called the Captain in accordance with standing instructions, and ordered Flight Sergeant Hunt to alert the stand-down watch of riggers. Allowing him one minute to get to the control car (his cabin was no more than 20 ft distant), the Captain would see at t=120 sec that the airspeed had dropped to 38 knots and the height was steady at a little over 1,400 ft with the nose only a couple of degrees up, but the elevators 8.5 degrees down. On being informed that this situation had evolved over more than two minutes he would probably deduce that the ship had suddenly become heavy due to some sort of damage and would take immediate steps to lighten her, with a view to slowing down and making repairs. The Chief Cox'n would by now have despatched the two spare Assistant Cox'ns and additional riggers to look for damage (the evidence is that there were at least two riggers in addition to Rigger Church in the fore part of the ship on impact). As for immediate action, the Captain could either drop water ballast or jettison emergency fuel. He might at this stage consider that it was premature to jettison fuel.

At t=150 sec (0206.30) the remote control was operated to drop a total of 2.75 tons of water from frames 6 and 11, more or less evenly disposed about the centre of buoyancy, thereby reducing the static heaviness of the ship from four tons to 1.25 tons. The computer showed conclusively that the aerodynamic effect of this was to cause the nose of the ship to drop. It was assumed that the height cox'n, being still unfamiliar with the "feel" of the ship, did not immediately apply corrective up-elevator.

At t=180sec (0207) the first dive can be said to have begun, for not only was the nose 2 degrees below the horizon but the ship was beginning

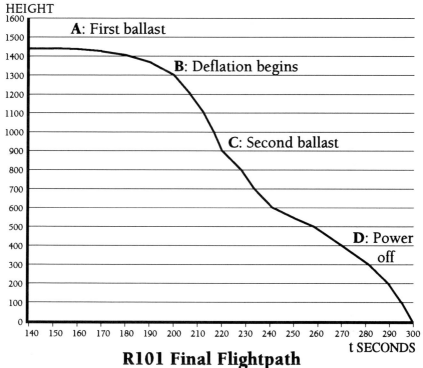

HEIGHT

A: First ballast

B: Deflation begins

C: Second ballast

D: Power off

t SECONDS

R101 Final Flightpath

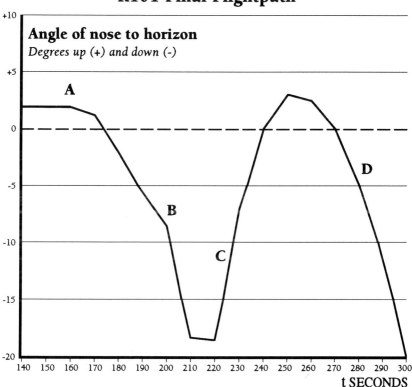

Angle of nose to horizon
Degrees up (+) and down (-)

A

B

C

D

t SECONDS

to lose height. Moreover, the incidence of the airflow was about to become negative.

At t=195 sec (0207.15), when the ship was pitched nose down 10 degrees and the airflow was impinging at an angle of 4 degrees on the top of the ship, a fifteen second gust, peaking at 24 knots with a downward component of 6 knots, was deemed to have struck her, impinging sharply on the upper surface of the nose cover and blowing directly into the cavity in the envelope with sufficient force to cause severe damage to the upper surfaces of gasbags 2 and 3. At this juncture the cox'n began to wind on up-elevator, first slowly, then, as it seemed to be ineffective, at maximum rate.

It was deduced from evidence submitted to the Court of Inquiry that deflation of the order of 7 tons of lift per gasbag per minute was within reason in such circumstances; in the computer study a figure of just under five tons per bag per minute was found to be enough to produce the observed result.

At t=198 sec this rate of loss of lift began in the three forward gasbags.

By t=210 sec (0207.30) the real emergency had begun: the ship had lost a further 2.5 tons of buoyancy in the nose and was losing it at a rate of nearly ten tons a minute; her nose was almost 19 degrees below the horizon and she was passing 1,100 ft, descending at the rate more than of 1,100 ft per minute. Because of the high rate of descent, however, the incidence of the air flow was once more positive, beginning to generate dynamic lift and a nose-up pitching moment. The nose held steady at this angle for about ten seconds despite the winding on of up-elevator at the maximum rate.

At t=220 sec, passing 900 ft, nose pitched 18 degrees down, the Captain was deemed to have decided to drop precious fuel from frames 3 and 5 – the only ballast forward of the centre of buoyancy that was under his immediate control. This was discharged between t=228 and t=232 sec. The response was immediate.

At t=240 sec (0208) the nose was virtually level and still rising, but the ship was descending bodily at 570 fpm as she passed through 600 ft. By then she was 4.3 tons statically heavy and severely out of trim by the nose. Although the ship was still going down rapidly, this marks the end of what has loosely been termed the 'first dive'. It can reasonably be argued that, the Chief Cox'n having alerted the off-duty watch and sent men out to look for trouble by t=150, the severe deflation of the gasbags could have been reported to the Captain within thirty or forty seconds of its happening. In less than thirty seconds after the end of the first dive the Chief Cox'n was heard to announce "We're down, lads". It is also relevant that during the steep phase of the first dive Rigger Church began to walk back from his forward station towards the control room and was subsequently despatched to drop emergency water ballast from the extreme nose of the ship, but was unable to reach it before the impact.

Assuming that at t=235 the Captain knew about the deflation of the forward gasbags, he would realise that their complete deflation would lose him a total of 13.5 tons of buoyancy on top of the heaviness of 1.5 tons attributable to the net effects of fuel consumption and rain absorption. He had started with 15.75 tons of jettisonable water and fuel. It would therefore be possible, by jettisoning all ballast, to establish virtually neutral buoyancy so that, needing only very little dynamic lift, he could slow down for damage limitation and take such further measures as were necessary, such as cutting away static fuel tanks, to keep the ship afloat. This would be the instinctive line of thinking of an airship pilot. His immediate problem, however, was that with the exception of one ton of emergency water ballast in the nose, all remaining water and fuel ballast tanks were aft of the centre of buoyancy.

The dropping of 4 tons had already checked the rate of descent and he would wish to augment this effect with the minimum adverse trim effect. At t=235, therefore, he was deemed to order the local release of water ballast at frames 0, 12 and 14, amounting to 2.5 tons disposed virtually evenly about the CB.

At t=240 sec the 1.5 tons began to go promptly from frames 12 and 14. We now know that Rigger Church was unable to reach the emergency water bags at frame 0, possibly because the gasbags 1 and 2, which would have become wholly deflated by t=250, had partially collapsed over the ladder giving access to the ballast bags on the mooring platform.

At t=250 sec the nose was just over 3 degrees above the horizon, the height 530 ft and rate of descent about 400 ft per min and decreasing. The airspeed was 37 knots. The nose now began to fall slowly even though elevator was hard up.

At t=265 sec the rate of descent began to increase again as she passed through 440 ft with her nose level but dropping. The second dive was beginning. Whether he knew or not that the ballast had not gone from frame 0, the Captain must have judged by t=265 that there was now no chance of keeping the ship afloat, because all the remaining ballast was aft of the CB and it would be impossible to bring the nose up if he released it. The obvious course left to him was to reduce the ship's speed and drop the 6 tons of ballast remaining, in an attempt to make a soft nose-down landing.

At t=270 sec the Chief Cox'n was despatched with the message "We're down, lads." At the same time, all the remaining fuel ballast amounting to 6 tons was discharged from frames 8A and 10.

At t=280 sec a reduction of power to one fifth was fed into the computer, since it is known that at least one engine was still running at fast cruise until impact. The forward gasbags were by now almost fully deflated and the net result was that the ship was virtually in static equilibrium (with one ton of water ballast still left at frame 0) as she passed down through 300 ft at a rate of about 700 fpm with her nose 5 degrees below the horizon. 10 seconds later it was 12 degrees down.

At t=300 sec (0209 hrs) *R101* struck the ground at an angle of 19 degrees nose-down. Her forward speed over the ground was 20.2 ft per sec (13.8 mph); the vertical speed of impact was 17 ft/sec. This was a fairly gentle impact, compatible with the site evidence, which indicated that the nose lifted just clear of the ground and the ship moved bodily forward some 90 ft without a significant change of attitude, to where the nose came to earth a second time and fire broke out.

From the beginning of the first dive at t=180 sec to the moment of impact the total loss of height was 1,400 ft, while the horizontal distance travelled was 3,100 ft, an average trajectory of 1:2.2 or 24 degrees. The steepest trajectory of the first dive was 47 degrees; the minimum downward trajectory during the so-called level phase was 11 degrees; and that of impact was 46 degrees.

At any stage of the flight the presence of gusts might have introduced short term modifications to the pitch angle of the ship and oscillations about the mean flightpath which would undoubtedly have given, albeit temporarily, false indications of the ship's "mean" behaviour and made it more difficult for the Captain and his Officers to judge the effects of command decisions. So great an expert as Dr Hugo Eckener pointed out that there were special difficulties in assessing the 'feel' of the elevator control of a ship that is at once statically heavy and trimmed heavy by the nose. When the outer cover ripped at 0204 the height cox'n could not have spent more than four minutes on the elevator wheel. Throughout the following 300 seconds the principal indicators of what was happening were the fluctuating readings of airspeed, height, pitch angle and rate of descent on primitive instruments. To the minor emergency of a torn cover was added the major emergency of deflation, both of them altering the handling characteristics of the ship. The rate of loss of lift from the forward gasbags was unprecedented. Moreover the Captain would have been aware that complete deflation of gasbags 1,2 and 3 would present him with a downward pitching moment and loss of lift close to, if not actually exceeding, the theoretical limit for the maintenance of level flight. To crown all, it proved impossible

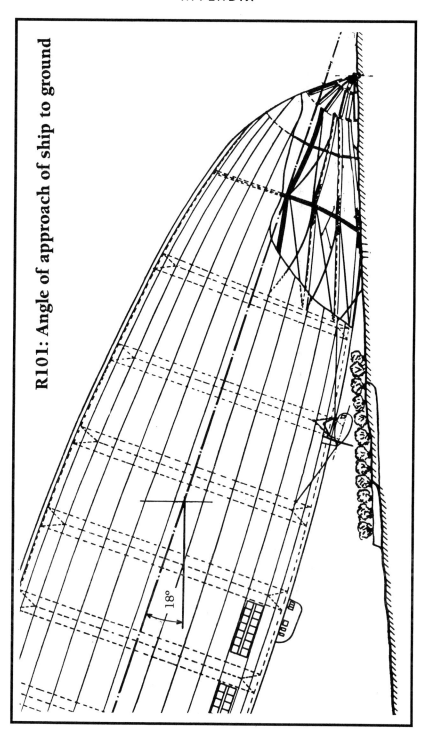

R101: Angle of approach of ship to ground

18°

to use the very substantial corrective moment of the emergency ton of ballast in the nose. In all these circumstances, no criticism can be levelled at the crew.

There is, it must be noted, ambiguity in my use of the term 'Captain' in this narrative. Had the ship's Captain, Flt Lieut Irwin, been acting as OOW from 0200 hrs, he might or might not have alerted Major Scott, the Officer in charge of the flight, as soon as the significant slowing down was observed between t=0 and t=70. Had he done so, then the subsequent command decisions would have been Scott's. If, on the other hand, any one of the other Officers had been OOW, then at t=70 he would have alerted Irwin, the Captain, in accordance with standing orders. Assuming Irwin's arrival in the control car by t=130 or so, the order to make the first drop of ballast must have been his own. If, then, he decided to call Scott, it is unlikely that the latter could have been present much before t=220 when the dive was at its steepest. It is pointless to conjecture further.

It has been speculated that the ship could have been kept in the air had those in command applied full engine power to counter the emergency. The obvious nodal points for doing this are:

1. To have used full power to assist the recovery from the first dive.
2. To have applied full power instead of cutting power after levelling out.

In dealing with Option 1 two constraints have to be considered:

(1) It is well documented that in earlier airships, the standard procedure, when a ship entered a steep dive, was to reduce power before trimming statically. In discussing the behaviour of R101 during the Hendon flights, Major Scott was reported to have said "that if a ship dived, the correct action to take was to stop all engines and if necessary release ballast to bring the ship up statically, as if an endeavour was made to bring the ship up by the elevators and full engine power the effect would be to accentuate the dive." For so long as the dive angle was increasing – that is, until t=210 sec – or being maintained – that is, until t=220 sec – no one would, therefore, contemplate increasing the power. With hindsight and the benefit of the theoretical work of Williams and Collar and their successors we know now that the doctrine was erroneous in the case of R101.

(2) The real emergency did not occur until the catastrophic deflation of the gasbags began at t=200 sec; Flt Sergt Hunt's warning "We're down, lads" indicates that the nature of the emergency was understood by about t=270 seconds. The optimising of several computer runs suggests the probability that the deflation could have been reported to the Captain about t=230 to 235 sec, which is probably the earliest moment at which the

severity of the emergency would have been recognised. But by then the nose was coming up rapidly, reaching level attitude at t=240.

If full power was to be ordered, therefore, the earliest possible time would be t=220 seconds, but it is more likely that the order would have been given coincidentally with the release of four tons of fuel ballast from frames 3 and 5 at t=230 sec. Allowing fifteen seconds for execution of the order through the five telegraphs, full thrust would have been available from t=245 sec, at which point the ship was about 600 ft above the ground and going down at about 750 ft per minute. Trial and error showed that unless, at the same instant, the Captain discharged a further 4 tons of fuel from frame 8A, close to the CB, the ship could not have recovered.

The computer run for the application of full power and the drop of 4 tons of fuel from frame 8A at t=245 sec, with elevators hard up, shows that the ship would have had a very severe impact with the ground in a slightly tail-down attitude at about t=370 seconds, unless Rigger Church had succeeded in dropping the one ton of water ballast from frame 0 before t=320 seconds at the latest. In the latter event, *provided that none of the remaining 3.5 tons of fuel and water ballast aft of the CB was released*, the rate of descent would reach zero at t= 360 sec with the ship 7.5 degrees nose up at 200 ft above the ground, her tailfin barely clearing it. Thereafter she would climb away at 42 knots, pitched 11 degrees nose up, elevators still hard up, to reach her original cruising height at t=560 sec (0213.20 hrs).

The point has to be made that at t=240 sec there would have been no need apparent to the Captain for applying full power, since he had sufficient ballast available to achieve slight positive buoyancy even with gasbags 1,2 and 3 fully deflated. It was only when it proved impossible to drop the ballast at frame 0 that the additional nose-up pitching moment provided by full power became necessary. By then only option 2 was available.

This option would have been to order full power instead of reduced power at t=270 sec. when the nose started to drop again after Rigger Church failed to reach frame 0 in time. A number of computer runs were made with the ship in various states of trim and heaviness, from which it was concluded that the very latest time for initiating a successful full power recovery was about t=255sec, and then only if (a) the ballast was dropped from frame 0 not later than t=320sec and (b) the ballast at frames 11, 12 and 14 was NOT dropped. Had all ballast been dropped, pull-out at full power would have been impossible.

General

My Father's Flying Log Book and manuscripts such as survived the War, as well as some family archives, form important sources of information. After the death of my Mother in 1932 I was absorbed into the family of Major Scott's Widow Jess, and in the remaining years of my minority two other airship Widows, Eve Atherstone and Florence Richmond also took a close interest in me. Eve, who later married Colonel Jack Waley Cohen, subsequently became a close personal friend. I therefore had the benefit, during my young manhood, of their memories and impressions, and access to many of the professional papers of both Major Scott and Colonel Richmond. In 1954, following a reading of Nevil Shute's *Sliderule* I corresponded about its airship chapters in some detail with Wing Commander R.S. Booth and recorded in my journal several very frank conversations about it with Mrs Eve Waley Cohen. The judgements I have formed and expressed on the basis of all this background information are, of course, wholly my own.

For the broad historical background up to 1919 I have relied on Raleigh and Jones *The War in the Air*.

My principal sources for the R101 story are the *Report of the R101 Inquiry*, the *Proceedings of the Court of Inquiry*, and the groups of individual papers submitted to the Court of Inquiry, and other related papers, in the Public Records Office series *Air5*. Other relevant airship files are contained in the PRO series *Air2* to *Air19*.

By far the most comprehensive single reference work for the story of *R100* and *R101* is Sir Peter Masefield's *To Ride the Storm*. Where the work itself has been used as a source, I have acknowledged it hereunder. Additionally, I found it a valuable reference book during the final revision of my manuscript, for rapidly and conveniently checking the facts which I had collected independently from original sources over a period of many years.

Following the publication of *To Ride The Storm* I discussed the relationships between its leading characters with the veteran airshipman, the late Lord Ventry, whom I had first met in the early 1930s. Again, the judgements formed are my own.

Chapter 1
The account of ballooning at Hurlingham is based on Chapter 2 of my Father's copy of *The Royal Naval Air Service Training Manual, November 1914.*

Chapter 2
For brief description of Submarine Scouts and their handling, see Meager, *My Airship Flights.*

Chapter 3
The description of *Coastals* and *Coastal Stars* and their handling is based on my Father's copy of the 1918 edition of the Airship Service Handbook for these airships, issued by the Admiralty.

The account of C20's adventures on 16th/17th September 1917 is based on Sinclair, *Airships in Peace and War.*

Chapter 4
For details of operations of R33, R36 and R38 see Sinclair, op. cit.; Hartcup, *The Achievement of the Airship*; Meager, op. cit.

Chapter 6
The views held by (Sir) Barnes Wallis are largely culled from Morpurgo, *Barnes Wallis.*

The quotations here and elsewhere from Col. Richmond's Diary relate to his Office Day Book, in the possession of the Royal Air Force Museum.

Chapter 7
For the story of the setting up of the Guild of Air Pilots and Air Navigators see Brown, *The History of the Guild of Air Pilots and Air Navigators.*

Chapter 8
Quotation from Hoare, Sir Samuel, *India by Air.*

Chapter 9
Account of the emergence of *R101* from her shed based on the diary of Lt Cdr Atherstone, quoted in Masefield, *To Ride the Storm.*

An outline of the first series of flights of *R101* is contained in *The Report of the R101 Inquiry*. The Flying Log of *R101* is in *PRO Air3/63.*

Chapter 10
Much in this chapter is based on Meager, *My Airship Flights.*

The Flying Log of *R100* is contained in *PRO Air3/59.*

Chapter 11
Booth's observations on behaviour of *R101* recorded in correspondence between Wg Cdr Booth and the author; also in *Proceedings of R101 Court of Inquiry.*

Meager's observations based on Meager, op.cit. and evidence given to Court of Inquiry.

Quotation from Mr McWade's report on leaking gasbags as reproduced in *Report of the R101 Inquiry*, which covers problems of the June flights in some detail. Booth's remarks on pitching movements of R101 quoted from *PRO Air5/1408*.

Chapter 12

An edited version of E.L. Johnston's account of *R100*'s voyage was published in *Aircraft Engineering* in October 1930.

N.S. Norway quoted from *Sliderule*.

Thunderstorm incident and Booth's comments contained in correspondence with author.

Chapter 13

Whilst the assessments of people in this chapter are my own, they are also based on talks or correspondence with Mrs Scott, Mrs Richmond, Mrs Waley Cohen (formerly Atherstone), Wg Cdr Booth, Lord Ventry and John Brancker (the late son of Sir Sefton). The factual material in the chapter is derived from P.R.O. documents relating to the Court of Inquiry, including the Minutes thereof.

Chapter 14

The quotation from Atherstone's diary is contained in the *Report of the R101 Inquiry*.

The letter from Major Villers to Sir John Simon, the President of the Court of Inquiry, is contained in the latter's notebook, ref *PRO Air5/911*. Apart from a personal letter from Major Teed who appeared as Counsel for the family of the ship's Captain, there is nothing else but a few doodles in this notebook.

Epilogue

The key evidence relating to the identification of bodies in the wreckage of *R101* is contained in the notebook of T.S.D. Collins (*PRO Air2/747*); the minutes of the Committee of Identification held at Beauvais on 6th October 1930, including a plot of body locations provided by the French Gendarmerie (*Air2/374*); and the notes on identification of bodies at the mortuary on 8th October (*Air2/374*). I also had a discussion with the late Lawrence A. Wingfield who unofficially accompanied the Air Ministry team to Beauvais on 5th October and was asked to help with identification. The evidence of the survivors is culled from the Minutes of the Court of Inquiry.

My conclusions as to the ship's behaviour on impact are derived from the official drawings showing the layout of the wreckage of *R101* and the suggested angle of approach to the ground, contained in *Air12/285-288*.

The computer study was carried out by Professor Alan Simpson PhD, DSc, FRAeS, FEng, and I am grateful to him for having been permitted to collaborate in the matter of operational inputs. The outputs are a matter of record, but I must bear responsibility for the conclusions reached from them, although they are based on detailed correspondence with Professor Simpson.

BIBLIOGRAPHY

Publications

Brown, D.B., *The History of the Guild of Air Pilots and Air Navigators*, published by The Guild, London 1967.

Burney, Sir Dennistoun, *The World, The Air and The Future*, Knopf, 1929.

Hartcup, Guy, *The Achievement of the Airship*, David & Charles, Newton Abbot 1974.

H.M. Stationery Office, *Report of the R101 Inquiry*, (Cmd 3825), London, 1931.

Higham, Robin, *The British Rigid Airship 1908-1931*, G.T. Foulis & Co, London 1961.

Hoare, Sir Samuel, *India by Air*, Longman's, Green & Co. Ltd, London 1927.

Jones, R. & Bell, A.H., *Experiments on a Model of the Airship R101 with Application to Determine Steady Motion*, Aeronautical Research Committee R&M No. 1400 May 1931, HMSO London 1932.

Masefield, Sir Peter G., *To Ride The Storm*, William Kimber, London, 1982.

Meager, Capt George, *My Airship Flights 1915-1930*, William Kimber, London 1970.

Morpurgo, J. E., *Barnes Wallis*, St Martin's Press, New York, 1972.

Raleigh, W. and Jones A. H., *The War in the Air*, Clarendon Press (6 volumes), 1922 on.

Shute, Nevil, *Sliderule*, William Heinemann Ltd, London 1954.

Sinclair, J.A., *Airships in Peace and War*, Rich & Cowan, 1934.

Spanner, E. F., *The Tragedy of R101*, Spanner, London, 1931.

Sprigg, Christopher, *The Airship*, Sampson Low, London, 1930.

Templewood, Viscount [Sir Samuel Hoare], *Empire of the Air*, Collins, London, 1957.

Williams, D.H. & Collar, A.R., *Calculation of the Motions of an Airship under Certain Conditions, Journal of Royal Aeronautical Society* vol xxxvii pp 35-75,
London Jan 1933.

Williams, T.B., *Airship Pilot No. 28*, William Kimber, London, 1974.

Public Record Office Documents

Air2/349	Airship Crew Licences.
Air2/364	Emergency Landing arrangements for India Flight.
Air2/373	Casualty Action, *R101*.
Air2/374	Identification of relics etc.
Air2/375/66289/30	
	Report of Preliminary *R101* Inquiry
Air2/493	Letters from the Public concerning conclusions of the *R101* Court of Inquiry.
Air2/747	*R101* - Coroner's Inquest.
Air2/1247	Investigation by Sir Bernard Spilsbury.
Air3/59	*R100* Flying Log.
Air3/63	*R101* Flying Log.
Air5/13	Responsibility of Major Scott vis-a-vis Ship's Captain.
Air5/14	Miscellaneous *R101* Papers.
Air5/380	RAW Preliminary Summary of Technical Information for the R101 Court of Inquiry.
Air5/902	Minutes of the *R101* Court of Inquiry.
Air5/903-906	Papers submitted to the *R101* Court of Inquiry.
Air5/910	Notes and Memoranda relating to possible causes of *R101* accident.
Air5/911	Sir John Simon's Notebook.
Air5/913	French Inquiry into *R101* accident.
Air5/919	Analysis of *R101* accident by Major P.L. Teed.
Air5/921	Papers prepared for Court of Inquiry but not submitted.
Air5/994	RAW Standing Orders.
Air11/160	Standing Orders and Instructions for Airship Crews.
Air11/167	Canadian Flight of *R100*.

Unpublished Papers

Auckland, M.F. & Light, J.C., *A Computer Simulation of the Final Flightpath of HMA R101*, Department of Aeronautical Engineering , University of Bristol, June 1984.

Richmond, Lt Col V.C., Office Day Book, Royal Air Force Museum Archives.